Catechetical Helps

for a new day

Revised and Expanded

By Edwin Kurth

Revised and Expanded
by Kenneth C. Wagener
and Rodney L. Rathmann

CONCORDIA PUBLISHING HOUSE • SAINT LOUIS

Catechetical Helps for a New Day
Revised and Expanded from *Catechetical Helps*
By Edwin Kurth

This edition published 2014 Concordia Publishing House
3558 S. Jefferson Ave., St. Louis, MO 63118-3968
1-800-325-3040 • www.cph.org

Text © 1961, 1970, 1997, 2014 Concordia Publishing House

Manufactured in the United States of America

2 3 4 5 6 7 8 9 10   23 22 21 20 19 18 17

Contents

Acknowledgments. 5

Introduction 7

Chapter 1: The First Commandment 19

Chapter 2: The Second Commandment 32

Chapter 3: The Third Commandment 40

Chapter 4: The Fourth Commandment 48

Chapter 5: The Fifth Commandment 55

Chapter 6: The Sixth Commandment 60

Chapter 7: The Seventh Commandment 67

Chapter 8: The Eighth Commandment 72

Chapter 9: The Ninth and Tenth Commandments. 78

Chapter 10: The Close of the Commandments;
Law and Gospel 83

Chapter 11: The Apostles' Creed. 92

Chapter 12: Angels and Human Beings 98

Chapter 13: The Second Article. 105

Chapter 14: The Second Article (Continued) 110

Chapter 15: The Second Article (Concluded) 118

Chapter 16: The Third Article 126

Chapter 17: The Holy Christian Church 134

Chapter 18: The Forgiveness of Sins (Justification) 140

Chapter 19: Prayer 147

Chapter 20: The Lord's Prayer 153

Chapter 21: The Sacrament of Holy Baptism 164

Chapter 22: Holy Baptism (Continued) 170

Chapter 23: The Office of the Keys 175

Chapter 24: Confession and Absolution 180

Chapter 25: The Sacrament of the Altar 185

Chapter 26: The Sacrament of the Altar (Continued) 189

Appendix 1

Martin Luther, His Life and Work 194
Drills for Books of the Bible 200
"Synod" 201
Lutheran Worship 201
Christian Symbols 205

Appendix 2

Luther's Small Catechism 212

Acknowledgments

The publisher acknowledges the following copyright holders:

ABINGDON PRESS

for the excerpt from *Feminine Faces*, by Clovis G. Chappell. Copyright © renewed 1969 by Clovis G. Chappell. Used by permission of Abingdon Press.

AUGSBURG FORTRESS

for the excerpt by Helmut Thielicke, reprinted from *How to Believe Again* by Helmut Thielicke, translated by H. George Anderson, copyright © 1972 by Fortress Press. Used by permission of Augsburg Fortress.

BAKER BOOK HOUSE

for the excerpts from *Illustrations for Biblical Preaching*, edited by Michael P. Green, copyright © 1982, 1985, 1989 by Michael P. Green.

for the excerpts from *Illustrations for Preaching and Teaching from "Leadership Journal,"* edited by Craig Brian Larson, copyright © 1993 by Christianity Today, Inc.

for the excerpts from *Contemporary Illustrations for Preachers, Teachers, and Writers*, edited by Craig Brian Larson, copyright © 1996 by Craig Brian Larson.

EDYTHE DRAPER

for excerpts from *Draper's Book of Quotations for the Christian World*, copyright © 1992 by Edythe Draper.

RESOURCE PUBLICATIONS

for excerpts from *Seasonal Illustrations for Preaching and Teaching*, by Donald L. Deffner, copyright © 1992 by Resource Publications, Inc. Reprinted with permission of Resource Publications, Inc., 160 E. Virginia St., #290, San Jose, CA 95112.

for excerpts from *Windows into the Lectionary*, by Donald L. Deffner, copyright © 1996 by Resource Publications, Inc. Reprinted with permission of Resource Publications, Inc., 160 E. Virginia St., #290, San Jose, CA 95112 (408-286-8505).

PACIFIC PRESS

for the excerpt by George Vandeman from *Planet in Rebellion*, by George Vandeman, used by permission from Pacific Press Publishing Association, Inc.

Each lesson in *Catechetical Helps* contains a sidebar referencing a relevant section of *Confirmation Builder*, a web application that provides teachers with PowerPoint slides, videos, discussion questions, and activities helpful in teaching Luther's Small Catechism.

Introduction

The Catechism

The Bible is the source of all Christian teaching ("doctrine") and living. The Christian faith is based only and entirely on the Bible.

Yet the Bible is a large book. In truth, it is a library of sixty-six books.

A catechism is a book of instruction in the form of questions and answers. Martin Luther's Small Catechism is a summary of the Bible. It helps us focus on the main teachings (doctrines) of the Bible.

The Catechism is an epitome and brief transcript of the entire Holy Scripture. (Martin Luther, What Luther Says, §358)

Dr. Martin Luther
Born Nov. 10, 1483
Died Feb. 18, 1546

Catechetical Helps is a study guide to the catechism, which presents "the chief parts of Christian doctrine."

Martin Luther wrote the catechism. But why did he write it?

In the early years of the sixteenth century, during a tour of congregations in Germany, Luther found that many people knew nothing at all about Christian doctrine. Even many pastors were unfit to teach, for they were not properly prepared to preach and teach God's Word. Yet all called themselves Christians and went to the Lord's Table (Holy Communion).

So, in 1529, Luther wrote his Small Catechism to help the people learn "the chief parts of Christian doctrine." It is called the *Small* Catechism because he also wrote another larger, more detailed exposition of Christian doctrine called the *Large* Catechism.

The Six Chief Parts

Luther's Catechism has Six Chief Parts:

Part 1. The Ten Commandments

Part 2. The Apostles' Creed

Part 3. The Lord's Prayer

Part 4. The Sacrament of Holy Baptism

Part 5. The Office of the Keys and Confession

Part 6. The Sacrament of the Altar

The Six Chief Parts of Christian Doctrine

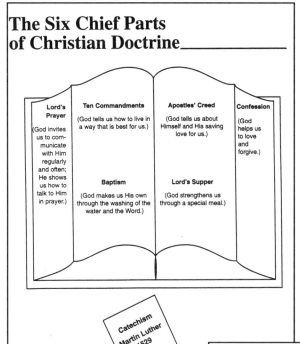

Lord's Prayer	Ten Commandments	Apostles' Creed	Confession
(God invites us to communicate with Him regularly and often; He shows us how to talk to Him in prayer.)	(God tells us how to live in a way that is best for us.)	(God tells us about Himself and His saving love for us.)	(God helps us to love and forgive.)
	Baptism (God makes us His own through the washing of the water and the Word.)	**Lord's Supper** (God strengthens us through a special meal.)	

Catechism
Martin Luther
1529

These chief parts of Christian doctrine are taken from the Bible.

The catechism offers a snapshot of Christian faith and life.

The Bible

Bible means "book." The Bible, the "Book of books," is the Word of God, God's written revelation to humankind. It is the source for all preaching, teaching, and practice in the Church. It is the one dependable guide for living, the one authority for Christian ministry and worship, the final standard for our knowledge of God and His salvation in Christ. The Bible is God's truth in human language.

Scripture is God's testimony concerning Himself.
(Martin Luther, What Luther Says, §167)

Means of Grace

Two Divisions

The Bible has two parts: the Old Testament and the New Testament.

Christ is the central figure of Scripture. His birth marks the division of time in Western civilization: BC and AD. *BC* stands for "Before Christ"—that is, before the incarnate Christ appeared on earth. *AD* stands for the Latin *Anno Domini*: "In the year of the Lord"—that is, when the Lord appeared on earth.

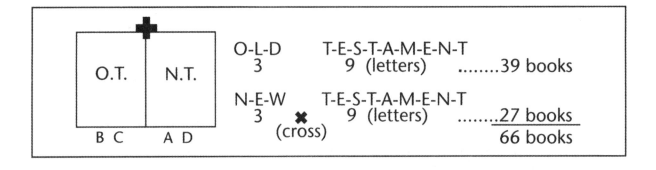

O-L-D	T-E-S-T-A-M-E-N-T			
3	9 (letters)		....	39 books
N-E-W	T-E-S-T-A-M-E-N-T			
3	✖ (cross)	9 (letters)	....	27 books
				66 books

O.T. | N.T.

B C | A D

The Testaments

A *testament* is like a will. It is an expression of an individual's intentions for children and heirs. A testament is often a written document to convey what's most important in life.

The Old and New Testaments are God's written will, His purpose and plan of salvation for the whole world.

The Old Testament contains thirty-nine books, the New Testament contains twenty-seven books.

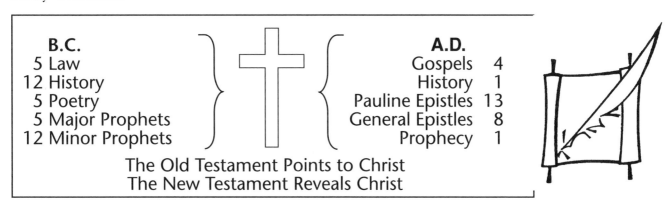

B.C.		**A.D.**	
5	Law	Gospels	4
12	History	History	1
5	Poetry	Pauline Epistles	13
5	Major Prophets	General Epistles	8
12	Minor Prophets	Prophecy	1

The Old Testament Points to Christ
The New Testament Reveals Christ

In the Old Testament the new lies hidden, in the New Testament the old is laid open. (St. Augustine)

Facts about the Bible

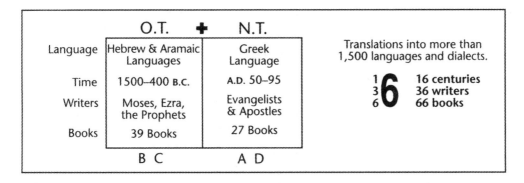

	O.T. ✝	N.T.
Language	Hebrew & Aramaic Languages	Greek Language
Time	1500–400 B.C.	A.D. 50–95
Writers	Moses, Ezra, the Prophets	Evangelists & Apostles
Books	39 Books	27 Books
	B C	A D

Translations into more than 1,500 languages and dialects.

16 centuries
36 writers
66 books

The Bible is a stream of running water, where alike the elephant may swim, and the lamb walk without losing its feet. (St. Gregory the Great)

Portions of the New Testament and the Bible have been translated into thousands of different languages. The entire Bible has been translated into hundreds of languages and dialects.

Verbal Inspiration

The Bible is inspired by God.

All Scripture is breathed out by God and profitable for teaching, for reproof, for correction, and for training in righteousness, that the man of God may be competent, equipped for every good work. (2 Timothy 3:16–17)

The Holy Spirit "breathed" into the writers the thoughts and words they were to write. (*Inspiration* means "breathed into.")

God told the writers	what to write when to write	*This book, the Holy Scripture, is the Holy Spirit's book … The Holy Spirit Himself and God, the Creator of all things, is the Author of this book. (What Luther Says, §169, 168)*

Illustrations of God inspiring the biblical writers:

1. The books of the Bible are God's CDs. The holy writers are God's loudspeakers.

2. As a musician breathes into an instrument and produces sound, so the Holy Spirit breathed into the writers and gave them utterance.

3. A secretary takes dictation. Who gives the thoughts and the words? Who signs his or her name to the work?

Because we are sinful human beings, we can't fully explain or understand the miraculous way in which God inspired the writers of Holy Scripture. Yet we marvel at the unity of God's Word, and we show great respect for it, because it points us to His Son, Jesus Christ.

Since "All Scripture is breathed out by God," the Bible is God's Word, His true, clear, and perfect Word.

The Bible is inerrant: it contains no errors.

The Bible is infallible: it cannot make mistakes; nor does it mislead humankind.

The Bible is reliable, trustworthy, and fully authoritative.

The Purpose of the Bible

The Bible's purpose is to reveal God's salvation in Jesus Christ.

Now Jesus did many other signs in the presence of the disciples, which are not written in this book; but these are written so that you may believe that Jesus is the Christ, the Son of God, and that by believing you may have life in His name. (John 20:30–31)

The Bible is like a road map showing us the way, Jesus Christ, who brings us to heaven. "I am the way, and the truth, and the life. No one comes to the Father except through Me" (John 14:6).

Interstate highways have signs along the road that report how many miles to a certain location: "Atlanta 52 Miles."

It would be foolish to park your car on the side of the road next to the sign and assume you are now at your destination. The sign serves to point the way. We travel the way to our final destination.

The Scriptures point to Christ, the way. By faith in Him, we travel through life toward God's free gift of salvation and eternal life in heaven.

Given the dangers associated with downhill skiing, it's hard to imagine people who are blind successfully navigating difficult courses, but blind skiers can learn to do slalom skiing in relative safety. It works like this: blind skiers and sighted skiers are paired up. The sighted skier skis beside the skier who is blind, directing the blind skier with words such as "Right!" "Left!" "Go straight!" Trusting their partner and the words the partner speaks, skiers who are blind are able to ski selected courses confidently and with ease. Working in this way, skiers who are blind are even able to compete in races. But if a blind skier would suddenly decide not to trust the words of his or her partner, the results could be deadly.

Like the skiers who are blind, each of us is blinded to God's plan of salvation. But we are not left alone. Jesus comes beside us. Through God's Word, He speaks to us, "I am the resurrection and the life. Whoever believes in Me, though he die, yet shall he live, and everyone who lives and believes in Me shall never die (John 11:25–26).

If someone considers the prophetic writings with all the diligence and reverence they are worth, while he reads and examines with great care, it is certain that in that very act he will be struck in his mind and senses by some more divine breath and will recognize that the books he reads have not been produced in a human way, but are words of God. (Origen)

How to Read the Bible

[Martin] Luther said that he studied the Bible the way he gathered apples. First, he shook the whole tree, that the ripest might fall. Then he climbed the tree and shook each limb, and when he had shaken each limb, he shook each branch, and after each branch every twig, and then he looked under each leaf.

Let us search the Bible as a whole, shake the whole trees, read it rapidly as we would any other book; then shake every limb, studying book after book. Then shake every branch, giving attention to the chapters (when they do not break the sense). Then shake every twig by careful study of the paragraphs and sentences[. We gain additional insights as we] look under every leaf by searching the meaning of the words. (Encyclopedia of Sermon Illustrations, 73)

We should not use the Bible

1. as only a storage container for souvenirs, clippings, and keepsakes;
2. as merely a table centerpiece;
3. as a charm to bring good luck to a household, like a horseshoe or rabbit's foot.

But we should

1. read the Bible;
2. learn it;
3. hear it preached;
4. believe it;
5. live according to it.

The Bible is alive, it speaks to me; it has feet, it runs after me; it has hands, it lays hold of me. (Martin Luther [attributed])

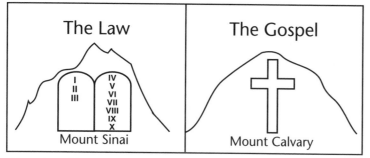

The Law — Mount Sinai — Exodus 20

The Gospel — Mount Calvary — John 3:16

Law and Gospel

Two Main Doctrines

The Bible is rightly "divided" into two main teachings: Law and Gospel.

These two doctrines stand out in the Bible like two mountain peaks.

The Difference between Law and Gospel

LAW

Tells what *we* are to do

Convicts us of sin

Preached to unrepentant
   sinners

Serves as a guide
for penitent believers

GOSPEL

Tells what *God* has done

Saves us from sin

Preached to troubled
   sinners

Creates a living faith

Aid to Memory

LAW	**S**hows	**O**ur	**S**in
GOSPEL	**S**hows	**O**ur	**S**avior

The G-O-S-P-E-L

in a sentence (also called "the Gospel in a nutshell").

G od so loved the world, that He gave His

O nly

S on, that whoever believes in Him should not

P erish but have

E ternal

L ife.

John 3:16

The word *Gospel* comes from the old English word *Godspell*.

Good news
Glad tidings } **that Jesus** **is** **my Savior**

Hymn

A mighty fortress is our God,
A trusty shield and weapon;
He helps us free from ev'ry need
That hath us now o'ertaken.
The old evil foe
    Now means deadly woe;
Deep guile and great might
Are his dread arms in fight;
On earth is not his equal.

The Word they still shall let remain
Nor any thanks have for it;
He's by our side upon the plain,
    With His good gifts and Spirit.
And take they our life,
Goods, fame, child, and wife,
Though these all be gone,
Our vict'ry has been won;
The kingdom ours remaineth.

Prayer

Almighty, everlasting God, Lord, Heavenly Father, whose Word is a lamp
to our feet and a light for our path: Open and enlighten our minds that we may
understand Your Word purely, clearly, and reverently, and fashion our lives according
to it, so that we may please You in all of our thoughts, words, and actions;
through Jesus Christ, Your Son, our Lord. Amen.

Bible Readings

2 Peter 1:16–21

_____

_____

Jeremiah 1:1–10

_____

_____

Ezekiel 2:1–5

_____

_____

John 5:36–47

_____

_____

Romans 3:19–28

_____

_____

Revelation 22:12–21

_____

_____

Deuteronomy 6:1–15

_____

_____

Catechetical Review

The Catechism

1. Which book is the source of all Christian doctrine? (The Bible.)

2. What is a doctrine? (A doctrine is a teaching.)

3. Which handbook presents the chief parts of Christian doctrine? (The catechism.)

4. Who wrote the catechism? (Dr. Martin Luther.)

5. When did he write it? (In 1529.)

6. Why did he write it? (The people knew so little of the Bible.)

7. Why is it called the _Small_ Catechism? (Luther also wrote a large one.)

8. Why is it called a _catechism_? (A catechism is a book of instruction in the form of questions and answers.)

9. What are the Six Chief Parts of Christian Doctrine?

   The Ten Commandments

   The Apostles' Creed

   The Lord's Prayer

   The Sacrament of Holy Baptism

   The Office of the Keys and Confession

   The Sacrament of the Altar

The Bible

1. Which book shows us the way of salvation? (The Bible.)

2. What is the meaning of the word _Bible_? (Book.)

3. Why is the Bible the best book? (It is the Word of God.)

4. What are the two parts of the Bible? (The Old Testament and the New Testament.)

5. What is the meaning of the word *testament*? (A covenant, an agreement.)

6. How many books has the Old Testament? (39.)

7. How many books has the New Testament? (27.)

8. How many books has the Bible? (66.)

9. During which space of time was the Bible written? (From 1500 BC to AD 100)

10. Who wrote the Old Testament? (Moses and the prophets.)

11. Who wrote the New Testament? (The evangelists and the apostles.)

12. In what languages was the Old Testament written? (Hebrew and Aramaic.)

13. In what language was the New Testament written? (Greek.)

14. Whose Word is the Bible, even though men wrote it? (The Bible is the Word of God.)

15. How do you explain this? ("For no prophecy was ever produced by the will of man, but men spoke from God as they were carried along by the Holy Spirit" [2 Peter 1:21]. The Holy Spirit breathed into the writers not only the thoughts but also the very words which they set down.)

16. How much of the Bible is inspired? ("All Scripture is breathed out by God" [2 Timothy 3:16].)

17. What is the purpose of the Bible? (To show us the way of salvation in Christ Jesus.)

18. How are we to use the Bible? (We should read the Bible, study it, hear it preached, believe it, and live according to it.)

Law and Gospel

1. What are the two chief doctrines of the Bible? (The Law and the Gospel.)

2. What is the Law? (The Law is the holy will of God.)

3. What does God tell us in the Law? (God tells us in the Law how we are to be, what we are to do, and what we are not to do.)

4. What is the Gospel? (The Gospel is the good news that Jesus is the Savior.)

5. What is the difference between the Law and the Gospel? (The Law shows us our sin; the Gospel shows us our Savior.)

6. Which Bible verse is known as the Gospel in a sentence? (John 3:16.)

Bible Passages

1. No prophecy of Scripture comes from someone's own interpretation. For no prophecy was ever produced by the will of man, but men spoke from God as they were carried along by the Holy Spirit. (2 Peter 1:20–21)

2. All Scripture is breathed out by God and profitable for teaching, for reproof, for correction, and for training in righteousness, that the man of God may be competent, equipped for every good work. (2 Timothy 3:16)

3. Now we have received not the spirit of the world, but the Spirit who is from God, that we might understand the things freely given us by God. And we impart this in words not taught by human wisdom but taught by the Spirit, interpreting spiritual truths to those who are spiritual. (1 Corinthians 2:12–13)

4. [Jesus] said, "Blessed rather are those who hear the word of God and keep it!" (Luke 11:28)

For Further Study

1. Study the Catechetical Review.
2. Memorize one or more Bible passages.
3. Memorize the first five books of the Bible.
4. Read Commandments 1–3 in the Appendix.

Books of the Bible

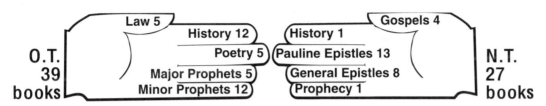

O.T. 39 books

Law 5
History 12
Poetry 5
Major Prophets 5
Minor Prophets 12

History 1
Pauline Epistles 13
General Epistles 8
Prophecy 1
Gospels 4

N.T. 27 books

OLD TESTAMENT

Pentateuch
Gen'-e-sis
Ex'-o-dus
Le-vit'-i-cus
Num'-bers
Deu-ter-on'-o-my

History
Josh'-u-a
Judg'-es
Ruth
1 and 2 Sam'-u-el
1 and 2 Kings
1 and 2 Chron'-i-cles
Ez'-ra
Ne-he-mi'-ah
Es'-ther

Poetry
Job
Psalms
Prov'-erbs
Ec-cle-si-as'-tes
Song of Sol'-o-mon

Major Prophets
I-sa'-iah
Jer-e-mi'-ah
Lam-en-ta'-tions
E-ze'-k-iel
Dan'-iel

Minor Prophets
Ho-se'-a
Jo'-el
A'-mos
O-ba-di'-ah
Jo'-nah
Mi'-cah
Na'-hum
Hab-ak'-kuk
Zeph-a-ni'-ah
Hag'-gai
Zech-a-ri'-ah
Mal'-a-chi

NEW TESTAMENT

Gospels
Mat'-thew
Mark
Luke
John

History
Acts

Paul's Letters
Ro'-mans
1 and 2 Co-rin'-thi-ans
Ga-la'-tians
E-phe'-sians
Phi-lip'-pi-ans
Co-los'-sians
1 and 2 Thes-sa-lo'-nians
1 and 2 Tim'-o-thy
Ti'-tus
Phi-le'-mon

General Letters
He'-brews
James
1 and 2 Pe'-ter
1, 2, and 3 John
Jude

Prophecy
Rev-e-la'-tion

The Five Areas of Congregational Life and Ministry

Through the years, life and ministry in the Christian Church has revolved around five important functions: *worship, nurture* (education), *fellowship, witness,* and *service.*

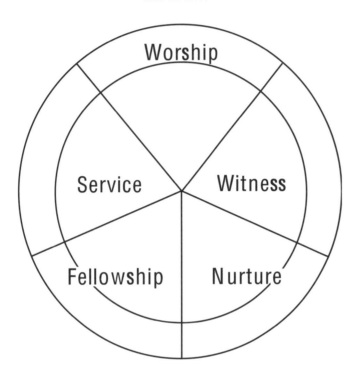

WORSHIP. God's people gather together to hear His Word, receive His forgiveness (absolution), and share in His Sacraments (Baptism and the Lord's Supper). We assemble to praise, pray, and give thanks for all of God's rich blessings to His dear children in Christ.

NURTURE. God's people gather to study His Word by the power of the Spirit. We are strengthened in our faith, empowered to live God-pleasing lives, and equipped for active participation in the ministry and mission of the congregation.

FELLOWSHIP. God's people gather together in the name and strength of Jesus Christ, the Lord and Savior. The Holy Spirit has placed us in a community of believers. As members of the family of God, we share a close relationship both with our Savior and with our fellow believers. Within this fellowship, we encourage and support one another and work together to accomplish our Lord's mission for His Church.

WITNESS. God's people are both equipped and enabled by the Holy Spirit to witness to the Good News of forgiveness, life, and salvation in Christ. We share our faith with others through our words and actions.

SERVICE. God's people are strengthened by His grace in Christ to care for our fellow human beings. We seek to serve people in all their needs—physical as well as spiritual. We carry the love and compassion of Jesus to our communities, cities, nation, and world.

The First Commandment

1

The Commandments: God's Law

Confirmation Builder—
Lesson 4

God reveals His will for His creation in the Law.

God Says: **L**ive **A**ccording to My **W**ill	**The Law tells us** **NO TRESPASSING** Under Penalty of Death

---

All souls are Mine; . . . the soul who sins shall die. (Ezekiel 18:4)

The Law Was Given Twice

The Law—the requirements of the Law—was first written into the heart of human beings. By nature, Adam and Eve knew right from wrong. Even today, every person has a natural knowledge of what the Law requires (Romans 2:14–15).

Through sin, however, the Law became blurred. Though we still know by nature that certain acts—for example, murder and robbery—are wrong, we do not know by nature that the desire to murder or steal is wrong. Our knowledge is imperfect. We see as through a foggy windshield.

Because of human sinfulness and the deliberate rejection of God's Word, God gave the Law a second time, on two tablets of stone. He gave His Law through Moses to the Israelites—and the whole world—about 1500 BC.

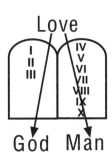

The Decalog is not of Moses, nor did God give it to him first. On the contrary, the Decalog belongs to the whole world; it was written and engraved in the minds of all human beings from the beginning of the world. (Martin Luther, What Luther Says, §2311)

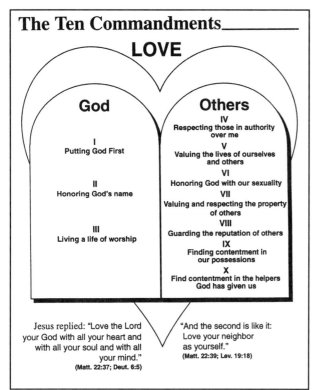

The Ten Commandments

LOVE

God

I
Putting God First

II
Honoring God's name

III
Living a life of worship

Others

IV
Respecting those in authority over me

V
Valuing the lives of ourselves and others

VI
Honoring God with our sexuality

VII
Valuing and respecting the property of others

VIII
Guarding the reputation of others

IX
Finding contentment in our possessions

X
Find contentment in the helpers God has given us

Jesus replied: "Love the Lord your God with all your heart and with all your soul and with all your mind." (Matt. 22:37; Deut. 6:5)

"And the second is like it: Love your neighbor as yourself." (Matt. 22:39; Lev. 19:18)

An interviewer once asked a number of people, "What do you think of the Ten Commandments?" One person just stared at the questioner and gasped, "Are you kidding?"

Another said, "Well, I don't take them literally."

One person replied with a laugh, "I think rules were meant to be broken."

Another said, "It's good that we don't have to keep them any more."

But one person replied, "I think God must be very concerned about the Ten Commandments to put them in the Bible twice." (Adapted from Seasonal Illustrations for Preaching and Teaching, *by Donald L. Deffner, p. 110)*

What Does the Law Require?

The requirement of the Law is *love.*

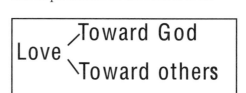

Love — Toward God / Toward others

"Teacher, which is the great commandment in the Law?" And [Jesus] said to him, "You shall love the Lord your God with all your heart and with all your soul and with all your mind. This is the great and first commandment. And a second is like it: You shall love your neighbor as yourself. On these two commandments depend all the Law and the Prophets." (Matthew 22:36–40)

One afternoon, Korean Airlines Flight 007 departed from Anchorage, Alaska, for Seoul, South Korea. The flight plan called for a direct route, but the aircraft's computer contained a one-and-a-half degree routing error. The navigation system was therefore inaccurate—a deadly problem for the crew and passengers.

As the plane flew over the Pacific Ocean, it increasingly strayed from its proper course. In time, the pilots encountered major complications. All aboard lost their lives because of a "minor error."

When it comes to God's Law, even our "minor errors" are deadly problems.

The First Commandment

You shall have no other gods.

What does this mean? We should fear, love, and trust in God above all things.

The First Commandment is the most important commandment, and therefore it stands at the beginning. God calls us to fear, love, and trust Him with all our heart, mind, and strength. All other commandments are based on, and flow from, the First Commandment.

The First Commandment is the standard, measure, rule, and strength of all the other Commandments. To it, as to a head, all the members are attached; in it they live and are active. (Martin Luther, What Luther Says, §2321)

There is only one God: The triune God. Besides Him, no other "god" exists. But sinful human beings *make* other gods for themselves. These other gods are known as idols—that is, "imitations."

The true God says, *"Beware of imitations!* Worship Me alone."

It is very easy to fall into idolatry, for all of us are idolaters by nature. Since idolatry is born in us, it pleases us very much. (Martin Luther, What Luther Says, §2105)

The Doctrine of God

God Exists

Every person believes in a Being higher than which nothing else exists. Some believe in Nature, others in Law, Chance, Fate, the Ground of Being, "the Man Upstairs," the Cosmic Principle, Allah, the Grand Architect of the Universe, the Great Designer, the Divine Presence, the Higher Self, or one of many other principles or objects. These are the various "gods" that human beings have created in the course of history.

Centuries ago, an Aztec king preserved his thoughts for the royal archive: "The gods that I am adoring, what are they but idols of stone without speech or feeling? They could not have made the beauty of the heaven, the sun, the moon, the stars, which light the earth, with its countless streams, its foundations and waters. . . . There must be some God, invisible and unknown, who is the universal creator" (Adapted from Encyclopedia of Sermon Illustrations, 555).

To praise You is the desire of man, a little piece of Your creation. You stir man to take pleasure in praising You, because You have made us for Yourself, and our heart is restless until it rests in You. (St. Augustine, Confessions)

Many people believe that God exists. Why?

Nature affirms "God exists!"

How can we account for the grandeur of the universe? What makes our solar system—the sun with its planets—so orderly and spectacular? Who—or what—brought forth the stars? the galaxies?

Who—or what—creates the mountains, gorges, oceans, and rivers?

Who calls forth life in all its wonderful variety and complexity?

Do we trace all things back to a "big bang" or "primeval soup"?

Many people answer, "There must be a God." The Bible answers simply and grandly, "In the beginning, God created the heavens and the earth."

Every created thing presupposes a creator: the watch a watchmaker, the ship a shipbuilder, the house an architect and builder. "For every house is built by someone, but the builder of all things is God" (Hebrews 3:4).

Humankind affirms "God exists!"

The belief in the existence of God is part of humankind's intuitive knowledge. Intuitions are fundamental thoughts, without which a person would not be rational. They embrace such general intuitive truths as the existence of matter or energy, mind, space, infinity, time, eternity, beauty, truth, cause, effect, and number. They cover also the axioms of mathematics, the sense of moral right and wrong, and the belief in a higher being.

You may see states without walls, without laws, without coins, without writing; but a people without a god, without prayers, without religious exercises and sacrifices, has no man seen. (Plutarch)
There never was any nation so barbarous, nor any people so savage, as to be without some notion of gods. (Cicero)

Civilizations of all times and places have acknowledged that a supreme being exists.

Conscience affirms "God exists!"

Conscience is "knowledge with" (*con* + *science*). By nature, human beings "know with" *someone* that certain deeds are wrong and will be punished. Where does this knowledge come from? Humankind is willingly or unwillingly admitting the existence of a moral order, a divine Judge. Conscience is the judge within human beings. (See Romans 2:14–15.)

The Bible affirms "God exists!"

Broadly speaking, there are two "books" through which God makes Himself known: The book of nature and the book of revelation.

Nature tells us	The Bible tells us
1. That God *is*	1. *Who* God is
2. That certain thoughts and actions are *wrong*	2. of God's forgiveness for human sin
	3. of God's eternal love in Christ
3. of God's justice and judgment	

The natural, or innate, knowledge of God may be compared to looking at a huge cave with a single candle. The supernatural, or revealed, knowledge of God may be compared to seeing the cave in the light of the sun. The Son of God reveals the Father.

No one has ever seen God; the only God, who is at the Father's side, He has made Him known. (John 1:18)

Who Is God

"God is Spirit" (John 4:24)—that is, a personal being without flesh and blood.

Human beings cannot draw or paint God. Sometimes God is pictured as an old man with a long, flowing beard, "the Ancient of Days," as in Michelangelo's

The Creation of Adam. But the picture is merely an artist's conception.

Air, ether, or gas is not spirit, for it is not a person. The angels are created spirits, without body and soul.

Attributes of God

An attribute is anything that can be said about a person or thing.

Eternal. God is without beginning and without end, like a ring or a circle.
There was never a time when God was not. He exists to all eternity.
How long is eternity? There is a little bird that returns every thousand years to a mountain of granite, wipes its beak on the mountaintop and flies away. When the little bird has worn down the mountain, a small fraction of eternity has passed—so the legend has it.

Eternity is another miracle we in this life cannot fully understand, for in the presence of God time as we know it does not exist.

- **Unchangeable.** God remains the same for all time; His will for His creation does not change from generation to generation.

- **Omnipotent.** *Omni* means "all." God is all-powerful, almighty. God made the world and preserves it. He parts the sea, stops the sun and moon in their courses, heals the sick, raises the dead, and gives eternal life.

- **Omniscient.** God is all-knowing. His knowledge and understanding is perfect and absolute. He knows everything about everything. He knows our every thought, word, and action. He understands our motives and plans. God's omniscience provokes both awe (fear) and comfort in human beings.

- **Omnipresent.** *Omnipresent* means "all-present." God is everywhere at the same time. Gravity, electromagnetic radiation, or cosmic rays are normally present all over the earth. God is always present.

- **Holy.** God is righteous, pure, without fault. Everything good and perfect comes from the Father, "with whom there is no variation or shadow due to change" (James 1:17).

- **Just.** God is fair and impartial. He rewards righteousness and punishes iniquity.

- **Faithful.** God keeps His promises.

- **Good.** God is kind. He desires our welfare.

- **Merciful.** God shows steadfast love and friendly compassion. His hands of mercy are always extended toward His creation.

- **Gracious.** God gives freely His undeserved kindness. He is rich in love and forgiveness.
- **Love**

The Only True God . . .

is the triune God.

There is only one God; but in this one divine Essence are three distinct, separate Persons: Father, Son, and Holy Spirit.

- The Father is God; the Son is God; the Holy Spirit is God. Yet there are not three Gods, but only one.

- The Father is eternal; the Son is eternal; the Holy Spirit is eternal. Yet there are not three eternal Beings, but only one.

- The Father is uncreated; the Son is uncreated; the Holy Spirit is uncreated. Yet there are not three uncreated Gods, but only one.

Each Person is not a "part" of God, so that the three together make the complete God, but each one is the full God.

Nor is each Person a different phase, aspect, or manifestation of God. Each Person is distinct.

There is no perfect analogy of the Holy Trinity anywhere in the realm of nature or reason.

Christians confess the mystery of the Trinity in Unity, and Unity in Trinity.

Imperfect Illustrations of the Trinity

1. **Three letters** form **one word**: G-O-D.

2. **The tree** has roots that draw in soil nutrients, a trunk that serves as a conduit, and leaves that absorb carbon dioxide and give off oxygen. Yet these three different parts with their different functions make up one tree.

3. **St. Patrick's example**: the shamrock.

4. **Hans Egede's example**: vapor, liquid, and solid are three "kinds" of water (mist, river, ice). Though water is present in these three ways, it is still always water: H_2O.

5 **Electricity** is light, heat, and power in one reality.

6. **Light** refracted through a prism or a dewdrop. Is light one color? What seems to be white is really a combination of all the colors of the rainbow.

7. **Triangle**. The sides and angles are equal; yet they are three distinct sides and angles.

8. **1 × 1 × 1 equals 1**.

Christians alone believe in the triune God. Religions that do not believe in the triune God are not Christian.

God Forbids

Idolatry.

Coarse idolatry is to worship any creature as God, or to believe in a god who is not the triune God.

Some civilizations worship human beings. In ancient times, kings and emperors were often worshiped as "gods" after their death. Some kings and emperors demanded to be worshiped as—and called!—"god" during their lifetime.

In modern times, fans of Elvis Presley have gathered to revere the rock-and-roll star as a "god." Worshipers raise their hands, spell and chant Presley's name, dance, and pray to "the King."

They believe that Elvis "watches over" them, and some claim to see him standing near an altar, decorated with candles, flowers, and music memorabilia.

Simple idolatry is to place something other than God first in your life. When we fear, love, or trust in ourselves or any other creature more than we fear, love, and trust in God, we are, simply, idolaters.

God Commands Us to *Fear* Him

The fear of God is reverence and spiritual worship of God. In this sense Scripture everywhere uses the expression "the fear of God." For the worship of God in its truest form does not consist in works, however great and holy, but in true and genuine reverence. (Martin Luther, What Luther Says, §1524)

Some people are afraid of driving over a bridge. Many will drive hours out of their way to avoid one. Others will try to cross but are consumed with fear in the middle of the bridge; they often cannot drive on. They block traffic.

Some years ago, *USA Today* reported that Michigan's Timid Motorist Program assists hundreds of drivers each year across the Mackinac Bridge, a five-mile-long bridge that rises two hundred feet above the water. At Maryland's Chesapeake Bay Bridge, more than four miles long and also two hundred feet above the water, thousands of people are helped across each year. For both locations, a bridge attendant, at the request of a driver, will get behind the wheel of the car and drive the vehicle safely over the bridge.

Some people "fear" bridges. They stand in awe of the bridge, its height and length, and have a sober respect while in its presence. God commands that we fear Him—that is, stand in awe of Him—and have a sober respect and reverence for His power, glory and grace. (Adapted from *USA Today*, as quoted in *Contemporary Illustrations for Preachers, Teachers, and Writers*, p. 71.)

Negative Examples

1. Abraham feared the Egyptian pharaoh more than God (Genesis 12:11–13).

2. King Jehoiachin feared Nebuchadnezzar more than he feared the living God (Jeremiah 22:25; see also 42:11).

3. Peter feared the crowds more than God; he denied the Savior (Luke 22:54–62).

God Commands Us to *Love* Him

[God] gave us His Son, poured out His great treasure most generously and sank and drowned all our sins and filth in the vast sea of His great goodness so that the heart cannot but let this great love and blessing draw it to love in return and then be prepared willingly to fulfill the divine commandments. Otherwise the heart cannot love; it must find that it has been loved first. One cannot love first. Therefore God comes, takes hold of the heart, and says: Learn to know Me. ["]Why, who are You?["] I am Christ; I have plunged into your wretchedness, have drowned your sin in My righteousness. This knowledge softens your heart. Therefore you cannot but turn to Him. In this way—when one learns what Christ is—love is taught. (Martin Luther, What Luther Says, §2564)

Negative Examples

1. The rich young man loved money and possessions more than Christ (Matthew 19:16–22).

2. The prophet Eli loved his sons more than he loved the Lord (1 Samuel 2:12–36).

God Commands Us to *Trust* Him

The three-year-old felt secure in his father's arms as Dad stood in the middle of the pool. But Dad, for fun, began walking slowly toward the deep end, gently chanting, "Deeper and deeper and deeper," as the water rose higher and higher on the child. The boy's face showed more and more panic, and he held all the more tightly to his father, who, of course, easily touched the bottom of the pool.

In truth, the child had no reason to be frightened or anxious. Though the water, even in the shallowest part, would have been over his head, his father had a secure grip even in the deepest parts. The child was safe in the strong arms of his father; he learned to trust his dad at all times and in all circumstances.

1. Goliath trusted in his own strength and ability. By God's grace and power, David was able to kill the Philistine warrior (1 Samuel 17).

2. Ananias and Sapphira trusted in their own ability to provide for their needs; they lied to God and to their fellow Christians (Acts 5:1–11).

Many people trust in their own resources to help through sickness and hardship; or trust their bank account ("In this God we trust"); or trust their own good works or accomplishments; or trust in superstitions and magical powers, such as knocking on wood, a rabbit's foot, amulets, luck rings, horseshoes, and crystals.

The First Commandment: Summary

1. Know God; that is, recognize Him as the triune God, Father, Son, and Holy Spirit, the Creator, Redeemer, and Sanctifier.

2. Acknowledge and believe in Him; that is, acknowledge His rightful claim on all creation and believe that He alone is God.

3. Fear, love, and trust in Him only.

Fear. We honor God according to the First Commandment, as by the Holy Spirit's power, **we fear to displease God by sinning.** Joseph, Daniel, and the three men in the fiery furnace all feared God. "The fear of the LORD is hatred of evil" (Proverbs 8:13).

Love. **We esteem Him as our highest good.** We love His Word, His ways, and His works in creating, saving, and preserving the world in Christ. We think more of God than we do of anyone or anything else.

Trust. **We rely on Him and expect help from Him.**

A little boy was unafraid as he walked through a dark tunnel, for he had hold of his father's hand; that was trust.

During a storm at sea, everyone on board ship was afraid except the pilot's son. When asked why he was not afraid, he said: "My father is at the wheel."

Job said, "Though He slay me, I will hope in Him," because He is God. (Job 13:15)

David trusted God when he fought against the giant (1 Samuel 17).

Hymn

Holy, holy, holy, Lord God Almighty!
Early in the morning our song shall rise to Thee.
Holy, holy, holy, merciful and mighty!
God in Three Persons, blessed Trinity!

Prayer

I believe in You, O God the Father, my Maker.
I believe in You, O God the Son, my Savior.
I believe in You, O God the Holy Spirit, my Helper.
Glory be to Thee, O Holy Trinity, One God, forever and ever.
Amen.

Bible Readings

Exodus 20:1–17

_____

_____

Matthew 22:34–40

_____

_____

Matthew 3:13–17

_____

_____

Psalm 19

_____

_____

Matthew 19:16–22

_____

_____

Daniel 3

_____

_____

Genesis 22:1–14

_____

_____

Catechetical Review

The Law

1. What is the Law? (The Law is the holy will of God.)

2. What does God tell us in the Law? (God tells us in the Law how we are to be, what we are to do, and what we are not to do.)

3. Where do you find the Law in summary or outline? (In the Ten Commandments.)

4. How often was the Law given? (The Law was given twice.)

5. When was the Law given for the first time? (At creation, God wrote the requirements of the Law into human hearts.)

6. What does this mean? (This means that Adam and Eve by nature knew right from wrong.)

7. Why was it necessary for the Law to be given a second time? (Humankind sinned; the knowledge of the Law thus became blurred.)

8. Through whom did God give the Law a second time? (Through Moses, on Mount Sinai, about 1500 BC)

9. What is the requirement of the First Table of the Law? (Love to God.)

10. What is the requirement of the Second Table of the Law? (Love to humanity.)

11. What, in one word, is the requirement of all the commandments? (Love.)

12. Who is obliged to keep these commandments? (Everyone.)

God and His Attributes

1. How do we know there is a God? (From nature, our conscience, and the Bible.)

2. Why can we not see God? ("God is spirit.")

3. What is a spirit? (A spirit is a personal being without flesh and blood.)

4. What does "God is eternal" mean? (He is without beginning and without end.)

5. What does "God is omnipotent" mean? (God can do everything.)

6. What does "God is omniscient" mean? (God knows all things, even what we think and say.)

7. Where is God? (God is everywhere [omnipresent]: in heaven, on earth, in this room, or wherever I am.)

8. Why can God do no wrong? (He is holy.)

9. Why can we always trust God? (He is faithful and keeps His promises.)

10. Why should we want to fear, love, and trust in God above all things? (He is our best Friend.)

The Triune God

1. Who is the only true God? (The only true God is the triune God.)

2. What does *triune* mean? (*Triune* means "three-in-one and one-in-three.")

3. How many Gods are there? (Only one.)

4. How many distinct Persons are there in the one divine Essence? (Three: Father, Son, and Holy Spirit.)

5. Who is the greatest of the three? (None; they are coequal in power and love.)

6. Can we fully understand the sublime mystery of the Trinity in Unity and Unity in Trinity? (No, but we believe it because the Bible teaches it.)

The First Commandment

1. What does the triune God command by the First Commandment? ("You shall have no other gods.")

2. Of what sin is that person guilty who worships other gods? (Idolatry.)

3. What are the two forms of idolatry? (Coarse and simple idolatry.)

4. When do we commit coarse idolatry? (When we worship any creature as God or believe in a god who is not the triune God.)

5. When do we commit simple idolatry? (When we love ourselves, others, or our possessions more than God.)

6. Of what are they guilty who reject Christ as God? (They are guilty of idolatry.)

7. What does God demand of us by every commandment? (To fear, love, and trust in Him.)

8. What does it mean to *fear* God? (To respect Him so much that we always want to do His will.)

9. What does it mean to *love* God? (To give Him first place in our lives; to give our whole heart to Him.)

10. What does it mean to *trust* God? (To rely on His help and guidance.)

11. Why would we have no trouble keeping the other nine commandments if we succeeded in keeping the First Commandment? (From the fear and love of God, the fulfillment of all commandments must flow.)

Bible Passages

1. [Jesus] said to him, "You shall love the Lord your God with all your heart and with all your soul and with all your mind. This is the great and first commandment." (Matthew 22:37–38)

2. And a second is like it: You shall love your neighbor as yourself. (Matthew 22:39)

3. Love does no wrong to a neighbor; therefore love is the fulfilling of the law. (Romans 13:10)

4. They will perish, but You will remain; they will all wear out like a garment. You will change them like a robe, and they will pass away, but You are the same, and Your years have no end. (Psalm 102:26–27)

5. "For nothing will be impossible with God." (Luke 1:37)

6. Lord, You know everything. (John 21:17)

7. Holy, holy, holy is the LORD of hosts; the whole earth is full of His glory! (Isaiah 6:3)

8. God is love. (1 John 4:8)

9. Hear, O Israel: The LORD our God, the LORD is one. (Deuteronomy 6:4)

10. For although there may be so-called gods in heaven or on earth—as indeed there are many "gods" and many "lords"—yet for us there is one God, the Father, from whom are all things and for whom we exist, and one Lord, Jesus Christ, through whom are all things and through whom we exist. (1 Corinthians 8:5–6)

11. "Go therefore and make disciples of all nations, baptizing them in the name of the Father and of the Son and of the Holy Spirit, teaching them to observe all that I have commanded you. And behold, I am with you always, to the end of the age." Matthew 28:19–20

12. Jesus said to him, "Be gone, Satan! For it is written, 'You shall worship the Lord your God and Him only shall you serve' " (Matthew 4:10)

13. "The Father judges no one, but has given all judgment to the Son, that all may honor the Son, just as they honor the Father. Whoever does not honor the Son does not honor the Father who sent Him." (John 5:22–23)

For Further Study

1. Study the Catechetical Review.

2. Memorize one or more Bible passages.

3. Memorize the order of the historical books of the Bible.

4. Read Commandments 4–6 in the Appendix.

2 The Second Commandment

The Second Commandment

You shall not misuse the name of the Lord your God.

What does this mean? We should fear and love God so that we do not curse, swear, use satanic arts, lie, or deceive by His name, but call upon it in every trouble, pray, praise, and give thanks.

> ## God's *Name:*
> ## Use with Respect

God's name describes Him.

Years ago, a name often identified a person with an occupation or other distinguishing mark: Mr. Miller was from a family of millers; Mrs. Taylor married into a family of tailors; Mr. Longfellow was tall. Most names today do not have such significance.

But God's names describe Him as He is. *God* means "the source and dispenser of all good."

- God Almighty: "El Shaddai" (Genesis 49:25).

- Yahweh: "I AM WHO I AM" (Exodus 3:14).

- Immanuel: "God with us" (Isaiah 7:14; Matthew 1:23)

- Jesus: "Savior" (Matthew 1:21)

- Christ: "The Anointed One" (Matthew 16:16)

We know and call on God by His name.

God's name stands for all that He is and does.

The flag stands for the country. Insult the flag and you insult the country.

God's name stands for God. Misuse the name and you insult God.

God forbids that human beings misuse His holy name.

The sun is always equally hot and luminous in itself, but it is not so to us. Sometimes it is hotter, and sometimes it is colder; sometimes brighter, sometimes less bright; and for hours each day we do not see it at all and are left in darkness and night.

So it is with God and His name. In itself, it is always holy, yet it is not always so among us. It is more revered, more hallowed at one time than at another, and by some it is not hallowed at all. [Our] prayer is that it be [holy,] revered [and honored among us always]—that we [give to God] the glory [and praise] due His name. (Encyclopedia of Sermon Illustrations, *395)*

Wrong Use of God's Name

God's name is used wrongly when we

1. *Curse*. Speak evil of God; wish evil to ourselves or to others.

Examples: "God damn you!" "Go to hell!" "I wish you all the *bad luck* in the world."

Shimei cursed David (2 Samuel 16:5–8).

"His blood be on us and on our children," shouted the crowd at Jesus' trial before Pilate (Matthew 27:25).

It's wrong to curse. To curse another is a sin against a human being made in the image of God (James 3:9). More seriously, it is a sin against the living God.

Cursing betrays a poverty of language.

Cursing is a poor public witness for Christ. When Peter wished to convince others that he was not one of the Lord's disciples, he cursed. Perhaps many people in the courtyard *were* convinced (Luke 22:54–62). When we curse, we may leave the same impression with our friends and neighbors.

Cursing is an insult to God.

Cursing God was punishable by death in the Old Testament (Leviticus 24:14). Even today, "the LORD will not hold anyone guiltless who misuses His name" (Exodus 20:7).

Let no corrupting talk come out of your mouths, but only such as is good for building up, as fits the occasion, that it may give grace to those who hear. (Ephesians 4:29)

---

2. *Swear*. To assert or declare under oath.

a. False oath. Perjury, a deliberate lie. Peter "began to invoke a curse on himself and to swear, 'I do not know this man of whom you speak'" (Mark 14:71). See also Leviticus 19:12.

b. Blasphemous oath. An oath to deny or blaspheme God or to deliberately sin against God's will and purposes. Some men conspired against the apostle Paul: they "bound themselves by an oath neither to eat nor drink till they had killed Paul" (Acts 23:12).

c. Frivolous oath. Thoughtless swearing, such as "Honest to God!" "Oh, Lord, no!" or "Lord, yes!"

Again you have heard that it was said to those of old, "You shall not swear falsely, but shall perform to the Lord what you have sworn." But I say to you, Do not take an oath at all, either by heaven, for it is the throne of God, or by the earth, for it is His footstool, or by Jerusalem, for it is the city of the great King. And do not take an oath by your head, for you cannot make one hair white or black. Let what you say be simply "Yes" or "No"; anything more than this comes from evil. (Matthew 5:33–37)

Lies and oaths are twins. A woman heard a speaker use an oath in almost every sentence. She thought, "This person apparently doesn't often tell the truth, because she is quite afraid we will not believe her."

d. Oaths in uncertain things. Herod swore he would give Salome anything she would ask. She asked for the head of John the Baptist (Matthew 14:6–9).

The examples of Abraham and of his servant (Genesis 24:3), of Paul (2 Corinthians 1:23), and of the Lord Jesus (Matthew 26:63) show that whenever the glory of God or the welfare of our neighbor demands it, we are justified, in God's eyes, in swearing.

To swear means to call upon God to witness the truth of what we say and to punish us if we do not tell the truth.

An oath is like a sword, to be used only at the command of the government, to defend oneself or one's neighbor.

3. *Use Satanic Arts.*

"I am the LORD; that is My name; My glory I give to no other, nor My praise to carved idols" (Isaiah 42:8).

Fortune-telling is wrong, whether by means of cards, astrology, phrenology (reading the bumps on your head), palmistry, crystal gazing, or spirit-messages. God in His love has veiled the future from our gaze. Anticipation of joy or sorrow decreases the one and increases the other.

A famous prince, when he was shown an astrologer's book with the day of his death written in it, replied: "Compare Psalm 31:15: 'My times are in Your hand; rescue me from the hand of my enemies and from my persecutors!'"

Other examples: Using part of God's Word as a charm against sickness; soothsayers, with their incantations.

Spiritism. The medium heals by mesmeric power, or in a trance he or she will discover the remedy for some disease. See Leviticus 19:31.

The so-called divine healing. God did not summarily promise us a double cure from sin and from sickness. Divine healers use His name without His command or promise.

Saul sought to consult the dead through the witch at Endor (1 Samuel 28).

4. *Lie.* To speak untruths.

5. *Deceive by His name.* To use religion as a cloak for hypocrisy.

To teach false doctrine as the Word of God; to pervert the Scriptures.

Example: Ananias and Sapphira (Acts 5:1–11). Church members who on Sunday sing, pray, and talk of applying God's Word in their lives and for the rest of the week are dishonest, corrupt, and evil.

The Right Use of God's Name

Isaac Newton never pronounced the name of God without lifting his hat. Robert Boyle never pronounced the name of God without a reverent pause. In times past, Christians regularly bowed their heads at the mention of the name of Jesus. We may and should use God's name in prayer and worship. Not to use God's name at all is a sin of omission.

Call upon it in every trouble. On difficult days, but also on good days. Make God your confidant, your trusted Friend. Some people call upon God's name only when they are in trouble.

A young woman in college might contact her parents only when she needs money. She misses many opportunities to share her other needs, to thank them for past blessings, and to draw close to her parents while she is away from home.

A young man has a close relationship with his parents. Even as an adult, he confides in his parents and goes for guidance, support, and help. He also shares with them his joys and successes.

Pray, praise. It is easier to pray than to praise. In times of great peril, national crises, or personal danger, Christians will individually and together in fellowship pray to the heavenly Father.

It was natural for George Washington to drop to his knees at Valley Forge and ask God for strength and courage. Abraham Lincoln often confessed that he spent much time in prayer because the responsibilities and challenges of his office were enormous.

A soldier who survived the infamous Bataan Death March during World War II was asked whether he prayed during the ordeal. He replied, "I guess everybody prayed there." While Charles Lindbergh was making his historic flight across the Atlantic, the fans at Yankee Stadium were asked to stand for two minutes to pray for his success. No one thought it strange.

To be a praying Christian does not simply mean to pray occasionally but to pray continually. No one can live by taking a breath only once in a while. A person cannot read by a light that flickers on and off. A ship cannot sail with only an occasional wind. A car cannot be driven regularly with only an occasional fill-up at the gas station. God invites us to "pray without ceasing" (1 Thessalonians 5:17).

It is at times more difficult to remember to praise God. Ten lepers met Jesus one day. They were in dire need of help. It was easy for them to pray, "Have mercy upon us." But only one remembered to return to render praise unto Christ. The Second Commandment enjoins us to pray *and* to praise.

Give thanks. The word *thank* is a distant relative to the Latin word "to know." In order to thank, one must know. The reason why many people—Christians too—fail to give thanks is that they do not know or reflect on their many blessings from God.

We can give thanks for many spiritual blessings: forgiveness of sins and reconciliation with the heavenly Father through the blood of Jesus, the new birth through Holy Baptism, the indwelling and gifts of the Holy Spirit, pardon and peace in the Lord's Supper, and the assurance of heaven.

The list below forms an acrostic of only some of God's rich blessings to us.

A stands for America, land that we love; anesthetic.

B—for books, beauty, Bible, Baptism.

C—for children, church.

D—for dawns, doctors.

E—for education, especially Christian education.

F—for friends, flowers, freedom, fun, father, faith, fire.

G—for God.

H—for hope, home, humor, hinges.

I—for immortality.

J—for Jesus.

K—for knowledge of God.

L—for life, love, light, law, labor, laughter.

M—for mother, memories, music, medicine.

N—for nature, night.

O—for opportunity.

P—for prayer, peace, progress.

Q—for questions and God's answers.

R—for romance.

S—for sorrow, sacrifice, sunsets, Sacrament of the Altar.

T—for truth, tomorrow.

U—for unity, especially the communion of saints.

V—for victories.

W—for worship, work, wages, wheels, water.

X—for all the X-tra things we forgot to mention.

Y—for yesterday, you.

Z—for zest.

Hymn

Take my life and let it be
Consecrated, Lord, to Thee;
Take my moments and my days;
Let them flow in ceaseless praise.

Prayer

We ask You, O Lord, that You would keep our tongues from evil and our lips from speaking deceit as we serve You in our daily lives. As Your holy angels always sing praises to You in heaven, may we, too, with our hearts and voices glorify You forever; through Jesus Christ, Your Son, our Lord. Amen.

Bible Readings

2 Samuel 16:5–13

_____

_____

Matthew 26:69–75

_____

_____

Matthew 14:1–12

_____

_____

1 Samuel 28:3–25

_____

_____

Matthew 7:15–20

_____

_____

Acts 5:1–11

_____

_____

Luke 17:11–19

_____

_____

Catechetical Review

1. What does God forbid by the Second Commandment? (God forbids us to misuse His name.)

2. What is God's name? (God's name is that by which He is called and known.)

3. How is God's name misused? (By cursing, swearing, using satanic arts, lying, or deceiving by His name.)

4. What is cursing by God's name? (Speaking evil of God, wishing evil to ourselves or to others.)

5. What is swearing by God's name? (Calling upon God to witness the truth of what we say and to punish us if we do not tell the truth.)

6. When may a Christian swear or take an oath? (Whenever the glory of God, the welfare of his neighbor, or the government demands it.)

7. What kind of swearing is forbidden? (False and unnecessary swearing.)

8. What are satanic arts? (Fortune-telling, etc.)

9. What is lying? (Telling untruths, half-truths, and falsehoods.)

10. What is deceiving by God's name? (Teaching false doctrine as the Word of God.)

11. What does God command in the Second Commandment? (He commands us to pray, praise, and give thanks.)

12. When shall we call upon God's name? (At all times, not only in times of trouble.)

Bible Passages

1. You shall not take the name of the LORD your God in vain, for the LORD will not hold him guiltless who takes His name in vain. (Exodus 20:7)

2. Speak to the people of Israel, saying, Whoever curses his God shall bear his sin. Whoever blasphemes the name of the LORD shall surely be put to death. (Leviticus 24:15–16)

3. With [the tongue] we bless our Lord and Father, and with it we curse people who are made in the likeness of God. From the same mouth come blessing and cursing. My brothers, these things ought not to be so. (James 3:9–10)

4. And thus Abraham, having patiently waited, obtained the promise. For people swear by something greater than themselves, and in all their disputes an oath is final for confirmation. So when God desired to show more convincingly to the heirs of the promise the unchangeable character of His purpose, He guaranteed it with an oath. (Hebrews 6:15–17)

5. Do not turn to mediums or necromancers; do not seek them out, and so make yourselves unclean by them: I am the LORD your God. (Leviticus 19:31)

6. Behold, I am against the prophets, declares the Lord, who use their tongues and declare, "declares the Lord." (Jeremiah 23:31)

7. This people honors Me with their lips, but their heart is far from Me. (Matthew 15:8)

8. Offer to God a sacrifice of thanksgiving, and perform your vows to the Most High, and call upon Me in the day of trouble; I will deliver you, and you shall glorify Me. (Psalm 50:14–15)

9. Ask, and it will be given to you; seek, and you will find; knock, and it will be opened to you. For everyone who asks receives, and the one who seeks finds, and to the one who knocks it will be opened. (Matthew 7:7–8)

10. Bless the Lord, O my soul, and all that is within me, bless His holy name! Bless the Lord, O my soul, and forget not all His benefits. (Psalm 103:1–2)

11. Oh give thanks to the Lord, for He is good; for His steadfast love endures forever! (Psalm 118:1)

For Further Study

1. Study the Catechetical Review.

2. Memorize one or more Bible passages.

3. Memorize the order of the poetry books of the Bible.

4. Read Commandments 7–10 in the Appendix.

3 The Third Commandment

Remember the Sabbath day by keeping it holy.

What does this mean? We should fear and love God so that we do not despise preaching and His Word, but hold it sacred and gladly hear and learn it.

> ## The Lord's Day
> ## Keep It Holy

God commands us to "observe" or "keep" the day of rest.

He invites us to be occupied in holy words, works, and life.

The command to Israel was this: Worship on the seventh day!

The command to the Church is this: Worship!

What is the Sabbath?

In ancient Israel, the Sabbath was the day of rest (*Sabbath* means "to cease, to stop"). The Sabbath was the seventh day; on the Sabbath, God rested from His work of creation.

And on the seventh day God finished His work that He had done, and He rested on the seventh day from all His work that He had done.

So God blessed the seventh day and made it holy, because on it God rested from all His work that He had done in creation. (Genesis 2:2–3)

The Sabbath was set apart as a special day of worship. For Christians, though, every day is a day of worship, set apart by the sacrificial work of Jesus for our forgiveness, life, and salvation. In Jesus, the Sabbath requirement is fulfilled. God's people receive their rest and renewal in Christ.

Christians are no longer obligated by the Law to keep the *seventh day* holy. Jesus' work on earth reveals God's will: He permitted His disciples to pick heads of grain on the Sabbath (Mark 2:23–28); He healed the sick and lame on the Sabbath (Mark 3:1–6); He allowed a restored paralytic to carry his mat on the Sabbath (John 5:1–11).

Jesus fulfills the Sabbath in His ministry, death, and resurrection. He is the Lord of the Sabbath.

Each day in itself has value. One day is as good as another (Romans 14:5–6).

We celebrate Sunday and other feasts not by divine command but in order to have time and opportunity for public worship. The moral content of the Third Commandment, however, remains for us.

God calls us to worship Him, to hear His Word, to remember daily our Baptism into Christ, and to receive the Lord's body and blood in Holy Communion.

Therefore let no one pass judgment on you in questions of food and drink, or with regard to a festival or a new moon or a Sabbath. These are a shadow of the things to come, but the substance belongs to Christ. (Colossians 2:16–17)

Sunday Is Now Our Sabbath Day

The early Christians chose Sunday as their holy day (Acts 20:7) because these things happened on the first day of the week:

1. God the Father began the creation of the world.

2. God the Son rose from the dead (Easter *Sunday*).

3. God the Holy Spirit founded the Christian Church (Pentecost). Pentecost is fifty days after the Sabbath of Passover week, or the first day of the week (Acts 2:1).

   (See also Acts 20:7; 1 Corinthians 16:2; and Revelation 1:10.)

Sunday reminds us of the Three Persons of the blessed Trinity and the work of creation, redemption, and sanctification.

Ways We Neglect the Sabbath

1. By not going to church at all

2. By going only on occasion; for example, only on Christmas and Easter

3. By going but not listening

   One man said he went to church for forty years, but never heard a sermon. When the minister started to preach, he would mentally review his last week's business and make plans for the coming week.

4. By going and listening but not believing

5. By going and listening and believing but not doing

Excuses! Excuses!

1. I don't have *time*. But you will have time to die.

2. I can read my Bible at *home*.

The story is told of a faithful church member who stopped attending worship services. When the pastor noticed the man had missed services for more than a month, he made a visit to the man's home.

It was a cold, wintery evening, and the pastor saw through the window the man at home alone, sitting in front of a blazing fire. The man welcomed the pastor inside, and together they walked toward the fireplace in the family room.

Before sitting down, the pastor picked up the iron poker and carefully moved a small piece of glowing wood to the front of the fireplace. The pastor sat down and began to ask the man about his family, his work, and his hobbies around the house. They chatted about sports, politics, and local events. After almost an hour, the pastor stood up, picked up the piece of wood in his hands, and held it out to the man.

"It's cold," he remarked. "Apart from the warmth of the fire, it's now cold."

The man paused. "Thank you, Pastor," he replied. "I understand. I'll see you in church on Sunday."

(Adapted from Illustrations for Biblical Preaching, *edited by Michael P. Green, Baker Book House, © 1982, 1985, 1989 by Michael P. Green, p. 60)*

Apart from Christ, from His Word and Sacraments, and from His Body, the Church, we are likely to grow cold. "Let us consider how to stir up one another to love and good works, not neglecting to meet together, as is the habit of some, but encouraging one another, and all the more as you see the Day drawing near" (Hebrews 10:24–25).

3. Going to church won't make me a better Christian.

God strengthens our faith through His Word. We live and grow as Christians only when we are connected to Christ. Jesus said, "I am the vine; you are the branches. Whoever abides in Me and I in him, he it is that bears much fruit, for apart from Me you can do nothing" (John 15:5).

4. I can worship God *in nature* or alone with my *golf clubs*.

As a matter of fact, most people don't worship when they are camping or hiking or enjoying God's creation. Furthermore, though nature tells you of God's majesty, power, and wisdom, nature does not tell us one word of His grace in Christ. "For a day in Your courts is better than a thousand elsewhere" (Psalm 84:10).

5. I already know everything that is preached.

We need regular nurturing from God's Word. Who among us refuses to eat something we recognize as having eaten before.

6. There are many *hypocrites* in the church.

Don't be surprised at that: Jesus said there will be weeds in the wheat fields (Matthew 13:24–30). Don't worry: the weeds will be sifted from the wheat at the great harvest. Naturally, every congregation is made up of imperfect people, of sinners. If all the members were perfect, who would be able to join the church? Jesus forgives our hypocrisy and tenderly invites us to gather together in worship.

7. I must prepare dinner for my family.

Eating on time is not so important as feeding your soul.

Several years ago, the *Chicago Tribune* reported that a business consultant surveyed 110 executives to find out what excuses they hear most from their employees.

Heading the list was "It's not my fault." A close second was "It's somebody else's fault."

Third was "Something else came up." Fourth was "I didn't have time," followed by "We've never done it that way before."

Other excuses were "No one told me to do it," "No one showed me how to do it," "I had too many interruptions," and "I'll get to it later."

Excuses don't impress anyone, least of all God.

Where's your priority? That's the question. The Lord Jesus made our redemption His first priority. He made no excuse for the work of salvation. He did not say, "The way is too long, and the cross is too heavy." Rather He said, "I love My people; therefore I will die for them."

By faith, we say, "I love my Savior. Therefore I will live for Him."

So today the Word itself, Baptism, and the Lord's Supper are our morning stars to which we turn our eyes as certain indications of the Sun of grace. For we can definitely assert that where the Lord's Supper, Baptism, and the Word are found, Christ, the remission of sins, and life eternal are found. (Martin Luther, What Luther Says, *§2862)*

We Keep the Third Commandment

1. By going to church; listening to, believing, and putting into practice God's Word; and receiving His Sacraments. (See Jesus' example in Luke 2:41–52 and Mary's in Luke 10:39.)

2. By praying and reading the Bible daily. (See the example of the Bereans in Acts 17:11.)

3. By supporting the work of the Church (Galatians 6:6–7).

4. By sharing the Gospel with others.

   Years ago, a ship on the Atlantic was in distress because its supply of fresh water had run out. The crew faced a horrible death from thirst, though water was all around!

   When hope was almost gone, they sighted a ship approaching in the distance. At once, they hoisted distress signals. But the only answer was "Dip it up!"

   "Dip it up?" What good would it be to dip up buckets of salt water?

   The crew signaled again, but got the same answer. Finally, in despair, they lowered a bucket.

   Imagine their amazement and joy when it turned out to be fresh water. They didn't know it, but they were at the mouth of the mighty Amazon, whose fresh water flows far out to sea.

   God's fresh water in His Word and Sacrament are always available in worship. Why do we neglect it? Why despair in life? "Dip it up!" (Adapted from Seasonal Illustrations for Preaching and Teaching, *pp. 114–15.)*

Hymn

O day of rest and gladness,
O day of joy and light,
O balm for care and sadness,
Most beautiful, most bright;
On you the high and lowly,
Through ages joined to bless,
Sing, "Holy, holy, holy,"
The triune God confess.

Prayer

Before worship:

O Lord, my creator, redeemer, and comforter, as I come to worship You in spirit and in truth, I humbly pray that You would open my heart to the preaching of Your Word so that I may repent of my sins, believe in Jesus Christ as my only Savior, and grow in grace and holiness. Hear me for the sake of His name. Amen. (*Lutheran Service Book*, inside front cover)

I come into Your house, O Lord, and worship You in Your holy place. Let me hear Your Word, believe Your promises, and confess Your name in my words and actions. Amen.

After worship:

Almighty and merciful God, I have again worshiped in Your presence and received both forgiveness for my many sins and the assurance of Your love in Jesus Christ. I thank You for this undeserved grace and ask You to keep me in faith until, with all Your saints, I inherit eternal salvation; through Jesus Christ, my Lord. Amen. (*Lutheran Service Book*, inside front cover)

Help us, O Lord, so that what we have heard and spoken today, we may believe in our hearts and always live in our lives, to Your glory. Amen.

Bible Readings

Acts 20:7–12

Luke 10:10–16

Matthew 7:24–27

Luke 8:4–15

_____

_____

James 1:21–27

_____

_____

Luke 10:38–42

_____

_____

Mark 12:41–44

_____

_____

Catechetical Review

1. What does God command in the Third Commandment? ("Remember the Sabbath day by keeping it holy.")

2. What is the Sabbath day? (A day of rest and worship.)

3. What day of the week did God set apart for the people of the Old Testament? (The seventh day, or Saturday.)

4. How did they keep the Sabbath holy? (By going to worship and refraining from work.)

5. Of what was the outward peace of that day to remind them? (Of the inward peace that Christ would bring through His cross.)

6. Why do we no longer observe the seventh day, as did the children of Israel before Christ? (Jesus fulfilled the Sabbath in His life, death, and resurrection. Christians are "free" in the Gospel to worship God on any and every day.)

7. What day do we commonly mean when we speak of the Sabbath? (We mean Sunday.)

8. Did God in the New Testament command us to keep any certain day holy? (No.)

9. Why, then, is one day in the week generally observed in a religious way? (That we might have time and opportunity for public worship.)

10. Why did the New Testament Christians choose Sunday as a worship day, or Sabbath? (Sunday reminded the Church of the first day of God's creative work, of the resurrection of Christ, and of the outpouring of the Holy Spirit, all of which occurred on the first day of the week.)

11. What does God forbid by the Third Commandment? (God forbids us to despise preaching and His Word.)

12. How do we misuse the day of worship? (By not coming to church at all, by coming only on occasion, by coming but not listening, by coming and listening but not believing, by coming and listening and believing but not doing.)

13. What should keep us from going to church? (Nothing on a regular basis.)

14. How do we remember the Sabbath day, to keep it holy? (By going to church, listening, believing, and doing.)

15. How else may we show our love for God's Word? (By faithful use of the Sacraments, by praying and reading the Bible daily, by supporting the work of the church, by sharing the Gospel with others.)

Bible Passages

1. For the Son of Man is lord of the Sabbath. (Matthew 12:8)

2. Therefore let no one pass judgment on you in questions of food and drink, or with regard to a festival or a new moon or a Sabbath. These are a shadow of the things to come, but the substance belongs to Christ. (Colossians 2:16–17)

3. Whoever is of God hears the words of God. (John 8:47)

4. Let the word of Christ dwell in you richly, teaching and admonishing one another in all wisdom, singing psalms and hymns and spiritual songs, with thankfulness in your hearts to God. (Colossians 3:16)

5. [Jesus] said, "Blessed rather are those who hear the word of God and keep it!" (Luke 11:28)

6. One who is taught the word must share all good things with the one who teaches. Do not be deceived: God is not mocked, for whatever one sows, that will he also reap. (Galatians 6:6–7)

7. Remember your leaders, those who spoke to you the word of God. Consider the outcome of their way of life, and imitate their faith. (Hebrews 13:7)

For Further Study

1. Study the Catechetical Review.

2. Memorize one or more Bible passages.

3. Memorize the order of the major-prophet books of the Bible.

4. Read Commandments 8–10 in the Appendix.

The Church Year

Two Main Divisions of the Church Year

The Church Year is divided into two parts:

1. The Time of Christmas and Easter (festival portion)

2. The Time of the Church (nonfestival portion)

The Time of Christmas and Easter extends from the First Sunday in Advent to Pentecost.

The Time of the Church extends from Trinity to the Sunday of the Fulfillment (Last Sunday after Pentecost). The Sundays in the Time of the Church are known as the Sundays after Pentecost.

1. The Time of Christmas and Easter

The Church celebrates three major festivals during this time: Christmas, Easter, and Pentecost. A number of lesser festivals also occur.

The Christmas Season

ADVENT. Four Sundays before Christmas. These Sundays remind us of Jesus' advent, or coming into the flesh, of His second advent, of His advent into our hearts through the spoken and visible (sacramental) Word. This season prepares us for Christmas.

CHRISTMAS. The Birth of Jesus, December 25.

THE CIRCUMCISION AND NAME OF JESUS, eight days after Christmas (January 1).

EPIPHANY. The manifestation of Christ to the Gentiles; Twelfth Night, or January 6. Commemorates the visit of the Wise Men.

The Easter Season

LENT. Forty days before Easter, exclusive of the Sundays (46 with the Sundays). However, the Sundays are not Sundays *of* Lent but Sundays *in* Lent.

ASH WEDNESDAY. First day of Lent.

HOLY WEEK. The week before Easter.

PALM SUNDAY or SUNDAY OF THE PASSION. First day of Holy Week. Commemorates Christ's triumphal entry into Jerusalem or the Passion.

MAUNDY THURSDAY. "Maundy," from the Latin *mandatum*. On this evening, Christ gave His disciples the "mandate," the command to "love one another as I have loved you" (John 15:12). It is also the night Jesus instituted the Lord's Supper. It is also known as Holy Thursday.

GOOD FRIDAY. God's Friday or the day when Christ died for our good— that is, for our forgiveness, life, and salvation.

EASTER. The day of Christ's resurrection.

The festivals of the Easter season include

ASCENSION. Forty days after Easter or ten days before Pentecost. Commemorates the coronation of Christ, His return to heaven as Savior and Lord.

PENTECOST. Fifty days after Easter. *Pentecost* means "fiftieth day."

2. The Time of the Church

TRINITY. The Sunday after Pentecost. All honor, praise, and glory is offered to the triune God for the work of redemption (remembered and celebrated from Advent to Pentecost).

From now on, the Sundays are called Sundays *after* Pentecost (e.g., The Second Sunday after Pentecost, The Third Sunday . . .) until Advent begins.

4 The Fourth Commandment

Confirmation Builder—
Lesson 7

Honor your father and your mother.

What does this mean? We should fear and love God so that we do not despise or anger our parents and other authorities, but honor them, serve and obey them, love and cherish them.

The First Table requires love toward God.

The Second Table requires love toward all people.

"Teacher, which is the great commandment in the Law?"

And [Jesus] said to him, "You shall love the Lord your God with all your heart and with all your soul and with all your mind. This is the great and first commandment. And a second is like it: You shall love your neighbor as yourself.

On these two commandments depend all the Law and the Prophets." (Matthew 22:36–40)

For Christians, everyone who has needs—physical, emotional, and spiritual—is our neighbor. Of course, some people are closer than others; for example, fellow members at church, relatives, community friends, and acquaintances. In many ways, Christian love and concern begins here *first.*

Yet the Lord Jesus calls us to love all people—even our enemies (Matthew 5:43–47; Luke 10:25–37).

So then, as we have opportunity, let us do good to everyone, and especially to those who are of the household of faith. (Galatians 6:10)

Peter Miller, a Baptist pastor during the American Revolution, lived in Ephrata, Pennsylvania, and enjoyed the friendship of George Washington.

In Ephrata also lived Michael Wittman, an evil-minded man who did all he could to oppose and humiliate the pastor.

One day, Wittman was arrested for treason and sentenced to die. Pastor Miller traveled seventy miles on foot to Philadelphia to plead for the life of the traitor.

"No," General Washington said, "I cannot grant you the life of your friend."

"My friend!" exclaimed the pastor. "He is my harshest critic and enemy."

When Washington learned the truth, he granted the pastor's request. Peter Miller took Michael Wittman home—no longer an enemy, but a friend. (Adapted from Illustrations for Preaching and Teaching from "Leadership Journal," *p. 142.)*

God Rules through Earthly Authority

God does not rule us directly but indirectly, through His representatives in home, church, school, work, and government.

We are called to honor and respect all lawful superiors as we would God, so long as they command nothing contrary to God's will.

In a word, next to the Gospel (ministry) . . . no better jewel, no greater treasure, no costlier gift, no finer foundation, no more precious possession, exists on earth than a government that administers and upholds justice. (Martin Luther, What Luther Says, *§1753)*

By His almighty power, God controls and rules the universe. On earth, God rules through parents, pastors, teachers, supervisors, and elected and appointed officials.

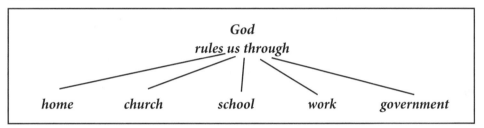

> **God**
> *rules us through*
>
> home   church   school   work   government

Authority
Show
Honor
Respect
Appreciation

- HOME. Parents: father and mother, or those who take their place as stepparents, grandparents, and guardians.

- CHURCH. Pastors, DCEs, deaconesses, and other church workers and leaders who serve Christ and His people.

- SCHOOL. All teachers and administrators in the schools, both in public and church day schools. The basic authority flows from the authority of parents.

- WORK. Supervisors, administrators, everyone who manages our work for the good of the company or organization.

- STATE. All elected and appointed officials, national, state, and local law-enforcement agencies, judges, and designated leaders.

Some time ago the Leaning Tower of Pisa began to lean too far. Seeing that the 180-foot-high tower would soon become dangerous, engineers designed a system to salvage the twelfth-century landmark by holding the lean constant.

First, the engineers injected super-cold liquid nitrogen into the ground around the tower to "freeze the area" and thereby minimize dangerous ground vibrations during their work and in future years. Then they installed cables to pull the structure more upright. The underground cables were expected to pull the tower toward center by at least one inch.

Left to itself, our world resembles the Leaning Tower of Pisa, tilting and heading toward catastrophe. To prevent total anarchy, God establishes governments to maintain order and stability. Authority and government function like the underground steel cables that hold up the Tower of Pisa. The tower still leans. It's not perfect. But the cables prevent total destruction.

We despise authority and the people whom God has placed over us

- by disobeying, talking back, resisting, and rebelling;
- by causing them grief and sorrow.

Some examples from the Bible:

1. The sons of Eli (1 Samuel 2:12, 23, 25).

2. Absalom tried to get the throne from his father David (2 Samuel 15).

3. The boys at Bethel and Elisha (2 Kings 2:23–25).

Some time ago, a man in West Haven, Connecticut, pulled up to an intersection in his car and thought he noticed a problem with his brakes. He shifted the car into park and got out to check the wheels. With no one in the driver's seat, the car suddenly slipped into reverse and took off backwards. The steering wheel spun, and the car began to circle round and round in the middle of the intersection.

The police and fire departments were called. The car kept circling faster and faster, blocking traffic for almost two hours. Finally, the police and fire officials devised a plan to "attack" the car from three sides with construction bulldozers. Soon the car was pinned down by the bulldozers. The firefighters then broke the driver's side window, reached in, and turned off the ignition.

Like a runaway car, people without respect for God's authority are out of control. They are a hazard to themselves and to others. God gives His Law and establishes authority for the good of His creation.

We honor the people whom God has placed over us

- by obeying;
- by loving;
- by serving.

The Fourth Commandment is the first and only commandment with a special promise added: "that it may go well with you and that you may live long in the land" (Ephesians 6:3). This shows the importance God attaches to the commandment.

In this way [God] sets father and mother apart, distinguishes them above all other persons on earth, and places them at His side. For to honor a person is a far higher matter than to love Him; because honor does not comprise love alone but also deference, humility, and awe, as if we were in the presence of majesty there hidden. Nor does honor require that we merely address parents kindly and reverently, but that, both in our hearts and in our actions, we show and make it clear that we esteem them highly and, next to God, consider them supreme. (Martin Luther, What Luther Says, *§3247)*

Reasons for keeping the Fourth Commandment:

1. The love and fear of God.

2. The promise of a long life, which means either length of years or the happiness we associate with a long life.

3. The curse pronounced against those who break this Commandment: "The eye that mocks a father and scorns to obey a mother will be picked out by the ravens of the valley and eaten by the vultures" (Proverbs 30:17).

4. The gratitude for benefits received from good parents.

Biblical examples of obedience and love:

1. **Joseph**. "Hurry and go up to my father and say to him, 'Thus says your son Joseph, God has made me lord of all Egypt. Come down to me; do not tarry" (Genesis 45:9; see also 46:29; 47:11–12).

2. **Solomon**. "Bathsheba went to King Solomon to speak to him on behalf of Adonijah. And the king rose to meet her and bowed down to her. Then he sat on his throne and had a seat brought for the king's mother, and she sat on his right" (1 Kings 2:19).

3. Elisha honored his mentor and teacher (2 Kings 2:12).

4. The Lord Jesus, who from the throne of His cross made provision for the earthly care of His mother (John 19:26–27).

Duties of Parents

Parents are to serve their children in five areas of life:

1. Physical

2. Intellectual

3. Emotional

4. Social

5. Spiritual

By God's design, parents are called to do the following:

1. Attend to the physical needs of their children: nutrition, clothing, shelter, medical and dental care, recreation, and fitness.

2. Train their children's minds, send them to school, help with homework, offer instruction and guidance in solving problems.

3. Provide support and encouragement as their children grow and mature, helping them to find their joy, encouragement, and sense of self in Jesus.

4. Model "social graces" and positive civic behavior for their children, encourage them to get along with people and to be responsible and active in community affairs.

5. Bring up their children up in the "discipline and instruction of the Lord" (Ephesians 6:4); share the Good News and love of Jesus; teach them to pray, to worship, to walk in God's ways. Where possible, Christian parents can send their children to a Christian day school, high school, and university. Christian parents will gladly bring their children to Sunday School and confirmation class and regularly worship as a family.

Hymn

Oh, blest the house, whate'er befall,
Where Jesus Christ is all in all!
A home that is not wholly His,
How sad and poor and dark it is!

Prayer

O Son of Mary: Consecrate our homes.

Son of David: Bless our government.

Son of Man: Rule the affairs of nations.

Son of God: Give us eternal life.

Almighty God, You have commanded us to honor our father and our mother. Give us Your goodness and grace in Christ, that we may love, respect, and obey our parents and all in authority. Be present in our homes and keep us from all harm and danger, that we may live together in peace and share Your blessings with all in need. In the name of Jesus, we pray. Amen.

Bible Readings

1 Samuel 2:12–36

_____

_____

2 Samuel 15:1–6

_____

_____

2 Kings 2:23–24

_____

_____

Ephesians 6:1–9

_____

_____

Luke 2:41–52

_____

_____

Genesis 46:28–34

_____

_____

_____

_____

Catechetical Review

1. What is the requirement of the Second Table of the Law? ("Love your neighbor as yourself.")

2. Who is your neighbor? (My neighbor is everyone who is in need of my love.)

3. Who, above many others, deserves your love? (My parents and others closest to me.)

4. What does God forbid by the Fourth Commandment? (God forbids me to despise my parents or other authorities.)

5. Who are your authorities? (All lawful superiors, such as father and mother, employers, government officials, teachers, and pastors.)

6. Why must we honor and obey all lawful authorities? (They rule over us in God's stead and are therefore His representatives.)

7. What is our duty toward our parents and authorities? (We should give them honor, serve and obey them, and hold them in love and esteem.)

8. When may we disobey our parents and authorities? (When they ask us to do what is against the will of God.)

9. What blessings does the Lord promise those who honor their father and mother? (Long life and happiness.)

10. What other reason have we for loving and serving our parents? (They have done so much for us.)

11 When especially do our father and mother need our love? (When they are old, lonely, or sick.)

12. Who is our perfect example in the keeping of the Fourth Commandment? (Our Lord Jesus.)

Bible Passages

1. So whatever you wish that others would do to you, do also to them, for this is the Law and the Prophets. (Matthew 7:12)

2. Children, obey your parents in everything, for this pleases the Lord. (Colossians 3:20)

3. The eye that mocks a father and scorns to obey a mother will be picked out by the ravens of the valley and eaten by the vultures. (Proverbs 30:17)

4. Servants, be subject to your masters with all respect, not only to the good and gentle but also to the unjust. (1 Peter 2:18)

5. Let every person be subject to the governing authorities. (Romans 13:1)

6. Obey your leaders and submit to them, for they are keeping watch over your souls, as those who will have to give an account. Let them do this with joy and not with groaning, for that would be of no advantage to you. (Hebrews 13:17)

7. Let them first learn to show godliness to their own household and to make some return to their parents, for this is pleasing in the sight of God. (1 Timothy 5:4)

8. You shall stand up before the gray head and honor the face of an old man, and you shall fear your God: I am the Lord. (Leviticus 19:32)

9. We must obey God rather than men. (Acts 5:29)

10. Listen to your father who gave you life, and do not despise your mother when she is old. (Proverbs 23:22)

For Further Study

1. Study the Catechetical Review.

2. Memorize one or more Bible passages.

3. Memorize the order of the minor-prophet books of the Bible.

4. Read the Close of the Commandments in the Appendix.

The Fifth Commandment

5

You shall not murder.

What does this mean? We should fear and love God so that we do not hurt or harm our neighbor in his body, but help and support him in every physical need.

LIFE Respect God's Gift

Life is our most valuable earthly possession.

To safeguard body and life, God gave the Fifth Commandment.

In truth, all human beings are murderers, for by "murder," God means

1. taking the life of a person;

2. hurting a person; and

3. hating and not helping a person.

You have heard that it was said to those of old, "You shall not murder; and whoever murders will be liable to judgment." But I say to you that everyone who is angry with his brother will be liable to judgment; whoever insults his brother will be liable to the council; and whoever says, "You fool!" will be liable to the hell of fire. (Matthew 5:21–22)

What Does God Forbid?

God forbids any action that takes or harms human life. The Bible recognizes three basic types of murder.

1. Literal:

- With one's own hands: for example, Cain murdered Abel (Genesis 4:8).

- Using others to murder at your request: for example, David arranged the death of Uriah (2 Samuel 11:15). Others guilty of this type of murder include Herod, Paul, and Judas.

- Causing an involuntary or accidental death: (Exodus 21:29; Deuteronomy 22:8).

- Taking one's own life (suicide): for example, Saul (1 Samuel 31); Judas (Matthew 27:5).

2. Indirect:

- Plotting or contributing to another's death: for example, Joseph's brothers (Genesis 37:17–35).

- Causing another person bodily harm: for example, Peter hurt Malchus (John 18:10).

3. Figurative:

- Neglecting to help and support others in need: for example, the priest and Levite toward the injured traveler (Luke 10:31–32).

- Hating others, neglecting their needs (1 John 3:15; Genesis 4:5–7).

There are glances of hatred that stab and raise no cry of murder. (George Eliot)

What Does God Say about Murder?

Abortion is murder (Jeremiah 1:5; Psalm 139:16).

The living but unborn are persons in the sight of God from the time of conception. Since abortion takes a human life, it is not a moral option except to prevent the death of another person, the mother. (Luther's Small Catechism with Explanation, Question 52)

Euthanasia is murder (Proverbs 6:16–17; 31:8).

Suicide is murder.

Murder is punishable by death (Genesis 9:6).

The government may use capital punishment upon murderers and other violent criminals (Romans 13:4).

Personal revenge, as well as gang or mob violence that results in death, is murder (Romans 12:19).

Accidental deaths (e.g., by gunfire or crashes) are not always not murder.

Taking an enemy soldier's life in war is not murder.

Legitimate self-defense is not murder.

What Does God Ask of His People?

We should help and befriend our neighbor

- in their physical needs: food, clothing, shelter;

- in their health needs;

- in their emotional needs.

In a French village years ago, the people gathered to plan a warm welcome for their new pastor. They decided that each would bring some new wine to pour into a large barrel; the barrel would then be presented as a gift to the pastor.

The blacksmith, a wise and frugal man, decided that since the rest were bringing wine, he could bring water. No one, he thought, would know the difference.

When the gift was presented and the pastor sampled the "wine," he found it was, in fact, pure water. All the villagers had been "wise and frugal." Every one depended on someone else to give generously (*Encyclopedia of Sermon Illustrations*).

Be kind to one another, tenderhearted, forgiving one another, as God in Christ forgave you. (Ephesians 4:32)

When Louis XII of France ascended the throne, he marked a black cross before the names of his enemies. They heard of it, took fright, and fled the country. But the king assured them of his grace, recalled them, and said, "I have put a cross before your names to remind you of the cross of Christ and His words spoken from the cross, 'Father, forgive them, for they know not what they do.'"

Care of the Body

As Christians, we are called by God to take good care of our body. Our life is a trust from God, an instrument for good; God invites us to use our body to His glory and for the benefit of others. St. Paul writes, "Do you not know that your body is a temple of the Holy Spirit within you, whom you have from God?" (1 Corinthians 6:19).

Because of God's grace, we can use His gift responsibly and wisely. We do not want to abuse our body by

- "burning the candle at both ends";

- neglecting regular dental and medical care;

- not allowing ourselves needed rest and recreation;

- using drugs not prescribed by a physician;

- using other products that could injure or ruin our health.

You are not your own, for you were bought with a price. So glorify God in your body. (1 Corinthians 6:19–20)

Hymn

Son of God, eternal Savior,
Source of life and truth and grace,
Word made flesh, whose birth among us,
Hallows all our human race,
You our head, who, throned in glory,
For Your own will ever plead:
Fill us with Your love and pity,
Heal our wrongs, and help our need.

Prayer

O Lord, our Refuge from the storm, hide us in Your own presence, we pray, and keep us safe from all danger, hardship, and destruction. By Your grace, make us strong in faith, that we may trust You through all adversity and reflect Your love in all circumstances. We ask this in the name of Jesus Christ, Your Son, our Lord. Amen.

Bible Readings

Genesis 4:1–15

_____

_____

Matthew 27:3–5

_____

_____

Matthew 26:51–52

_____

_____

Genesis 37

_____

_____

Luke 10:25–37

_____

_____

Matthew 8:5–13

_____

_____

Genesis 45:1–16

_____

_____

Catechetical Review

1. What does the Fifth Commandment say? (You shall not murder.)

2. What great sin does God forbid by the Fifth Commandment? (The sin of taking human life, literally, indirectly, and figuratively.)

3. How does God permit a murderer to be punished? (With death.)

4. Who has the right to punish a murderer with death? (The government.)

5. What else, besides killing a person, does God forbid by the Fifth Commandment? (Hurting a person or hating a person.)

6. Why should you take good care of your body? (My body is a sacred trust from the Lord and should be used for His kingdom and the good of others.)

7. How do you take good care of your body? (By keeping it as clean, healthy, and strong as I can.)

8. Can you hurt or harm your neighbor without striking a blow? (Yes, when my words and actions bring pain or hardship to another person.)

9. Is quarreling a sin against the Fifth Commandment? (Yes; God forbids all quarreling, nagging, teasing, angry words, hateful looks, and envy in our hearts.)

10. What should we do if we have hurt or harmed our neighbor in his or her body? (We should repent and, as far as possible, make good the wrong.)

11. What is our duty toward our neighbor? (To help and befriend our neighbor in every bodily need.)

12. In what way can we help and befriend our neighbor? (By being peaceable, kind, and obliging.)

Bible Passages

1. Whoever sheds the blood of man, by man shall his blood be shed, for God made man in His own image. (Genesis 9:6)

2. All who take the sword will perish by the sword. (Matthew 26:52)

3. Everyone who hates his brother is a murderer, and you know that no murderer has eternal life abiding in him. (1 John 3:15)

4. Out of the heart come evil thoughts, murder, adultery, sexual immorality, theft, false witness, slander. (Matthew 15:19)

5. If your enemy is hungry, feed him; if he is thirsty, give him something to drink; for by so doing you will heap burning coals on his head. (Romans 12:20)

6. Blessed are the meek, for they shall inherit the earth. Blessed are those who hunger and thirst for righteousness, for they shall be satisfied. Blessed are the merciful, for they shall receive mercy. Blessed are the pure in heart, for they shall see God. Blessed are the peacemakers, for they shall be called sons of God. (Matthew 5:5–9)

For Further Study

1. Study the Catechetical Review.

2. Memorize one or more Bible passages.

3. Review the books of the Old Testament: Genesis to Malachi

4. Memorize Commandments 1–3 in the Appendix.

6 The Sixth Commandment

You shall not commit adultery.

What does this mean? We should fear and love God so that we lead a sexually pure and decent life in what we say and do, and husband and wife love and honor each other.

God's Gift of Sexuality

Next to life itself, the most valuable earthly blessing we have is God's gift of relationships.

In particular, marriage is a blessing from God. God establishes and blesses the relationship between husband and wife, a relationship that includes sexual intimacy and fulfillment.

God gives the Sixth Commandment to protect and nurture both husband and wife, and to provide stable families, communities, and nations.

> ### Sexual Purity and Decency— Treasure It!

Marriage

Marriage was instituted by God.

The man said, "This at last is bone of my bones and flesh of my flesh; she shall be called Woman, because she was taken out of Man. Therefore a man shall leave his father and his mother and hold fast to his wife, and they shall become one flesh." (Genesis 2:23–24)

Marriage is

- established by God for the good of humankind;
- constituted by one man and one woman;
- by mutual consent;
- a life-long union;
- usually celebrated in a public service or ceremony;
- subject to the laws of the state; and
- often blessed with children.

A husband's duty is to love, honor, and respect his wife. A wife's duty is to love, honor, and respect her husband, and to regard him as God's chosen representative in their family.

Marriage is not for a moment; it is for a lifetime. It requires long and serious preparation. It is not to be leaped into, but entered with solemn steps of deliberation. For one of the most intimate and difficult of human relationships is that of marriage. (Gina Cerminara, Draper's Book of Quotations for the Christian World, *§7641).*

The Blessings of Christian Marriage

*That God Himself established marriage and pronounced it good also means that He created it for the good of humanity. He is at work in marriage to accomplish His purposes. In marriage God intends to provide for (1) the relation of man and woman in mutual love (Gen. 2:18); (2) the procreation of children (Gen. 1:28); and (3) the partial remedy for sinful lust (1 Cor. 7:2). Both the fourth and sixth commandments presume and support these purposes of marriage in human life." (*Human Sexuality: A Theological Perspective, Commission on Theology and Church Relations, The Lutheran Church—Missouri Synod, 1981)*

A Christian View of Sexuality

As redeemed children of God, Christians desire to honor God with our lives in every way—including sexuality. In the Sixth Commandment, God calls us to

- rejoice that He has created us male and female;

- affirm that our sexual identity as male and female is good and pleasing to our heavenly Father;

- see marriage as a lifelong relationship, expressed in mutual commitment to His plan and purpose for creation;

- recognize that He wills and commands that sexual intercourse be reserved for marriage alone;

- understand that sexual love is a blessing from God for human pleasure and fulfillment, as well as for human procreation.

Two are better than one, because they have a good reward for their toil. For if they fall, one will lift up his fellow. But woe to him who is alone when he falls and has not another to lift him up!

Again, if two lie together, they keep warm, but how can one keep warm alone? And though a man might prevail against one who is alone, two will withstand him—a threefold cord is not quickly broken. (Ecclesiastes 4:9–12)

A braid appears to contain only two strands of hair. But it is impossible to create a braid with only two strands. If the two could be put together at all, they would quickly unravel.

Here is the mystery: What looks like two strands requires a third. The third strand, though not immediately evident, keeps all the strands tightly woven.

In a Christian marriage, God's gracious presence, like the third strand in a braid, holds husband and wife together. (Adapted from Illustrations for Preaching and Teaching from "Leadership Journal," *p. 149.)*

When Marriage Fails: Divorce

God intends for marriage to be a lifelong relationship. God forbids divorce except for unfaithfulness: adultery and/or intentional desertion.

Through marriage, a husband and wife are joined together as "one flesh" (Genesis 2:24). If a husband or wife withdraws love from his or her spouse for another person, by that act of unfaithfulness he or she divorces from the spouse. The innocent party may go to court and ask that it be publicly known that the spouse has divorced himself or herself privately.

Dissolving a marriage is a serious matter. Psychiatrists, psychologists, and marriage and family counselors report that divorce is similar to the emotional impact of losing a spouse in death.

Christianity teaches that marriage is for life. . . . Churches all agree with one another about marriage a great deal more than any of them agrees with the outside world. I mean, they all regard divorce as something like cutting up a living body, as a kind of surgical operation. Some of them think the operation so violent that it cannot be done at all; others admit it as a desperate remedy in extreme cases. They are all agreed that it is more like having both your legs cut off than it is like dissolving a business partnership or even deserting a regiment. (C. S. Lewis, Joyful Christian, *p. 200)*

What is the Christian's responsibility? To lead a sexually pure and decent life in word and action, in thought and desire.

God calls us, in other words, to avoid adultery.

What does it mean to adulterate a thing? It means to mix it with inferior substances. Pure flour mixed with some inferior stuff becomes adulterated flour. When an article is adulterated, it has lost its purity, it becomes spoiled. God wants us to avoid everything by which our sexual purity is spoiled or adulterated. The opposite of sexual purity is sexual adulteration, or adultery.

Keep Yourself Pure

In what you think . . .

Finally, brothers, whatever is true, whatever is honorable, whatever is just, whatever is pure, whatever is lovely, whatever is commendable, if there is any excellence, if there is anything worthy of praise, think about these things. (Philippians 4:8)

One must live the way one thinks or end up thinking the way one has lived. (Paul Bourget)

Cogitatio, imaginatio, delectatio, assentio.
Thought; Imagination; Fantasizing; Assent.

This is the whole history of the fall into sin.

In a movie, some shipwrecked men are left drifting aimlessly on the ocean in a lifeboat. As the days pass under the scorching sun, their rations of food and fresh water give out. The men grow deliriously thirsty. One night while the others are asleep, one man ignores all previous warnings and gulps down some salt water. He quickly dies.

Ocean water contains seven times more salt than the human body can safely ingest. A person dehydrates because the kidneys demand extra water to flush the overload of salt. The more salt water someone drinks, the thirstier he gets. He actually dies of thirst.

When we lust, we become like this man. We thirst desperately for something that looks like what we want. We don't realize, however, that it is precisely the opposite of what we really need. In fact, it can kill us. (Adapted from Illustrations for Preaching and Teaching from "Leadership Journal," *p. 147.)*

Our body is "the temple of the Holy Spirit"

In what you see . . .

Be on guard against lewd and suggestive pictures, magazines, movies, and immodest dress.

A mother visited her son at college. She found obscene posters hung in his dormitory room While he was away for a few minutes, she hung up her favorite portrait of Christ. When she returned some weeks later, she found all the other posters removed.

In what you hear . . .

Do not listen to obscene lyrics, lewd jokes, rumors, and gossip. These are like sparks that kindle unholy fires.

In what you say . . .

Sex is like fire. In [its proper place,] the fireplace, it's warm and delightful. Outside [its proper place,] it's destructive and uncontrollable." (Illustrations for Biblical Preaching, *p. 333)*

Sexually Pure and Decent

How can a young man keep his way pure? By guarding it according to Your word. (Psalm 119:9)

---

1. Read the Word of God. Joseph thought of God's will (Genesis 39:9).

2. Pray for God's strength, wisdom, and guidance. When alone, pray "O Lord, help me through Christ to overcome this temptation." Or, "Create in me a clean heart, O God" (Psalm 51:10).

3. Work hard, play hard. Idleness is the devil's workshop.

4. Stay away from bad situations; avoid friends and acquaintances who may have a bad influence on you. "Do not be deceived: 'Bad company ruins good morals'" (1 Corinthians 15:33).

5. Worship regularly, gather with Christian friends for fun and recreation.

6. Exercise moderation in all circumstances.

Hymn

Oh, blest that house where faith is found
And all in hope and love abound;
They trust their God and serve Him still
And do in all His holy will!

Prayer

Almighty, eternal God, in Christ You have revealed the mystery of the ages and brought life and salvation to our world. We pray, cleanse the foolish and sinful desires of our hearts, and purify us that we might live to Your glory in all our relationships. By the power of Your Holy Spirit, let us serve You, heavenly Father, in purity, honesty, and integrity; through Jesus Christ, Your Son, our Lord. Amen.

Bible Readings

Genesis 2:18–25

John 2:1–11

Ephesians 5:22–33

Matthew 5:27–32

Genesis 39:1–20

Mark 6:16–28

Proverbs 23:29–35

Catechetical Review

1. What does God forbid by the Sixth Commandment? (God forbids all unfaithfulness—sexual impurity and indecency—in marriage as well as all sexual impurity and indecency.)

2. Who instituted marriage? (God Himself instituted marriage.)

3. For what purpose did God institute marriage? (For the sake of children, mutual companionship, and to restrain immorality.)

4. How many persons form the wedding contract? (Two: one man and one woman.)

5. How long is this union to last? (This union is to last for life.)

6. What is the only scriptural ground for divorce? (Unfaithfulness; that is, through adultery or intentional desertion.)

7. How is marriage to be entered into? (Freely, deliberately, reverently, and with proper fear, love, and trust toward God.)

8. Who ordinarily should perform a Christian marriage? (The pastor.)

9. What is the responsibility of the husband toward his wife? (To love, honor, and respect her.)

10. What is the responsibility of the wife toward her husband? (To love, honor, and respect him, and to regard him as God's chosen representative in their family.)

11. What is the responsibility of all persons, whether married or unmarried? (To lead a sexually pure and decent life in word and action, thought and desire.)

12. What are some dangers to purity? (Indecent materials, videos, shows; bad companions; immodest dress; idleness.)

13. What are some helps to purity? (God's Word and prayer; the Lord's Supper; activity; moderation in fear of God.)

14. Why is it important to watch over our thoughts and desires? (Thoughts and desires give way to deeds.)

Bible Passages

1. [Jesus said,] "Have you not read that He who created them from the beginning made them male and female, and said, 'Therefore a man shall leave his father and his mother and hold fast to his wife, and the two shall become one flesh'? So they are no longer two but one flesh. What therefore God has joined together, let not man separate." (Matthew 19:4–6)

2. [Jesus said,] "I say to you: whoever divorces his wife, except for sexual immorality, and marries another, commits adultery." (Matthew 19:9)

3. Flee from sexual immorality. Every other sin a person commits is outside the body, but the sexually immoral person sins against his own body. (1 Corinthians 6:18)

4. Keep yourself pure. (1 Timothy 5:22)

5. Flee youthful passions and pursue righteousness, faith, love, and peace, along with those who call on the Lord from a pure heart. (2 Timothy 2:22)

6. Do you not know that your body is a temple of the Holy Spirit within you, whom you have from God? You are not your own, for you were bought with a price. So glorify God in your body. (1 Corinthians 6:19–20)

7. [Jesus said,] "You have heard that it was said, 'You shall not commit adultery.' But I say to you that everyone who looks at a woman with lustful intent has already committed adultery with her in his heart." (Matthew 5:27–28)

8. My son, if sinners entice you, do not consent. (Proverbs 1:10)

9. How then can I do this great wickedness and sin against God? (Genesis 39:9)

10. Create in me a clean heart, O God, and renew a right spirit within me. (Psalm 51:10–11)

For Further Study

1. Study the Catechetical Review.

2. Memorize one or more Bible passages.

3. Memorize the order of the Gospels and the historical book of the New Testament.

4. Memorize Commandments 4–6 in the Appendix.

The Seventh Commandment

You shall not steal.

What does this mean? We should fear and love God so that we do not take our neighbor's money or possessions, or get them in any dishonest way, but help him to improve and protect his possessions and income.

Respect for Others

All earthly goods and possessions really belong to God. In His goodness and mercy, He distributes these among people—to some people more, to some less.

We often affirm, "I own this." "She owns that." For practical and legal purposes, these statements are true.

In reality, however, God owns everything. We are only caretakers, stewards, administrators of God's gracious gifts to His creation.

> *The earth is the LORD's and the fullness thereof, the world and those who dwell therein, for He has founded it upon the seas and established it upon the rivers.*
> *(Psalm 24:1–2)*

As stewards, we may use the possessions God has entrusted to us as we wish, as long as we do not contradict God's purposes. We may keep, sell, trade, or give away our possessions. But God commands us never to step over the line between what is ours and what belongs to our neighbor.

God commands all people, "You shall not steal."

It is not our right or prerogative to inquire how anyone acquired his or her possessions. It is never right to take what does not rightfully belong to another person, nor can we ever justify taking anything that does not properly belong to us.

The picture shows the arrangement God commands us to respect and live by.

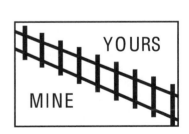

Stealing

1. **Robbery** is stealing by force, as with gun, knife, or other deadly weapon. The traveler on the road to Jericho was beaten (Luke 10:30).

2. **Theft** is stealing by stealth: breaking into a house, shoplifting, pilfering, cheating on taxes and reports. (Gehazi [2 Kings 5:20–24] misrepresented his master, Elisha, to get riches from Naaman).

3. **Usury** is stealing by overcharging, charging excess interest, or by paying wages that are too low.

4. **Fraud** is stealing through false advertising or sales (i.e., cheating). See Leviticus 19:35.

5. **Covetousness** is the desire to have or acquire improperly, the wish to "get something" at the expense of someone else. Gambling is the lust for possessions without personal responsibility.

6. **Envy** is to begrudge other people their rightful possessions or happiness.

7. **Partnership with thieves** is also stealing. See Proverbs 29:24.

8. **Laziness** is an unwillingness to be responsible in our daily work and obligations. See 2 Thessalonians 3:10.

9. **"Robbing God."** Poor stewardship of God's gifts is theft against God. "Will man rob God? Yet you are robbing Me. But you say, 'How have we robbed You?' In your tithes and contributions" (Malachi 3:8).

God commands us to give faithfully, willingly to Him.

Just Retribution

Here and Hereafter

1. One thief through another.

2. Unhappy in the possession of stolen goods.

3. Detection and sentence. The bridge that led from the court where men were tried to the "Tombs" in New York City was known as "The Bridge of Sighs."

4. "The way of transgressors is hard" (Proverbs 13:15 KJV). Crime does not pay.

We Honor God according to the Seventh Commandment When We Help Our Neighbor Improve and Protect His Property and Business

1. **To improve** by advice, encouragement. Not a knocker of the firm you work for; faithful in discharge of duties. If able, offer loan of money.

Abraham gave Lot the choice (Genesis 13:9). Joseph advised his brothers how to act before Pharaoh that they might receive the land of Goshen. (Genesis 46:31–34).

At Wittenberg, a student did not have money for his trip home. At last, he asked Luther for some, but Luther had none at the time. "O God, where shall I seek help?" Luther's eye fell on a gold-lined silver goblet that he had recently received as a gift from the Elector. He gave that to the student.

2. **To protect property** from destruction by fire and various forms of vandalism, as breaking windows, or tearing up hymnals in church, picking flowers, walking on lawns; Halloween pranks.

To protect business from undermining influences and slanderers.

Have you always helped your neighbor?

Have you ever stolen? Ever thought of stealing? Ever borrowed without returning? Then you are a thief in the sight of God.

Hymn

God of grace and God of glory,
    On Your people pour Your pow'r;
Crown Your ancient church's story;
    Bring its bud to glorious flow'r.
Grant us wisdom, grant us courage
    For the facing of this hour,
For the facing of this hour.

Prayer

O Lord our God, You have commanded that we should receive Your many blessings with thankful and generous hearts. Give us Your grace, we pray, to use all of our talents and abilities for Your glory and for the good of others. Help us to respect the gifts and possessions You have given to others, so that we might encourage all people to trust Your mercy and love in Jesus Christ our Lord. In His name, we pray. Amen.

Bible Readings

1 Corinthians 6:20

_____

_____

John 12:1–8

_____

_____

2 Kings 5:20–27

_____

_____

Luke 19:1–10

_____

_____

Leviticus 6:1–7

_____

_____

Genesis 13:1–12

_____

_____

_____

_____

Catechetical Review

1. What does God forbid by the Seventh Commandment? (God forbids us to take our neighbor's money or goods, or to obtain anything by dishonest means or actions.)

2. Who really owns all money and goods? (God owns everything.)

3. What then is our relationship to money and goods? (We are stewards.)

4. What is a steward? (A steward is a caretaker of someone else's possessions.)

5. Why is it important that we use God's possessions in the way He wants us to use them? (We must at the Last Day give a report on how we used His gifts.)

6. For what purposes should we use God's gifts? (For supporting ourselves, our loved ones, the poor and needy, church, and missions.)

7. What is required in stewards? ("It is required of stewards that they be found trustworthy" [1 Corinthians 4:2].)

8. Who are unfaithful stewards? (Misers, spendthrifts, idlers, gamblers; those who do not support the church according to their means.)

9. What forms of stealing are forbidden? (Taking what belongs to the home, school, church, store, or to a person buying or hiding stolen goods; keeping what we borrowed; cheating; damaging property; participating in illegal and dishonest ventures by helping a thief.)

10. What must we do if we have stolen? (We must confess our wrong, return the stolen goods, and steal no more.)

11. Why should we be careful not to steal even in a small way? (Bad beginnings often lead to big bad endings.)

12. What is our duty toward our neighbor? (To help him to improve and protect his property and business.)

Bible Passages

1. Let the thief no longer steal, but rather let him labor, doing honest work with his own hands, so that he may have something to share with anyone in need. (Ephesians 4:28)

2. Give to the one who begs from you, and do not refuse the one who would borrow from you. (Matthew 5:42)

3. Whoever is generous to the poor lends to the LORD, and He will repay him for his deed. (Proverbs 19:17)

4. For even when we were with you, we would give you this command: If anyone is not willing to work, let him not eat." (2 Thessalonians 3:10)

5. The wicked borrows but does not pay back, but the righteous is generous and gives. (Psalm 37:21)

6. The partner of a thief hates his own life; he hears the curse, but discloses nothing. (Proverbs 29:24)

For Further Study

1. Study the Catechetical Review.

2. Memorize one or more Bible passages.

3. Memorize the order of Paul's Letters in the New Testament.

4. Memorize Commandments 7–10 in the Appendix.

8 The Eighth Commandment

Confirmation Builder—
Lesson 11

You shall not give false testimony against your neighbor.

What does this mean? We should fear and love God so that we do not tell lies about our neighbor, betray him, slander him, or hurt his reputation, but defend him, speak well of him, and explain everything in the kindest way.

> ## A GOOD NAME
> ### Respect and Defend It

The Second Table of the Law

Commandment	Purpose
4	To protect family
5	To protect life
6	To protect marriage
7	To protect property
8	To protect reputation

Family, life, marriage, and property are God's gifts to humankind; each is necessary to life.

A good name is also necessary for our earthly life. To safeguard reputation, God gave the Eighth Commandment.

A young man supposedly went to the Greek philosopher Socrates to learn public speaking. On being introduced, he talked so incessantly and so disrespectfully of others that Socrates immediately demanded twice his ordinary fee. "Why charge me double?" the young man rudely asked. Socrates replied, "I must teach you twice: first how to control your tongue, and second how to speak." (Adapted from Illustrations for Biblical Preaching, *p. 378)*

There is nothing about a man or in him which can do greater and more extensive good or harm in spiritual or in secular matters than the tongue, although it is the smallest and weakest of his members. (Martin Luther, What Luther Says, *§4278)*

The ability to communicate with words is one of God's many blessings to the world. "Language is the Rubicon that divides human beings from animals" (Max Mueller). "Speech is civilization itself" (Thomas Mann). Language and speech are gifts that can be used to great good, but also to great evil.

Every kind of beast and bird, of reptile and sea creature, can be tamed and has been tamed by mankind, but no human being can tame the tongue. It is a restless evil, full of deadly poison. (James 3:7–8)

GUARD YOUR TONGUE

A spoken word is like a stone cast into the water, it forms circles that keep on widening.

A young man during the Middle Ages went to a monk, saying, "I have sinned by telling slanderous statements about someone. What should I do now?" The monk replied, "Put a feather on every doorstep in town." The young man did it. He then returned to the monk, wondering if there was anything else that he should do. The monk said, "Go back and pick up all the feathers." The young man replied, "That's impossible! By now the wind will have blown them all over town." The monk replied, "So has your slanderous word become impossible to retrieve." (Adapted from Illustrations for Biblical Preaching, *p. 175)*

Mark Twain remarked, "One of the striking differences between a cat and a lie is that a cat has only nine lives."

"How great a forest is set ablaze by such a small fire!" Because a cow kicked over a lamp, the city of Chicago went up in flames.

An old saying notes, "After two years of life, we learn to talk; but then we spend the rest of our days on earth trying to control our mouth."

The tongue is a small but exceedingly unruly member. We can tame horses with bits, and turn ships that are driven by fierce winds with a small rudder, but the tongue can no man tame.

Stolen property may be returned, but a shattered reputation cannot always be restored. Slander is, in many ways, worse than theft.

God Forbids False Testimony in

1. courts of law;

2. daily conversation;

3. school and work environments; and

4. church.

In Court

Here are several examples of how one may violate the Eighth Commandment in a court of law:

- The JUDGE who renders an unjust verdict (e.g., Pontius Pilate)

- The WITNESSES who pervert or misrepresent the truth or who withhold facts (e.g., the false witnesses against Jesus in Matthew 26:59–61 and against Naboth in 1 Kings 21:13)

- The JUDGE or members of the JURY who accept bribes (e.g., Felix in Acts 24:25–26)

- The LAWYER who, though aware of his client's guilt, knowingly presents falsified evidence or perjured testimony

In Daily Life, School, Work, and Church

We do NOT, out of a deceitful heart, honor God in these ways:

- Tell lies: speak falsehoods, withhold truth

    —Gehazi (2 Kings 5:22, 25)
    —What kinds of "lies" do people tell? Social, business, professional, and "white" lies. Each is a lie—a falsehood or withholding of the truth.

- Betray others through acts of treachery, disloyalty, or breaking faith with someone to hurt or kill

    —Delilah betrayed Samson to the Philistines (Judges 16:18).
    —Judas betrayed Jesus (Matthew 26:14–16).

- Slander others: to spread lies, false reports, to defame and libel.

    —Absalom sought to turn the hearts of the people away from his father (2 Samuel 15:1–6).
    —A group of fourth-graders in a Chicago school once accused a substitute teacher of sexual abuse. By evening, the story had become a lead topic of TV and radio news reports and in local papers. The school board promised a complete investigation.
    The next day police investigators interviewed fourteen of the children, and authorities quickly determined the charges were false. Apparently, the children made their false accusation because the substitute teacher threatened to report the class for unruliness.
    —Slander is a vicious act—a crime—that does lasting harm.

- Hurt one's reputation: to injure or destroy a person's position, status, or character in the eyes of others.

We DO honor God according to the Eighth Commandment in these ways:

- Defend our neighbors: Take their part, especially in their absence. Don't lend an ear to gossip. The ear can sin as well as the tongue. Martin Luther said this: "The slanderer has the devil on the tongue, and the listener has him in the ear."

- Speak well of our neighbors. Point out their good traits. Jonathan pointed out the good traits of David (1 Samuel 19:4). People spoke well of the centurion (Luke 7:4–5).

- Explain everything in the kindest way: To "put the best construction" on her words and actions.

    —Alexander the Great is said to have held one ear closed when someone was denounced in his presence; it was, he insisted, reserved for the accused.
    —A woman once brought a complaint to the king about her neighbor. The king said, "That is none of my business." The woman answered, "But, my lord, he speaks evil of you." "Then that is none of your business," the king answered.

A gossip is a person who loves to engage in idle talk, groundless rumor, and mischievous tattle. Envy is the mother of gossip.

Our neighbor's faults fill a little bag; but we see the bag in front of us, and so we readily see his or her mistakes.

Surely no human being has kept the Eighth Commandment. We are eager to hear "bad news" and rumors about other people, and we have readily gossiped against family members, friends, and neighbors. We have all violated God's commandment against false testimony.

Our Lord Jesus Christ, by His innocent suffering and death, has atoned for our many sins.

He committed no sin, neither was deceit found in His mouth. When He was reviled, He did not revile in return; when He suffered, He did not threaten, but continued entrusting Himself to Him who judges justly. He Himself bore our sins in His body on the tree, that we might die to sin and live to righteousness. By His wounds you have been healed. (1 Peter 2:22–24)

In Christ, we are forgiven; let us learn of His grace, His strength, His example.

Hymn

Let us ever walk with Jesus,
    Follow His example pure,
Through a world that would deceive us
    And to sin our spirits lure.
Onward in His footsteps treading,
    Pilgrims here, our home above,
Full of faith and hope and love,
Let us do our Father's bidding.
Faithful Lord, with me abide,
I shall follow where You guide.

Prayer

Almighty God, You have sent the Spirit of truth to us to guide us into all truth. Rule in our hearts, we pray, by Your grace and power, that we may be truthful in our thoughts, words, and actions. Keep us, merciful Lord, in Your fatherly care and protection, that no fear or sinful ambition may make us deceitful in our speech or behavior. Cleanse us, we ask, from everything false and wrong, and bring us into the freedom of Your Good News in Christ Jesus our Lord, in whose name we pray. Amen.

Bible Readings

1 Kings 21:1–16

_____

_____

1 Samuel 22:6–19

_____

_____

Matthew 26:59–61

_____

_____

2 Samuel 15:1–6

_____

_____

James 3

_____

_____

1 Samuel 19:1–7

_____

_____

Luke 7:4–5

_____

_____

_____

Catechetical Review

1. What does God forbid by the Eighth Commandment? (God forbids us to give false testimony against our neighbor.)

2. When do we "give false testimony"? (When we tell lies about, betray, slander, or hurt our neighbor's reputation.)

3. What does it mean to "tell lies about" our neighbor? (To spread a false statement or to withhold the truth.)

4. What does it mean to "betray" our neighbor? (To reveal that which our neighbor has told us in secret.)

5. What does it mean to "slander" our neighbor? (To spread evil about our neighbor.)

6. Where is this sin of giving false testimony commonly committed? (In courts, daily conversation, school, work, and church.)

7. What is our duty toward our neighbor? (To defend and speak well of him or her, and to explain everything in the kindest way.)

8. When do we "defend" our neighbor? (When we speak up for him or her, especially when our neighbor is unable to provide a defense.)

9. When do we "speak well of" our neighbor? (When we point out his or her good points and intentions.)

10. When do we "explain everything in the kindest way"? (When we put the best construction on his or her words and actions.)

Bible Passages

1. A false witness will not go unpunished, and he who breathes out lies will not escape. (Proverbs 19:5)

2. Whoever goes about slandering reveals secrets, but he who is trustworthy in spirit keeps a thing covered. (Proverbs 11:13)

3. Humble yourselves before the Lord, and He will exalt you. Do not speak evil against one another, brothers. The one who speaks against a brother or judges his brother speaks evil against the law and judges the law. But if you judge the law, you are not a doer of the law but a judge. (James 4:10–11)

4. "Judge not, and you will not be judged; condemn not, and you will not be condemned; forgive, and you will be forgiven." (Luke 6:37)

5. Love bears all things, believes all things, hopes all things, endures all things. (1 Corinthians 13:7)

For Further Study

1. Study the Catechetical Review.

2. Memorize one or more Bible passages.

3. Memorize the order of the General Epistles (letters) in the New Testament.

4. Memorize the Close of the Commandments in the Appendix.

9 The Ninth and Tenth Commandments

Confirmation Builder—
Lessons 12 and 13

The Ninth Commandment

You shall not covet your neighbor's house.

What does this mean? We should fear and love God so that we do not scheme to get our neighbor's inheritance or house, or get it in a way which only appears right, but help and be of service to him in keeping it.

The Tenth Commandment

You shall not covet your neighbor's wife, or his manservant or maidservant, his ox or donkey, or anything that belongs to your neighbor.

What does this mean? We should fear and love God so that we do not entice or force away our neighbor's wife, workers, or animals, or turn them against him, but urge them to stay and do their duty.

```
LUST
Beware of Fire
```

Both commandments are about unrestrained desire. To *covet* is to have a sinful desire for anyone or anything that belongs to our neighbor.

It is not wrong to desire—covet—spiritual or earthly blessings. It is wrong, however, to covet what God has not intended to give us or what God has forbidden. It is wrong to covet what belongs to someone else.

Eve, together with her husband, **Adam**, ate the fruit of the tree of the knowledge of good and evil; she coveted "wisdom" (Genesis 3:6).

Ahab wished to have Naboth's vineyard. His wish was not wrong in itself; the king first offered Naboth a fair price for the land. When Naboth refused to part with his inheritance, however, Ahab was wrong to covet the property. "I wish to have that vineyard at any cost," said Ahab, in effect. "If I can't get it by fair means I will arrange to take it by force" (1 Kings 21:1–16).

David lusted after Bathsheba. He coveted another man's wife. David, too, arranged for Uriah's death in order to take Bathsheba as his wife (2 Samuel 11:2–4).

Paul wished to have a servant run his errands and wait on him during his captivity in Rome. But he *did not* wish to have Onesimus, for Paul knew that Onesimus belonged to Philemon. So Paul sent Onesimus back to Philemon. Read the Epistle to Philemon.

What then shall we say? That the law is sin? By no means! Yet if it had not been for the law, I would not have known sin. For I would not have known what it is to covet if the law had not said, "You shall not covet." But sin, seizing an opportunity through the commandment, produced in me all kinds of covetousness. (Romans 7:7–8)

When Pompeii was being excavated, there was found a body that had been embalmed by the ashes of Vesuvius. It was that of a woman. Her feet were turned toward the city gate, but her face was turned backward toward something that lay just beyond her outstretched hands.

The prize for which those frozen fingers were reaching was a bag of pearls. Maybe she herself had dropped them as she was fleeing for her life. Perhaps she had found them where they had been dropped by another. Though death was hard at her heels, and life was beckoning to her beyond the city gates, she could not shake off their spell. She had to return to pick them up, with death her reward.

To covet is often to choose death. (Adapted from Feminine Faces, *by Clovis G. Chappell)*

A child shoved his hand in the opening of a very expensive Chinese vase. When he could not pull it out again, he raised a frightful cry. His parents tried desperately to help the child, but they also could not remove the boy's hand from inside the vase.

Finally, there was nothing left to do but to break the beautiful, expensive vase. And when the father smashed it with a hammer blow, it became clear why the child had been hopelessly stuck. His fist grasped a mere quarter which he had seen in the bottom of the vase. He had grabbed it tightly, and in his childish ignorance, was unwilling to let it go. (Adapted from How to Believe Again *by Helmut Thielicke)*

The Ninth and Tenth Commandments remind us that

1. evil desire—coveting—is truly sin;

2. every human being lives with evil desires—covetousness.

What God Forbids

- Scheming to get our neighbor's property or possessions.

  —An adviser once tried to persuade a general not to begin a war with the ancient Romans. "When you have conquered Rome," he asked the general, "What will you do next?"
  "I will conquer Sicily."
  "And when you have conquered Sicily?"
  "Then I will cross over to Africa and conquer it."
  "And when you have conquered Africa?"
  "Then I will conquer Spain . . . and then Greece . . . and then Macedonia," came the general's reply. "Then we will sit down and enjoy ourselves."
  "Sir," responded the adviser, "Why not sit down in your own kingdom and be content with everything you have now?"

- Getting something in a way that only appears right.

- Enticing or forcing away our neighbor's spouse, friends, workers, or anything that belongs to our neighbor.

God Calls Us

- To help and be of service to all people.

- To encourage others to be faithful in their relationships and duties.

- To be content and grateful for His many blessings and helpful to our neighbor with regard to his or her possessions, spouse, and workers.

—A couple who had lived in the same house for 30 years grew tired of their surroundings. "Let's sell and move!" they decided together. So they listed their house with a Realtor, who immediately began to write an elaborate listing for the newspaper and realty network.

Before the agent turned in the description, however, she showed the ad to the couple. It was a glowing description of their home, noting the excellent location, solid brick exterior, comfortable rooms, large lot, and many other valuable features.

The couple looked at each other. "On second thought," the wife replied, "we really are happy here. I'm not sure we would be content in another home."

Hymn

Now thank we all our God
    With hearts and hand and voices,
Who wondrous things has done,
    In whom His world rejoices;
Who from our mother's arms
    Has blest us on our way
With countless gifts of love
And still is ours today.

Prayer

Almighty God, everlasting Father, we thank You for the many blessings of our earthly life, all gifts from Your gracious hand.

Give us Your grace and strength, that we may be content in all situations. Help us to rejoice with others in their success and joy, that we might radiate the love of Christ, who has loved us and redeemed us for all eternity. In His name we pray. Amen.

Bible Readings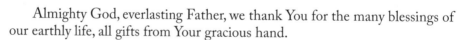

2 Samuel 11:2–4

_____

_____

2 Samuel 15:1–6

_____

_____

Epistle to Philemon

_____

_____

Matthew 6:19–23

_____

_____

Genesis 19

_____

_____

Luke 19:41–44

_____

_____

Matthew 7:24, 25

_____

_____

Catechetical Review

1. What does God forbid by the Ninth and Tenth Commandments? (God forbids us to covet.)

2. What does *covet* mean? (*Covet* generally means "passionately wish to have.")

3. Is it always wrong to passionately wish for something? (No, but it is wrong to wish to have something at someone else's expense.)

4. What, for instance, should we not wish to have at the expense of our neighbor? (A person's house, spouse, friends and workers, animals, or personal property.)

5. Why does God forbid us to covet? (He wants us to be satisfied with what He gives us.)

6. What attitude of heart makes for peace of mind? ("Godliness with contentment" makes for peace of mind.)

7. What does God mean by, "You shall not covet"? (We should not have evil desires, but only holy desires, in our heart.)

8. How should we not feel toward our neighbor when he has something we cannot have? (We should not feel envious of him.)

9. What should be our attitude toward our neighbor when God has blessed him with material gifts? (We should be happy with him, and help him that he might enjoy his blessings.)

10. In whom should we find our great delight? ("Delight yourself in the LORD, and He will give you the desires of your heart" [Psalm 37:4].)

Bible Passages

1. For we brought nothing into the world, and we cannot take anything out of the world. But if we have food and clothing, with these we will be content. (1 Timothy 6:7–8)

2. What then shall we say? That the law is sin? By no means! Yet if it had not been for the law, I would not have known sin. For I would not have known what it is to covet if the law had not said, "You shall not covet." (Romans 7:7)

3. Speak to all the congregation of the people of Israel and say to them, You shall be holy, for I the Lord your God am holy. (Leviticus 19:2)

4. Delight yourself in the Lord, and He will give you the desires of your heart. (Psalm 37:4)

5. For you were called to freedom, brothers. Only do not use your freedom as an opportunity for the flesh, but through love serve one another. (Galatians 5:13)

6. Have nothing to do with irreverent, silly myths. Rather train yourself for godliness; for while bodily training is of some value, godliness is of value in every way, as it holds promise for the present life and also for the life to come. (1 Timothy 4:7–8)

For Further Study

1. Study the Catechetical Review.

2. Memorize one or more Bible passages.

3. Review the order of all the books of the New Testament.

4. Review the Ten Commandments in the Appendix.

The Close of the Commandments; Law and Gospel

10

Confirmation Builder—
Lessons 10 and 3

The Close of the Commandments

What does God say about all these commandments? He says: "I, the Lord your God, am a jealous God, punishing the children for the sin of the fathers to the third and fourth generation of those who hate Me, but showing love to a thousand generations of those who love Me and keep My commandments." (Exodus 20:5–6)

What does this mean? God threatens to punish all who break these commandments. Therefore, we should fear His wrath and not do anything against them. But He promises grace and every blessing to all who keep these commandments. Therefore, we should also love and trust in Him and gladly do what He commands.

IF YOU DISOBEY {	Your father Your government Your God	} **what results?** {	Wrath Punishment Death

---

God Is a Jealous God
This Means:
God Demands First Place in Our Lives

A campus pastor was calling on a brilliant graduate student at the university. The young woman had attended chapel service with her friends. When the pastor visited her, she recalled how she had tried to find God all her life, but without success. "Every night for nine years, I read my Bible," she said, "and prayed for faith. But God never gave it to me."

Then, quietly, the pastor asked, "Did you ever pray for forgiveness?"

The young woman was silent for a moment. She then remarked, "No," and went on to explain that she had never broken any of the Ten Commandments. Surprised by her comment, the pastor went through the commandments, beginning with the last.

No, she had never coveted. No, she had never given false testimony, or stolen anything, or committed adultery. She had never killed anyone, disobeyed or failed to honor her parents, or taken God's name in vain.

Finally, the pastor asked, "Is there anything—anything at all—which you would place before God in life?"

She paused. "If anything got in the way of my career, it would have to go." (Adapted from Seasonal Illustrations for Preaching and Teaching, *pp. 39–40)*

God is a jealous God. He insists on being obeyed, for He is our Creator, Preserver, Redeemer, and Sanctifier. He holds property rights in us.

Visiting the Iniquity
This Means:
God Punishes Sins

If children also hate God, God will punish them, not only for their sins but *also* for the sins committed by their parents, grandparents, and other ancestors.

Who Can Keep the Law Perfectly?
NO ONE!

Many people believe and say, "I don't have to go to church. I don't need Christ or organized religion. If I do what is right, that's enough in God's eyes."

In a sense, that's true. If we do what is right—*always* do what is right—God will be satisfied with our life. But here's the question: "Can we do what is right—*always* right—according to God's standard?"

In the light of the Ten Commandments, ask yourself: Can I keep God's Law perfectly? If I try real hard—extra hard—for a whole week, could I live up to God's standards? If I locked myself up in a cell all my life, could I escape sinning?

It is impossible for human beings to fully obey the Law!

For whoever keeps the whole law but fails in one point has become accountable for all of it. For He who said, "Do not commit adultery," also said, "Do not murder." If you do not commit adultery but do murder, you have become a transgressor of the law. (James 2:10–11)

- *The Law is like a priceless painting.* One spot or blemish on the canvas affects the whole picture.

- *The Law is like a chain.* Each part is integrally connected to the next part. If a person dangles from a chain connected to a large tree, does it really matter which link breaks?

When people say, "I don't need Christ," they make the mistake of comparing themselves with other people. And because they perceive themselves as being as good or better than others, they reason that they are entitled to God's blessings. But we all fall short in comparison with God's holiness.

Luke 18:9–14 tells about two men in the temple. The Pharisee made the mistake of comparing himself with other people. He said, "God, I thank You that I am not like other men." But the tax collector recognized the presence of holy God in the temple. He cried out in humility and shame, "God, be merciful to me, a sinner!"

- *The Law is like a smartphone screen.* It is very bright in a dark room, but in bright sunlight, it seems to go dark. Our deeds done in this dark world may be bright and noteworthy, but in the light of God's holiness they are as a "polluted garment" (Isaiah 64:6).

Now, if no one can keep the Law, why then did God give it? Was it given just to torment human beings? No, the Law serves a purpose—a threefold purpose: as a *curb*, a *mirror*, and a *guide rule*.

The Purposes of the Law

CURB—The Law checks the coarse outbursts of sin.

A curb keeps cars from running onto sidewalks and lawns. In the days of the wild west, people regularly carried and used guns. Shootings were common until the government stepped in. People may still have had the intention of shooting up the town, but they were afraid of punishment. The law checked the coarse outbursts of sin.

The red light says stop—in the name of the law.

MIRROR—The Law shows us our true condition. It shows us that we have been made dirty by sin.

The apostle Paul said this in his letter to the Roman Christians: "If it had not been for the law, I would not have known sin" (7:7).

And "through the law comes knowledge of sin" (3:20).

The Law shows Christians which works please God. To please God, we don't have to torture our bodies or go into a monastery, as Luther did at one time. In faith, through Christ, we want to do His will as revealed in the Commandments.

GUIDE—The Law shows us how to live.

In North Dakota, where blizzards rage, farmers sometimes stretch guidelines from the house to the barn. The line shows them where to walk when blizzards make it impossible to see. So too the Law in the Christian's life.

In baseball, rule books are used. The Law is the Christian's rule book. "Your word is a lamp to my feet and a light to my path" (Psalm 119:105).

What Is Sin?

1. Sin is *missing the mark*.

The picture is that of an archer, aiming his arrow at the target. He draws the string back, lets go—whoosh! The arrow flies through the air; it misses. The archer "sinned." Ancient Greeks might say, "He missed the mark."

The target God has set up for us is perfection. "You shall be holy, for I the Lord your God am holy" (Leviticus 19:2). "You therefore must be perfect, as your heavenly Father is perfect" (Matthew 5:48). Anything less than perfect is "sin." It is "missing the mark."

2. Sin is *transgression*—that is, *stepping over the line.*

3. Sin is *iniquity*—that is, *unevenness.*

We are all builders. Every one is building a structure we call "our life." Every thought, word, or action is a brick added to the walls of this building. The plumb line of the Law shows what kind of structure we are building: is it level?

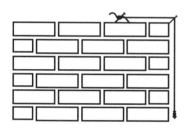

Our life is like a road. We travel down the road every day. Is it a smooth road, even, without bumps or potholes or broken pieces? Are all parts up to standard—perfectly level? Whatever defects we find along the road are "un-equity," iniquity. Is your life a perfect road?

4. Sin is wickedness, crookedness. We wind aside from the straight path, we turn away, we fail to take the right road.

Is our life a straight path without any curves or crooks or bends? To turn aside from God's ways, either to the right or to the left, is wickedness. Is there any zigzag in your life?

5. Sin is guile: deception, insincerity, being one person on the inside and another on the outside.

6. Sin is lawlessness.

Everyone who makes a practice of sinning also practices lawlessness; sin is lawlessness. (1 John 3:4)

Other words include *offense, wrongdoing, immorality, misdeed, evil, corruption, ungodliness, impurity, affront to God.* All sin is a departure from God's Word and will.

Can anyone list every sin?

No! In addition to idolatry, disobedience, murder, unfaithfulness, theft, lying, envy, and greed, there are disputes, contentions, strife, anger, violence . . .

All are thoughts and actions against God's Law, rebellion against His will.

Now the works of the flesh are evident: sexual immorality, impurity, sensuality, idolatry, sorcery, enmity, strife, jealousy, fits of anger, rivalries, dissensions, divisions, envy, drunkenness, orgies, and things like these. I warn you, as I warned you before, that those who do such things will not inherit the kingdom of God. (Galatians 5:19–21)

The Punishment of Sin: "The Wages of Sin Is Death" (Romans 6:23)

- Sin and death are merely different stages or phases of one and the same thing.

- Sin is death begun; death is sin finished, worked out to its logical conclusion.

- Sin is death in the green; death is sin dead ripe.

- Sin is the seed; death is the fruit of that seed.

The root and source of all sin is unbelief or the turning away from God, just as, on the other hand, the source and root of all righteousness is faith. (Martin Luther, What Luther Says, §4185)

- Sin is a dying away from God; they that sin die unto God and gravitate toward that place where death reigns. That is hell. Hell is the place where spiritual death reigns, where God is excluded.

The wages of sin is DEATH—spiritual, temporal, eternal.

Two Kinds of Sin

If we could perfectly *keep* the Law, we could be *saved* by the Law—that is, by our own good works, by our own efforts and achievement and character. We cannot, however, keep the Law; we cannot be saved by the Law.

How then are we saved? We are saved by Jesus, who kept the Law for us perfectly, and offered Himself as the once-for-all sacrifice for our sins.

[He] was delivered up for our trespasses and raised for our justification. (Romans 4:25)

A father said to his younger son, "Cut and stack this wood today."

The boy tries to obey his father, but he is too weak; he can hardly begin the task. Along comes his older brother and says, "Step aside, I'll do it for you." And he does.

Now, when the father comes home, will he punish the younger son for disobeying him? No! The work was completed. The father's command was fulfilled—*only, of course, by the older son in his brother's place.*

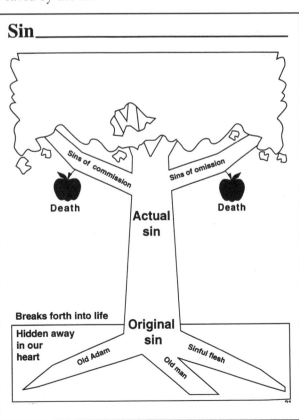

The Difference between Law and Gospel

	Law	Gospel
teaches	• what to do • what not to do	• what God has done for our salvation • what God still does to bring us salvation
shows	• us our sin • the wrath of God	• our Savior • the grace of God
must be proclaimed to	• all people, but especially to the impenitent	• sinners who are troubled because of their sins

GOOD NEWS

We are freed from the guilt, the punishment, and the power of sin and are saved eternally because of Christ's keeping the Law and His suffering and death for us.

The heavenly Father says to us, "Live according to My Word." As sinful human beings, we try, but we are too weak; in fact, too rebellious. Along comes our Brother, Jesus Christ, and says, "I'll fulfill the Father's command for you." And He does.

Jesus actively obeyed His Father. His perfect obedience is part of His saving work for us, and through faith in Him, we are considered righteous before God.

Therefore, we are saved by Christ, who kept the Law in our stead and gave up His life as an atoning sacrifice for our sins (1 John 2:2). Through Baptism, He places His righteousness on us like a white garment.

Hymn

Jesus, Thy blood and righteousness,
My beauty are, my glorious dress;
Midst flaming worlds, in these arrayed,
With joy shall I lift up my head.

Prayer

Almighty and everlasting God, of Your great mercy in Jesus Christ You have granted us forgiveness of sin and all things pertaining to life and godliness. Therefore send us Your Holy Spirit that He may so rule our hearts that we, being ever mindful for Your fatherly mercy, may strive to overcome the world and, serving You in holiness and pureness of living, may give You continual thanks for all Your goodness; through Jesus Christ, our Lord. Amen.

Bible Readings

Genesis 3:1–7

Genesis 5:3

_____

_____

1 Timothy 1:5–11

_____

_____

Romans 6:12–23

_____

_____

Luke 12:35–48

_____

_____

Galatians 3:1–13

_____

_____

Romans 5:12–21

_____

_____

Catechetical Review

1. What does the Close of the Commandments contain? (A threat and a promise.)

2. What is God's threat upon those who fail to keep these Commandments? (Death and damnation.)

3. What is God's promise to those who keep His Commandments? (Grace and every blessing.)

4. What kind of obedience does God require of us? (A perfect obedience.)

5. Who can keep God's Law perfectly? (No human being.)

6. For what purpose, then, was the Law given? (The Law serves as a curb, a mirror, and a guide.)

7. How does the Law serve as a curb? (The Law checks the coarse outbursts of sin.)

8. How does the Law serve as a mirror? (The Law shows us that our heart is sinful.)

9. How does the Law serve as a guide? (The Law shows Christians how God desires to guide us in our daily life.)

10. Of what are we guilty when we depart from these rules? (We are guilty of sin.)

11. What is sin? ("Sin is lawlessness"; that is, being and living without the Law in our thoughts, words, and actions (1 John 3:4).)

12. What are the two kinds of sin? (Original and actual sin.)

13. What is original sin? (Original sin is that sin with which we were born, which we had at our "origin.")

14. What is actual sin? (Actual sin is every sinful act against the Law in thoughts, desires, words, or behavior.)

15. What is the wages of sin? ("The wages of sin is death" [Romans 6:23].)

16. Of what does the study of God's Law convince us? (That we cannot keep the Law, and that we are therefore lost and condemned sinners.)

Martin Luther's Christian Questions

Do you believe that you are a sinner? Yes, I believe it; I am a sinner.

How do you know this? From the Ten Commandments, which I have not kept.

Are you sorry for your sins? Yes, I am sorry that I have sinned against God.

What have you deserved from God because of your sins? His wrath and displeasure, temporal death, and eternal damnation.

Do you hope to be saved? Yes, that is my hope.

In whom then do you trust? In my dear Lord Jesus Christ.

Who is Christ? The Son of God, true God and man.

What has Christ done for you that you trust in Him? He died for me and shed His blood for me on the cross for the forgiveness of sins.

What motivated Christ to die and make full payment for your sins?

His great love for His Father and for me and other sinners, as it is written in John 14; Romans 5; Galatians 2; and Ephesians 5.

Bible Passages

1. The soul who sins shall die. (Ezekiel 18:20)

2. For the wages of sin is death, but the free gift of God is eternal life in Christ Jesus our Lord. (Romans 6:23)

3. You therefore must be perfect, as your heavenly Father is perfect. (Matthew 5:48)

4. For whoever keeps the whole law but fails in one point has become accountable for all of it. (James 2:10)

5. Surely there is not a righteous man on earth who does good and never sins. (Ecclesiastes 7:20)

6. We have all become like one who is unclean, and all our righteous deeds are like a polluted garment. We all fade like a leaf, and our iniquities, like the wind, take us away. (Isaiah 64:6)

7. For by works of the law no human being will be justified in His sight, since through the law comes knowledge of sin. (Romans 3:20)

8. Your word is a lamp to my feet and a light to my path. (Psalm 119:105)

9. Behold, I was brought forth in iniquity, and in sin did my mother conceive me. (Psalm 51:5)

10. Then desire when it has conceived gives birth to sin, and sin when it is fully grown brings forth death. (James 1:15)

11. So whoever knows the right thing to do and fails to do it, for him it is sin. (James 4:17)

12. Now it is evident that no one is justified before God by the law, for "The righteous shall live by faith." (Galatians 3:11)

13. Christ redeemed us from the curse of the law by becoming a curse for us—for it is written, "Cursed is everyone who is hanged on a tree." (Galatians 3:13)

For Further Study

1. Study the Catechetical Review.

2. Memorize one or more Bible passages.

3. Review the books of the Bible.

4. Review the Close of the Commandments in the Appendix.

11 The Apostles' Creed

Confirmation Builder—Lessons 15 and 16

Creeds

A creed is a statement of what one believes, teaches, and confesses.

Speaking a creed together is a sign of personal faith and congregational unity. A creed gives public witness to God's truth revealed in Holy Scripture.

In one respect, a creed is similar to the Christian flag. Both are symbols of what we believe. Saying the creed is like holding high the flag.

The Christian flag has three colors; the Creed has three Articles:

- The Blue Rectangle, symbol of the Father's faithfulness;

- The Red Cross, symbol of the Savior's atoning blood;

- The White Field, the sanctifying power of the Holy Spirit.

The Apostles' Creed

The best-known creed of the Christian Church is the Apostles' Creed. This creed is a summary of what the apostles believed and taught the early Christians.

A legend from long ago suggests that the apostles gathered together after Pentecost to write down "the basics" of their faith in Jesus, with each apostle contributing a clause. The result was the *Apostles' Creed*. In the Middle Ages, the creed was often known as the *Twelve Articles*.

It is not likely that the apostles actually composed the creed. But the creed contains what the apostles believed, for we find much the same statements of faith in their inspired writings.

The Apostles' Creed is very old. From the Bible and the writings of the Church Fathers, we learn that candidates for Baptism were required to make a confession of their faith and state briefly what they believed regarding God the Creator, Jesus the Savior, and the Holy Spirit the Sanctifier. Some type of creed or confession was undoubtedly in use. The Apostles' Creed is an explanation of the trinitarian faith given in and confessed at Baptism.

This confession of faith we did not make or invent, neither did the fathers of the church before us. But as the bee gathers the honey from many a beautiful and delicious flower, so this creed has been collected in commendable brevity from the books of the beloved prophets and apostles, that is, from the entire Holy Scriptures, for children and plain Christians. It is, therefore, justly called the Apostles' Creed. (Martin Luther, What Luther Says, *§1040)*

The word *creed* is from the Latin *credo:* "I believe."

The First Article

Creation

I believe in God the Father Almighty, Maker of heaven and earth.

What does this mean?

I believe that God has made me and all creatures; that He has given me my body and soul, eyes, ears, and all my members, my reason and all my senses, and still takes care of them.

He also gives me clothing and shoes, food and drink, house and home, wife and children, land, animals, and all I have. He richly and daily provides me with all that I need to support this body and life.

He defends me against all danger and guards and protects me from all evil.

All this He does only out of fatherly, divine goodness and mercy, without any merit or worthiness in me. For all that it is my duty to thank and praise, serve and obey Him.

This is most certainly true.

> # I Believe

We say "I" believe, for no one can be saved by another person's faith; each one must believe for himself or herself.

We can neither eat nor sleep nor learn for others. Neither can we believe for someone else.

Some may say, "My parents were devout Christians." Or, "My family has always believed in God."

Salvation is always personal. Each person says for himself or herself, "I believe."

If you confess with your mouth that Jesus is Lord and believe in your heart that God raised Him from the dead, you will be saved. For with the heart one believes and is justified, and with the mouth one confesses and is saved. (Romans 10:9–10)

Believe means "to trust"—"to take God at His word"

Believe means to

- **know** (with your mind);
- **assent** (with your lips);
- **trust** (with your heart).

Let's say that I *know* that George Washington existed. I assent to the fact that he was a living, breathing human being. But do I trust him for my salvation? No!

I know the history of Christ's life and death. I assent to it as historically true. Trust, or saving faith, goes one step farther. I fully trust Christ for complete forgiveness and salvation.

Christian faith is not merely knowledge and assent, but trust in Jesus as Savior and Lord.

Faith is not only to think of Christ that He was born of the Virgin, suffered, was crucified, rose, ascended to heaven. But faith dwells in a heart that embraces and grasps the Son of God . . . and firmly holds that God gave His only-begotten Son into death for us and has so loved us that for His sake we should not perish but have eternal life. (Martin Luther, What Luther Says, *§1375—see also §1376)*

True faith is the reliance on the word and promise of God. Reliance on anything else is not faith but superstition. Some say it does not matter so much *what* you believe, just *that* you believe. If that were true, we might then say, "It does not matter so much *what* you eat, just *so* you eat."

It does, however, matter what we eat. And the Bible reveals that what we believe matters: About Jesus, the author of Acts records, "There is salvation in no one else, for there is no other name under heaven given among men by which we must be saved" (4:12).

God the Father

The First Person of the Holy Trinity is called the Father because He is

- the Father of our Lord Jesus Christ (John 17:1–26; Ephesians 1:3);

- the Father of all human beings; that is, the one Creator (Acts 17:24–29);

- the Father of His children in Christ Jesus (Romans 4:11; Galatians 3:26).

Is it possible to have the "brotherhood" of human beings without the Fatherhood of God? The Bible teaches the Fatherhood of God and the "brotherhood" of Christians. There can be no brothers and sisters in Christ without one Father.

Trying to build the brotherhood of man without the fatherhood of God is like trying to make a wheel without a hub. (Irene Dunne, from Draper's Book of Quotations for the Christian World*)*

Almighty

God is all-powerful. His rule and majesty are without limit.

A smart phone or tablet can hold a lot of information—seemingly without limit. But when the battery dies, there is no power and no information, no matter how many buttons you push.

The story is told of visitors who were touring an old corn mill. The mill was powered by a river that ran right next to the large water wheels. But all the wheels were silent and still. "Where is the power?" someone asked the guide.
The guide pointed to a large handle on the wall. He invited one of the visitors to pull it down. Immediately, the wheels began to turn and the whole mill was alive with activity.

When God speaks, the universe is alive with activity. He is called "Almighty," "Maker" because by His word **He made all things out of nothing**. God said, "Let there be" and there was! (Genesis 1). In the beginning, God—not evolution—created all things.

Maker of Heaven and Earth

By heaven and earth, we mean **all creatures, visible and invisible**.

There are three orders of creatures:

1. All body and no soul—animals

2. All soul and no body—angels

3. Both body and soul—man *No wonder*

What does it mean to have a god? Or, what is God? Answer: A god means that from which we are to expect all good and in which we are to take refuge in all distress. So, to have a God is nothing other than trusting and believing Him with the heart. I have often said that the confidence and faith of the heart alone make both God and an idol. If your faith and trust is right, then your god is also true. (Martin Luther, Large Catechism I 1–3)

Hymn

Praise to the Lord, the Almighty, the King of creation!
O my soul, praise Him, for He is your health and salvation!
Let all who hear Now to His temple draw near,
Joining in glad adoration!

Prayer

We bless You, Almighty Father, for You have made all things in heaven and on earth, both visible and invisible. Keep us safe, we ask You, by Your mighty power and help us to walk everyday in Your fatherly mercy and goodness; through Jesus Christ, Your Son, our Lord. Amen.

Bible Readings

Psalm 8

_____

_____

Hebrews 11:1–3

_____

_____

Luke 7:1–10

_____

_____

John 4:46–54

_____

_____

John 1:1–5

_____

_____

Genesis 1

_____

_____

Psalm 95

_____

_____

Catechetical Review

The Creed

1. What is a creed? (A creed is a statement of what one believes.)

2. How many universal Christian creeds are there? (Three: the Apostles' Creed, the Nicene Creed [formulated in AD 325], and the Athanasian Creed [AD 600].)

3. In what worship service do we commonly use the Apostles' Creed? (At services without Holy Communion and Baptisms.)

4. When do we commonly use the Nicene Creed? (At festival services and Holy Communion.)

5. When particularly do we use the Athanasian Creed? (On Trinity Sunday.)

6. Why is the first creed called the Apostles' Creed? (It contains essentially what the apostles believed.)

7. Why is the Apostles' Creed divided into three articles? (There is one article for each of the Three Persons of the Holy Trinity: the Father, the Son, and the Holy Spirit.)

8. Which work is ascribed to each Person by way of preeminence? (To the Father, the work of creation; to the Son, the work of redemption; to the Holy Spirit, the work of sanctification.)

The First Article

1. Why do you say "*I* believe" and not "*We* believe"? (I must believe for myself if I am to be saved.)

2. What does it mean to believe in God? (To believe in God means to know, assent to, and trust in God.)

3. Why is God called the Father? (He is the Father of our Lord Jesus Christ, and He is our Father by faith in Jesus.)

4. Why is God called "almighty" and "maker"? (He made heaven and earth out of nothing, by His almighty power.)

5. What do we understand by "heaven and earth"? All creatures, visible and invisible.

Bible Passages

1. The righteous shall live by his faith. (Habakkuk 2:4)

2. But I trust in you, O Lord; I say, "You are my God." (Psalm 31:14)

3. For this reason I bow my knees before the Father, from whom every family in heaven and on earth is named. (Ephesians 3:14–15)

4. Have we not all one Father? Has not one God created us? Why then are we faithless to one another, profaning the covenant of our fathers? (Malachi 2:10)

5. For in Christ Jesus you are all sons of God, through faith. (Galatians 3:26)

6. In the beginning, God created the heavens and the earth. (Genesis 1:1)

7. For by Him all things were created, in heaven and on earth, visible and invisible, whether thrones or dominions or rulers or authorities—all things were created through Him and for Him. (Colossians 1:16)

For Further Study

1. Study the Catechetical Review.

2. Memorize and learn to use all the Bible passages, or the following:
   No. _____

3. Memorize the Apostles' Creed.

12 Angels and Human Beings

The Good Angels

The foremost beings among the invisible creatures are the angels.

1. The angels are **personal spirits**.

2. They are **invisible**, though they may temporarily assume visible forms. Pictures are meant to symbolize certain characteristics of their nature. Wings suggest rapidity of movement; white garments, purity. Angels are sometimes depicted as youths in order to emphasize their chastity; at other times as men in order to stress their strength and prowess.

3. They are **sexless, sinless, deathless.** They neither marry nor are given in marriage. They are innumerable, grouped in ranks. Some have names (Gabriel, Michael). They are confirmed in their bliss (perfection).

4. Their work is to serve God and His children.

5. *Angel* means "messenger."

   [Jesus said,] "See that you do not despise one of these little ones. For I tell you that in heaven their angels always see the face of My Father who is in heaven." (Matthew 18:10; see also Psalm 34:7; 91:11)

The Evil Angels

The angels were all made holy. Satan was even of high rank in heaven. We do not know why, but we do know that some angels rebelled against God and His truth and became the fallen spirits.

God did not create the devils; they made themselves evil. As rebels and anarchists, they were outlawed from heaven and are now without hope of redemption. They are "living evildoers," enemies of God and man, constituting the "powers of darkness."

The evil angels are many; they are cunning and powerful. We cannot overcome them by our own strength. We can, however, overcome them through Jesus' strength and mercy.

- **Genesis 3:1–5.** Sin was brought into the world by the devil.

- **Matthew 4:1–11.** Jesus used the Word of God against Satan.

- **Revelation 20:10.** At the end of history, Satan is judged and eternally tormented.

Human Beings

The foremost beings among the visible creatures are humans. Why? They have

1. speech;

2. reason; animals have only instinct—a marvelous gift from God—but only human beings have ability to think, plan, speak, and act with logic and critical reflection;

Man differs from the animals in that he asks himself questions. He asks them about the world and about himself, about the meaning of things, the meaning of disease and healing, life and death. He is conscious of his weakness, of his responsibility, and of his shortcomings, and he asks himself if there is any way out. I know that it is in fact God who puts these questions to him, that it is God who is speaking to him, even though he may not realize it. (Paul Tournier, from Draper's Book of Quotations for the Christian World*)*

---

3. an immortal soul;

4. a unique body;

5. dominion over every living creature (Genesis 1:28);

6. the image and likeness of God (Genesis 1:26); that is, human beings were able to know, love, trust, and obey God perfectly.

The "Image of God"

What is meant by the "image of God"?

Adam's mind was illuminated, so that he knew God, knew himself, knew the mysteries of nature.

Adam's will ran parallel to God's will.

Adam's heart loved God and everything that is good, noble, and praiseworthy.

The image of God in which Adam was made was something most beautiful and noble. The leprosy of sin adhered neither to his reason nor to his will. But, within and without, all his senses were pure. His intellect was very clear, his memory very good, and his will very sincere. His conscience was clean and secure, without any fear of death and without any care. To these inner perfections came also that beautiful and superb strength of the body and all its members by which he surpassed all the other animate creatures in nature." (Martin Luther, What Luther Says, *§2738)*

But in the fall, the divine image was lost in human beings, so that today our

- mind is clouded—by nature, we do not and cannot know God;

- will runs counter to God's will—by nature, we do not and cannot please God;

- heart is evil—by nature, we rebel against God and disobey His Word.

No human being can restore the image of God. Only God can restore His image in His children. While we live on earth, Christians cannot attain complete knowledge and righteousness of life. But the beginning is made in Christ.

Do not lie to one another, seeing that you have put off the old self with its practices and have put on the new self, which is being renewed in knowledge after the image of its creator. (Colossians 3:9–10)

In heaven, however, the divine image shall be fully restored.

Luther's Explanation of the First Article

God has made me . . .

not evolution, not random chance, not impersonal forces of nature. God is my Maker. I am a fallen saint, not a cultured brute; I am a withered flower, not a cultivated weed.

"God has given me my body and soul, eyes, ears, and all my members, my reason, and all my senses."

I walk, run, laugh, cry, think, talk, work, sleep, hear, see, taste, smell, and feel. What great blessings!

He preserves me—

The clock maker makes his clock, winds it up, and leaves it to run on its own. The shipbuilder builds and launches his ship, and others navigate it. The world, however, is not like a clock or ship, an object constructed by God and then dismissed from His hands (Deism). God does not simply from time to time review and repair His creation. Rather, God takes an active interest and role in the preservation of the universe and in my personal well-being. He gives me life's necessities and luxuries. Even though I work for these and in a sense "earn" them, I know that God gives me health, strength, ability, and a clear mind to work and receive His blessings.

In 1937, Walt Disney released Snow White, *the first full-length animated movie. Producing an animated movie was a gargantuan task. Disney artists drew over a million pictures. Each picture flashed onto the screen for less than a quarter of a second.*

As we watch the movie run at regular speed, it seems so simple. We have no idea of all that goes into it.

Our lives are like that movie. God puts infinite thought, skill, and attention into every detail. His love is constantly present. Yet as our lives run at "regular speed," we have no idea how much God's providence fills every second. (Adapted from USA Today, *as quoted in* Contemporary Illustrations for Preachers, Teachers, and Writers, *p. 193.)*

A young girl asked her mother, "Where did you get that delicious bread?" Her mother replied, "From the store." "Where did the store get it?" "From the bakery." "Where did the bakery get it?" "From the mill, where grains are stored and prepared." "Where did the mill get it?" "From the farmer." "Where did the farmer get it?" "From the seeds planted in the ground." "How did the ground do all this?" "By God's grace and providence."

Where do we get "all things"? *From God.*

He defends me—

There is no chance, lawlessness, or caprice in my life. All happenings are marshaled under the law of His love.

Why? Because **He loves me**. "All this He does only out of fatherly, divine goodness and mercy."

In response, I thank and praise (tell others), serve and obey Him.

Symbol of
St. Michael
and All Angels

$$\boxed{\text{This Is Most Certainly True}}$$

Hymn

Ye watchers and ye holy ones,
    Bright seraphs, cherubim, and thrones,
Raise the glad strain: "Alleluia!"
Cry out, dominions, princedoms, pow'rs,
    Virtues, archangels, angels' choirs:
"Alleluia, alleluia! Alleluia, alleluia, alleluia!"

Prayers

Be here with us every day,
In our work and in our play
When we learn and when we pray;
Hear us, Holy Jesus.
When we lie asleep at night,
Ever may Your angels bright
Keep us safe till morning light;
Hear us, Holy Jesus. Amen.

Bible Readings

2 Kings 19:35–36

_____

_____

Acts 12:1–19

_____

_____

Jude 6

_____

_____

Genesis 19:1–16

_____

_____

1 Kings 17

_____

_____

Exodus 2:1–10

_____

_____

Psalm 103

_____

_____

Catechetical Review

Angels

1. What are the foremost beings among God's invisible creatures? (The angels.)

2. How were all angels when God first made them? (They were all good.)

3. How did some angels become evil? (They rebelled and fell away from God.)

4. What are the fallen angels called, since they are "the evil ones"? (They are called "devils.")

5. Did God make the devils? (No, God made only good angels.)

6. Whose fault was it that certain good angels became devils? (It was their own fault.)

7. How do the evil angels try to harm us? (They try to lead us away from God and into sin.)

8. What should we do to resist the evil angels? (Watch and pray, and, through Christ's strength, say no to temptation.)

9. Describe the good angels. (The good angels are lovely and happy spirits.)

10. What else can you say about the good angels? (They are sinless, sexless, and deathless.)

11. What is the work of the good angels? (The good angels serve God and help His children.)

12. Why should we not be afraid even when we are alone at night? (God's angels are watching over us.)

13. What prayer may we speak to God every morning and night? ("My heavenly Father, let Your holy angel be with me, that the evil foe may have no power over me. Amen.")

Human Beings

1. Who is foremost among God's visible creatures? (Human beings.)

2. Why are human beings the highest of God's creation on earth? (Because they are made in the divine image.)

3. What does this mean that humans are made in the divine image? (Adam and Eve were made without sin, to know, fear, love, trust, and obey God.)

4. Do we still possess the divine image? (No, not since the fall.)

5. In whom is the divine image partly renewed? (In God's redeemed children; that is, in Christians.)

6. When will the divine image be restored fully? (In heaven.)

Preservation

1. What does God still do for you besides having created you? (He preserves me.)

2. What does God give you for your preservation? (Everything I need for this life.)

3. Why does God give you so much good? (He is the kindest of fathers.)

4. What does God continually do for your well-being? (He defends me against all dangers and guards and protects me from all evil.)

5. What moves God to do all this for you? ("All this He does only out of fatherly, divine goodness and mercy, without any merit or worthiness in me.")

6. How do you then respond to God? ("For all this it is my duty to thank and praise, serve and obey Him.")

Bible Passages

1. Are [angels] not all ministering spirits sent out to serve for the sake of those who are to inherit salvation? (Hebrews 1:14)

2. Be sober-minded; be watchful. Your adversary the devil prowls around like a roaring lion, seeking someone to devour. Resist him, firm in your faith, knowing that the same kinds of suffering are being experienced by your brotherhood throughout the world. (1 Peter 5:8–9)

3. For He will command His angels concerning you to guard you in all your ways. On their hands they will bear you up, lest you strike your foot against a stone. (Psalm 91:11–12)

4. The Lord God formed the man of dust from the ground and breathed into his nostrils the breath of life, and the man became a living creature. (Genesis 2:7)

5. So God created man in His own image, in the image of God He created him, male and female He created them. (Genesis 1:27)

6. And to put on the new self, created after the likeness of God in true righteousness and holiness. (Ephesians 4:24)

7. He is the radiance of the glory of God and the exact imprint of His nature, and He upholds the universe by the word of His power. (Hebrews 1:3)

8. The eyes of all look to You, and You give them their food in due season. You open Your hand; You satisfy the desire of every living thing. (Psalm 145:15–16)

9. Casting all your anxieties on Him, because He cares for you. (1 Peter 5:7)

10. My times are in Your hand; rescue me from the hand of my enemies and from my persecutors! (Psalm 31:15)

11. Oh give thanks to the LORD, for He is good; for His steadfast love endures forever! (Psalms 118:1)

For Further Study

1. Study the Catechetical Review.

2. Memorize one or more Bible passages.

3. Memorize Luther's Explanation to the First Article.

The Second Article

Redemption

Confirmation Builder—
Lesson 17

And in Jesus Christ, His only Son, our Lord, who was conceived by the Holy Spirit, born of the Virgin Mary, suffered under Pontius Pilate, was crucified, died and was buried. He descended into hell. The third day He rose again from the dead. He ascended into heaven and sits at the right hand of God the Father Almighty. From thence He will come to judge the living and the dead.

What does this mean? I believe that Jesus Christ, true God, begotten of the Father from eternity, and also true man, born of the Virgin Mary, is my Lord,

who has redeemed me, a lost and condemned person, purchased and won me from all sins, from death, and from the power of the devil; not with gold or silver, but with His holy, precious blood and with His innocent suffering and death, that I may be His own and live under Him in His kingdom, and serve Him in everlasting righteousness, innocence, and blessedness, just as He is risen from the dead, lives and reigns to all eternity.

This is most certainly true.

Summary

Two Names	Jesus Christ
Two Natures	Son of God—divine Son of Man—human
Two Names Explained	Jesus = Savior Christ = anointed
Threefold Office	To be our Prophet, Priest, and King
His Work	To save us from . . .
The Unholy Three	Sin, Death, and the Devil

His Names

Jesus Means "Savior"

There are many "saviors." Doctors save health, lawyers save their client's reputation, lifeguards save drowning victims. But Jesus saves "His people from their sins."

Artists who have grasped the true meaning of the life of Christ have painted the baby Jesus lying in a cradle with the cross over His head. This portrait recognizes that from the day of His birth the Lord Jesus Christ knew the cross as His reason for coming to earth. His sacrificial death was His ultimate goal in life; He meant to crown His life by dying on the cross. The angel said to Joseph: "[Mary] will bear a son, and you shall call His name Jesus, for He will save His people from their sins (Matthew 1:21).

Christ (Greek) or *Messiah* (Hebrew) Means "the Anointed One"

Christ is not really a name but a title, like *governor* or *president*. It indicates that Jesus held public offices—prophet, priest, and king.

In the Old Testament, priests and kings were anointed. Aaron and his sons were anointed. Samuel anointed Saul; that is, he poured fragrant oil over his head. By this sign, all the people knew that Saul was chosen for the work of a king. Samuel also anointed David. Prophets, too, were anointed. So Christ was anointed—chosen, consecrated, or set apart—for a specific work, a threefold work, that of Prophet, Priest, and King. He was anointed, however, not with oil, but with the Holy Spirit without measure, at the time of His Baptism.

And when Jesus was baptized, immediately He went up from the water, and behold, the heavens were opened to Him, and He saw the Spirit of God descending like a dove and coming to rest on Him. (Matthew 3:16)

His Natures

DIVINE	**and**	**HUMAN**
GOD		**MAN**
He is true God, begotten of the Father from eternity.		He is true man, born of the Virgin Mary.
He has divine names and divine attributes and does divine works.		He lives as a true man, with human feelings and actions.
He receives divine honor and glory.		
Two natures in one person: some imperfect illustrations are iron and heat, body and life, glass and light.		

Christ Is True God

The Son of God, and God the Son. St. John writes, "No one has ever seen God; the only God, who is at the Father's side, He has made Him known" (1:18).

Only God has divine names. If Christ has divine names, then He is true God.

Only God has divine attributes. If Christ has divine attributes, then He is true God.

Only God can do divine works. If Christ does divine works, then He is true God.

He Had to Be True God

to overcome sin, death, and the devil for us.

Christ Is True Man

Born of a woman (Galatians 4:4), sent in the likeness of sinful man (Romans 8:3), found in appearance as a man (Philippians 2:8), He called Himself "the Son of Man." He is flesh of our flesh, bone of our bone. He had our wants and desires, our hunger and thirst, our sense of pleasure and pain, all without sinning. He ate the bread of His own earning. He grew in stature and wisdom, hungered and ate, thirsted and drank, worked and wearied, walked and slept, rejoiced and wept, suffered and died, and so we rightly call Him "the man Christ Jesus."

He Had to Be True Man

- to be under the Law and fulfill it for us (active obedience);

- to be able to suffer and die in our place, as our substitute (passive obedience).

Hymn

Oh, for a thousand tongues to sing
My great Redeemer's praise,
The glories of my God and King,
The triumphs of His grace!

Prayer

O Lord Immanuel, Son of God and Son of Man, we thank You that Your name is Jesus, the Savior of all people. To You alone we confess all our sins; we pray: "have mercy upon us." In Your great love, give us pardon and peace and the joy of salvation. We ask this in Your name. Amen.

Bible Readings

Psalm 2

Luke 7:11–17

_____

_____

Matthew 14:13–21

_____

_____

Luke 8:22–25

_____

_____

John 11:35–36

_____

_____

Colossians 1:12–20

_____

_____

Philippians 2:5–11

_____

_____

Catechetical Review

1. Do you hope to be saved? (Yes, such is my hope.)

2. In whom, then, do you trust? (In my dear Lord Jesus Christ.)

3. What does the name *Jesus* mean? (*Jesus* means "Savior.")

4. What does the title *Christ* or (in Hebrew) *Messiah* mean? (*Christ* and *Messiah* mean "the Anointed One.")

5. Who is Jesus Christ? (Jesus Christ is true God and true man, my Savior.)

6. What two natures are united in Him? (The divine nature and the human nature.)

7. Why do you believe that Jesus Christ is true God? (He was begotten of the Father from eternity.)

8. Why do you believe that Jesus Christ is true man? (He was born of the Virgin Mary.)

9. Why was it necessary for our Savior to be true God? (So that He might live, fulfill the Law, suffer, and die as a ransom for me and all people, and thus overcome sin, death, and the devil.)

10. Why was it necessary for our Savior to be true man? (So that He might fulfill the Law and suffer and die for me.)

11. What has Christ done for you that you trust in Him? (He died for me and shed His blood for me on the cross for the forgiveness of sins.)

Bible Passages

1. And this is eternal life, that they know You the only true God, and Jesus Christ whom You have sent. (John 17:3)

2. She will bear a son, and you shall call His name Jesus, for He will save His people from their sins. (Matthew 1:21)

3. How God anointed Jesus of Nazareth with the Holy Spirit and with power. He went about doing good and healing all who were oppressed by the devil, for God was with Him. (Acts 10:38)

4. Great indeed, we confess, is the mystery of godliness: He was manifested in the flesh, vindicated by the Spirit, seen by angels, proclaimed among the nations, believed on in the world, taken up in glory. (1 Timothy 3:16)

5. For in Him the whole fullness of deity dwells bodily. (Colossians 2:9)

6. But if we walk in the light, as He is in the light, we have fellowship with one another, and the blood of Jesus His Son cleanses us from all sin. (1 John 1:7)

7. He was still speaking when, behold, a bright cloud overshadowed them, and a voice from the cloud said, "This is My Beloved Son, with whom I am well pleased; listen to Him." (Matthew 17:5)

8. We know that the Son of God has come and has given us understanding, so that we may know Him who is true; and we are in Him who is true, in His Son Jesus Christ. He is the true God and eternal life. (1 John 5:20)

9. That all may honor the Son, just as they honor the Father. Whoever does not honor the Son does not honor the Father who sent Him. (John 5:23)

10. For there is one God, and there is one mediator between God and men, the man Christ Jesus. (1 Timothy 2:5)

For Further Study

1. Study the Catechetical Review.

2. Memorize one or more Bible passages.

3. Memorize the Second Article.

14 The Second Article (Continued)

Christ's Work

Prophet

The work of a prophet in the Old Testament was to preach—to proclaim God's Word to people. A prophet might also, by inspiration of the Holy Spirit, announce future events (predictions).

Christ as a prophet preached and still preaches, namely, through His ministers.

Priest

The work of the priest in the Old Testament was to make sacrifices for sins and to intercede for God's people and the world.

Christ, as our Priest, did not sacrifice a bull or turtledove or lamb, but He sacrificed Himself as the Lamb of God on the altar of the cross.

As our Priest, He also pleads for us. He is our Advocate.

As our Priest, He fulfilled the Law in our stead perfectly.

King

The work of a king is to rule.

Christ is a king. He rules over everything and especially over the Christian Church.

He is King over the

- Kingdom of Power—world;

- Kingdom of Grace—Church;

- Kingdom of Glory—heaven.

His States—Humiliation and Exaltation

Step 1

He Was Conceived [formed in the Womb] **by the Holy Spirit**

Joseph was the foster father and guardian of Jesus, but not His real father. His real Father is God.

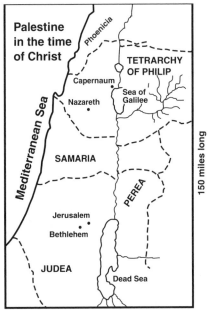

Step 2

Born of the Virgin Mary

Here is a brief summary of His life:

As a Child. The Holy Spirit, Mary, Joseph, Bethlehem, shepherds, Magi, Simeon, Herod, the massacre of the innocents, flight to Egypt, return to Nazareth.

As a Youth. Visits to the temple, became a "son of the Law" at age twelve; loved the Scriptures; grew in wisdom and stature, in favor with God and man; keen observer of nature, judging from His later parables; assisted His foster father in his carpenter shop.

As a Man. John (Baptism); devil (temptation in wilderness); twelve disciples; miracles on sick, afflicted, dead, demon-possessed, nature; preached and taught; the years of popularity but also opposition; Judas; Caiaphas; Pilate.

Step 3

Suffered under Pontius Pilate

Maundy Thursday, the institution of the Lord's Supper, Garden of Gethsemane, betrayal by Judas Iscariot, arrest, trial before Annas and Caiaphas, two sessions of the Jewish Council (Sanhedrin), Good Friday morning at six before Pilate, to Herod, back again, scourging, crown of thorns, mock scepter, buffeting, the journey to Calvary by the Way of Sorrows.

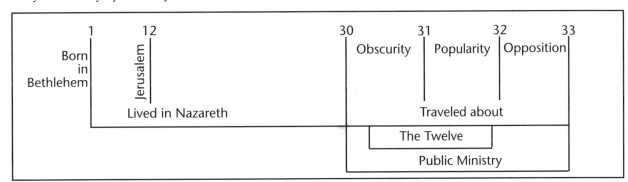

Step 4

Was Crucified

Calvary or, in Aramaic, Golgotha, the place of the skull; at the crucifixion, the transverse bar was laid on ground and the victim was laid on it; a spike driven first through one hand and then the other; the victim was hoisted and fastened by means of ropes to upright post; one nail through each foot, or a long spike through both; in the middle of the post was a wooden pin to support the main weight of the body, but this pin also served to keep the body in the same cramped position; the Roman statesman Cicero said that crucifixion should never come near the eyes and ears of a Roman, much less to his person, but crucifixion came to Jesus; crucified in the midst of two malefactors, as the chief sinner; and so He bore the iniquity of us all; from 9 to 3 on cross, a darkness from 12 to 3; seven words from the cross.

Step 5

Died

Physically. Soldiers did not break His legs; centurion pierced His side with a spear.

Legally. When Pilate learned from the centurion that Jesus had died, he gave the body of Jesus to Nicodemus and to Joseph of Arimathea.

Step 6

and Was Buried

The bodies of the crucified would be dumped on the garbage pile in the Valley of Hinnom, but Jesus was buried with the rich—the Virgin-born was placed in the virgin tomb that belonged to Joseph; His body did not see corruption.

Why Did Jesus Humble Himself?

Christ humbled Himself in order to redeem sinful human beings. *Redeem* means to "buy back." In ancient times, a person could "redeem" (buy) the freedom of a slave from slavery. The life of the slave was *redeemed*. Sometimes people redeem for others what that person has pawned; that is, they purchase back what someone else bought. Jesus is our *Redeemer*. He bought back our lives from the devil, the world, and our own sinful flesh with His holy, precious blood.

Peter the Great of Russia laid aside his royal garments, dressed in the clothes of a workman, went to Holland and England, and hired himself out as a carpenter, in order to learn the art of shipbuilding. He did this for the sake of his people, that he might supply, in the way of knowledge, what they lacked. So, on a far grander scale, the King of heaven vacated His throne for a season, laid aside His lustrous garments, clothed Himself in the humble garments of mortal man and became a carpenter. He did this for the sake of His people, to rebuild their broken lives.

A young boy spent an entire year constructing a model ship, similar to a great ship that was docked in his town's harbor. Every sail was intricately cut and sewn, exactly to scale and perfectly placed. Every plank was carved and fastened precisely. Finally the time came for the grand launching on a small creek near his home. During the first few moments, the ship slid gracefully over the water and rode the slow current. But then, without warning, the current quickened and a gust of wind pushed the boat down the creek. The boy was unable to keep up with the ship's pace. It soon sailed out of sight in the widening stream. The boy was crushed.

Some months later, the boy spotted a magnificent model ship in the front window of an antique shop—his ship! The very work of art he had fashioned was for sale. The price was steep, and even though it belonged to him already, he was willing to pay anything to get it back. He scraped together every last penny he had to buy the ship again.

The whole world is God's by right of creation. He made it, and everything was "very good," precisely as He wanted it. Sin destroyed His perfect creation. So God redeemed us—He bought us back again—in the death of His only Son. We are His twice—created and rescued in Christ.

From What Has Christ Redeemed You?

From the unholy three—sin, death, and the devil.

- He redeemed me from the punishment of sin, taking the blame and guilt upon Himself.

- He redeemed me from the sting of death, taking away the fear of natural death and the punishment of eternal death.

- He redeemed me from the ownership of Satan, giving me power to resist temptation.

Now, if you are asked, "What do you believe in the Second Article about Jesus Christ?" answer briefly,
"I believe that Jesus Christ, God's true Son, has become my Lord."
"But what does it mean to become Lord?"
"It is this. He has redeemed me from sin, from the devil, from death, and from all evil. For before I did not have a Lord or King, but was captive under the devil's power, condemned to death, stuck in sin and blindness."

For when we had been created by God the Father and had received from Him all kinds of good, the devil came and led us into disobedience, sin, death, and all evil [Genesis 3]. So we fell under God's wrath and displeasure and were doomed to eternal damnation, just as we had merited and deserved. There was no counsel, help, or comfort until this only and eternal Son of God—in His immeasurable goodness—had compassion upon our misery and wretchedness. He came from heaven to help us [John 1:9]. So those tyrants and jailers are all expelled now. In their place has come Jesus Christ, Lord of life, righteousness, every blessing, and salvation. He has delivered us poor, lost people from hell's jaws, has won us, has made us free [Romans 8:1–2], and has brought us again into the Father's favor and grace. He has taken us as His own property under His shelter and protection [Psalm 61:3–4] so that He may govern us by His righteousness, wisdom, power, life, and blessedness. (Martin Luther, Large Catechism, II 27–30)

He Died for Me

The price He paid for my redemption was His holy, precious blood, and His innocent suffering and death.

Blood is life. In the Old Testament, sacrifices included the shedding of blood. Christ, the perfect Sacrifice, shed His blood to give forgiveness, life, and salvation to the world.

Indeed, under the law almost everything is purified with blood, and without the shedding of blood there is no forgiveness of sins. (Hebrews 9:22)

A farmer was found kneeling at a soldier's grave near Nashville, Tennessee. The cemetery caretaker came to him and said, "Why do you pay so much attention to this grave? Was your son buried here?" "No," he said. "During the war, my family were all sick. I was drafted, but I could not leave my wife and children. One of my neighbors came over and said, 'I will go for you; I have no family.' He went in my place. He was seriously wounded and taken to the hospital, but soon died. I come here often that I might remember this simple truth, 'He died for me.'"

Christ was our Substitute. He went forth to fight our battles. He died—*for us!* But He was also raised to life for our life and salvation.

On May 21, 1946, a young scientist, Louis Slotin, was carrying out an experiment at Los Alamos, New Mexico, in preparation for the testing of an atomic bomb in the South Pacific.

Though he had done the experiment many times, the scientist's screwdriver slipped at a critical moment. The two hemispheres of radioactive uranium came too close together. Instantly the room was filled with a dazzling bluish haze. Instead of ducking and possibly saving himself, Slotin tore the two hemispheres apart with his hands. He thus interrupted the chain reaction.

On the way to the hospital, he confided to his companion, "You will all come through all right. But I don't have a chance at all." It was only too true. He died nine days later.

Two thousand years ago, the Son of God walked directly into sin's deadly radiation and took up the cross in His hands. In His death, He broke the chain reaction—sin, death, eternal separation from God. He gave His life for me. (Adapted from Planet in Rebellion*)*

The story is told of the pelican that dwells in the remote regions of Africa. The mother pelican loves her tender young and cares and toils for their good. She brings them water from distant watering holes and fishes the seas for their food. In times of severe famine, the pelican feeds her young with her own blood; by feeding them, however, she dies.

Christ died that we might have life. He shed His blood willingly, and sprinkled us that we might be forgiven, secure in the promise of resurrection and eternal life.

As our "Vicar," or Substitute, Jesus made us "at one" with God. He effected our "at-one-ment." We refer to this so great sacrifice in our stead as the *vicarious atonement.*

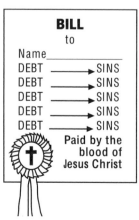

BILL
to
Name_____
DEBT ———→ SINS
DEBT ———→ SINS
DEBT ———→ SINS
DEBT ———→ SINS
DEBT ———→ SINS
Paid by the blood of Jesus Christ

Hymn

My faith looks up to Thee,
Thou Lamb of Calvary,
Savior divine.
Now hear me while I pray;
Take all my guilt away;
O let me from this day
Be wholly Thine!

Prayer

All thanks to You, my Lord Jesus Christ,

For all pain and insults You endured for me—scourging, ridicule, and crucifixion;

For all the benefits You have given me—forgiveness, life, and salvation.

You are my most merciful Redeemer, Friend, and Brother. May I trust You every day, love You in every way, and follow You through every joy and sorrow. In Your name I pray. Amen.

Bible Readings

Matthew 4:17

John 1:35–36

Psalm 24

Matthew 1:18–25

Luke 2:1–20

Matthew 27:11–26

_____

_____

John 19:17–42

_____

_____

Catechetical Review

1. For what threefold office was Christ anointed? (To be our Prophet, Priest, and King.)

2. In what respect was He a prophet? (He preached during His earthly ministry and still preaches today through His ministers.)

3. A Priest? (He sacrificed Himself on the altar of the cross, and He prays for us.)

4. A King? (He rules over the world and especially over His Church.)

5. What two states do we distinguish in Christ's performance of His threefold office? (The State of Humiliation and the State of Exaltation.)

6. What are the steps in the State of Humiliation? (He was conceived by the Holy Spirit; born of the Virgin Mary; suffered under Pontius Pilate; was crucified, died, and buried.)

7. By whom was Jesus conceived? (Jesus was conceived by the Holy Spirit.)

8. Of whom was He born? (Jesus was born of the Virgin Mary.)

9. Was Joseph His real father? (No, Joseph was only His foster father.)

10. Where was Jesus born? (In Bethlehem.)

11. For what purpose was Jesus born? (To save His people from their sins.)

12. Where did Jesus live most of the time? (In Nazareth.)

13. At what age did He begin His public ministry? (Around 30. [Luke 3:23]).

14. What names are sometimes given to the three years of His public ministry? (Obscurity, popularity, and opposition.)

15. In what ways did Jesus prove that He is the Son of God? (By His words and by His works.)

16. What is meant by the expression "suffered under Pontius Pilate"? (Jesus was crowned with thorns, scourged, and ridiculed.)

17. Why did Jesus die on the cross? (To redeem me, a lost and condemned creature.)

18. From what has Jesus redeemed you? (From the dominion and punishment of sin, the sting of death, and the ownership of Satan.)

19. What price did Jesus pay for your redemption? (His holy, precious blood.)

20. For what purpose has Jesus redeemed you? ("That I may be His own and live under Him in His kingdom, and serve Him in everlasting righteousness, innocence, and blessedness.")

Bible Passages

1. The one who hears you hears Me, and the one who rejects you rejects Me, and the one who rejects Me rejects Him who sent Me. (Luke 10:16; Prophet)

2. For I delivered to you as of first importance what I also received: that Christ died for our sins in accordance with the Scriptures. (1 Corinthians 15:3; Priest)

3. And Jesus came and said to them, "All authority in heaven and on earth has been given to Me." (Matthew 28:18; King)

4. And the angel answered her, "The Holy Spirit will come upon you, and the power of the Most High will overshadow you; therefore the child to be born will be called holy—the Son of God." (Luke 1:35)

5. Therefore the Lord Himself will give you a sign. Behold, the virgin shall conceive and bear a son, and shall call His name Immanuel. (Isaiah 7:14)

6. For our sake He made Him to be sin who knew no sin, so that in Him we might become the righteousness of God. (2 Corinthians 5:21)

7. The next day he saw Jesus coming toward him, and said, "Behold, the Lamb of God, who takes away the sin of the world!" (John 1:29)

8. But if we walk in the light, as He is in the light, we have fellowship with one another, and the blood of Jesus His Son cleanses us from all sin. (1 John 1:7)

For Further Study

1. Study the Catechetical Review.

2. Memorize one or more Bible passages.

3. Memorize Luther's explanation to the Second Article.

15 The Second Article (Concluded)

State of Exaltation

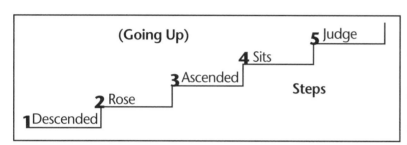

Step 1

He Descended into Hell (1 Peter 3:18–19)

Jesus descended into hell to show Himself as Conqueror of sin, death, evil, and Satan. We, too, can now triumph over Satan and hell through our Substitute and Champion.

False teachings regarding Christ's descent into hell:

a. That the soul of Jesus went down into "Limbo," the place where the souls of the "righteous" who had died before Christ were kept until His coming.

b. That "hell" was merely the grave.

c. That Christ wished to give the condemned unbelievers a "second chance" for repentance and salvation.

d. That He suffered the torments of hell in His descent.

Step 2

1st Day	2nd Day	3rd Day
6 P.M.	6 P.M.	6 P.M.
Friday	Saturday	Sunday
The Third Day		

The Third Day He Rose Again from the Dead

The Jewish nation referred to part of a day as a "day." Their day began at 6 p.m.—that is, at sundown. "And there was evening and there was morning, the first day" (Genesis 1:5).

He Rose Again

The disciples had no doubt that Jesus rose bodily from the grave. At first, they were disinclined to believe. But by the power of the Holy Spirit, the many infallible proofs at last convinced them and changed them from doubting, fearful men and women to bold witnesses. The Bible records at least nine appearances of the risen Jesus to His disciples:

1. To Mary Magdalene (John 20).

2. To the women at the tomb (Matthew 28).

3. To Peter (Luke 24:34; 1 Corinthians 15:5).

4. To James (1 Corinthians 15:7).

5. To the disciples of Emmaus, Easter afternoon (Luke 24).

6. To the disciples, Easter evening, with Thomas absent (John 20).

7. To the disciples and Thomas (John 20).

8. To the seven by the sea; the miraculous catch of fish (John 21).

9. To the eleven on the mountain (Matthew 28). This possibly included some of the five hundred mentioned by Paul (1 Corinthians 15:6).

With a Glorified Body

His body had not seen corruption. It was raised free from the weakness of human flesh.

It was the same body, for He talked and walked with the disciples, and they recognized Him. He ate with them not for the sake of sustenance but for the purpose of identification. He showed them His hands, feet, and side, and let them handle Him.

It was the same body, only different. Mary Magdalene at first mistook Him for the gardener. The seven by the sea did not recognize Him until after the miraculous catch of fish. He walked those seven miles from Jerusalem to Emmaus. Think of the hideous torture inflicted upon Him by the scourge, thorns, buffeting, nails, and spear. His body was now no longer subject to pain. His body was not hampered by time or space. He passed through the tomb without even disturbing the grave clothes. The stone was rolled away not to let Christ out but to let the disciples in. He descended into hell; disappeared at Emmaus; entered the closed room of the disciples; ascended into heaven. His body was different.

Reasons for Believing in the Historical Fact of Christ's Bodily Resurrection from the Dead

1. **Christ Himself spoke frequently of His resurrection.** (See Luke 9:22; 18:31–33; 24:46.) He is the Lord, the Son of God, whose word is trustworthy.

2. **The disciples are reliable, accurate historians,** both able and willing to tell the truth. It is absurd to say that they were deceived, for they refused to believe in their Master's resurrection until He showed Himself alive by many infallible proofs. Thomas, for instance, did not say, "I am willing to believe *if . . .*" He said, "Unless I see in His hands the mark of the nails and place my finger into the mark of the nails, and place my hand into His side, *I will never believe*" (John 20:25, emphasis added). He was determined *not to believe.*

It is equally absurd to say that the disciples palmed off a deliberate lie upon posterity. It is easy to understand that people will lie in order to advance their careers; to gain prestige, power, and financial success; or even to escape punishment or pain. But no sensible person will tell a lie that will bring him or her dishonor, persecution, and death. What earthly advantages could the disciples possibly hope to gain by spreading a lie that Jesus rose again? None! It's not at all reasonable to believe that the disciples fabricated the story of the resurrection in order to be martyred for Jesus.

3. How can history account for the **changed behavior** of the disciples if not upon the basis of the resurrection? Almost overnight, the disciples were changed from timid men and women in seclusion to people of deep conviction and courage. What happened to bring about this change? Only one explanation is satisfactory: the disciples were positive that Jesus, who was dead on Good Friday, was now alive on Easter Day. No one could shake their confidence. They held fast to this truth as if the hope of heaven depended upon it. *And it did.*

4. **The observance of Sunday** is another argument in favor of the resurrection. It takes a lot to get people to change the calendar. For centuries, God's people observed the seventh day as a holy day. Now, suddenly, they switched to Sunday. Why? An extraordinary event must have taken place to bring about this change—the resurrection of Jesus Christ!

5. The miracle of **Christianity** rests upon a living Lord, not upon a dead teacher or philosopher from long ago.

What His Resurrection Shows

1. **That Christ is the Son of God** and that His doctrine is the truth. No man can say, "Destroy this temple, and in three days I will raise it up," and make good his claim.

Only God has power over death.

If Christ has power over death, then Christ must be God.

2. **That God accepted the sacrifice of His Son for the reconciliation of the world.**

3. **That all believers shall rise to eternal life.** To the question, "Shall a person live again?" the believing heart answers, "Yes!" As the snake continues to live even though it has shed its skin, as the musician retains her skill though her flute break, as the snail creeps forth and leaves its vacant shell behind, so will humans live even though they die.

Jesus said to her, "I am the resurrection and the life. Whoever believes in Me, though he die, yet shall he live, and everyone who lives and believes in Me shall never die. Do you believe this? (John 11:25–26)

The human heart says, "Look how the pomegranate bursts its shell! Look how the egg produces its young! Look how the lily comes to life out of an ugly bulb! These are imperfect symbols of the promise of resurrection.

Look at the butterfly. First, there is the larva, representing the lowly condition of mortal humans on this earth. Next, the seemingly lifeless pupa lying in its chrysalis—how like the human body in the grave! Finally, the butterfly bursts its shell, emerges, dries its wings, and soars heavenward with a beautiful new body.

Cicero, the Roman statesman, noted in his writings that nothing is more established in history than belief in the immortality of the soul. The Greeks, as well as the Romans, placed lighted candles in the tombs of their dead. The Persians often left their graves partly open. Egyptians, too, believed in the afterlife. Even the most barbarous nations and civilizations had customs that expressed or implied the hope of life after death.

These customs, however, are a frail foundation upon which to build the hope of the resurrection. Likewise, the universal longing of the human race after immortality is not the strongest proof. We turn to Jesus and ask Him, "If a person dies, shall he live again?"

We hear Him say, "Come to My tomb, come see where My body lay. There is the stone slab, there are the graveclothes. But do you seek Me? I am risen! Why do you look for the living among the dead? I am the resurrection and the life."

Thanks be to God, who gives us the victory through our Lord Jesus Christ (1 Corinthians 15:57).

Step 3

He Ascended into Heaven

This was Christ's exaltation. He came from heaven; He returns to heaven to resume His place as Lord. He had died once; He will not die again. Instead, He visibly ascended on high to prepare a place for us. His ascension is a pledge of our destiny. Heaven is our home.

We should learn to bring our eyes, our hearts, and souls to bear upon yonder life in heaven and in a lively hope await it with joy. (Martin Luther, What Luther Says, *§1891)*

Step 4

And Sits at the Right Hand of God, the Father Almighty

Christ occupies the seat of honor and majesty and exercises divine power. The "right hand" is a symbol of power, partnership, and honor. "John is my right-hand man." The apostles in Jerusalem extended "the right hand of fellowship" to Paul and Barnabas (Galatians 2:9). Solomon seated his mother to his right; that is, in the place of honor (1 Kings 2:19)

The LORD says to my Lord: "Sit at My right hand, until I make Your enemies Your footstool. (Psalm 110:1)

Step 5

From Thence He Will Come to Judge the Living and the Dead

Christ will come

a. *suddenly*, without warning, "as a thief"—we should always be prepared;

b. *visibly*—"every eye will see Him" (Revelation 1:7);

c. *in glory*—not in poverty and lowliness, as at Bethlehem;

d. *to judge*—the first time, He came to save.

A man was brought into court. His lawyer successfully pleaded his case, and he was released. Later, the lawyer became a judge, and the man was brought again into court. The man said confidently to his former lawyer, "Your Honor, you know me; you once pleaded my case." The judge said, "But now I am your judge."

Believers in Christ need not fear the judgment. For us, the Last Day signifies a consummation. We need not fear the signs that precede the second coming. When the trees in the springtime begin to shoot forth, we feel no fear, for they signal the approach of summer. We know that winter, with its blasts and chills, will soon be past. Summer and luxurious warmth will soon engulf us. The birds will return and fill the air with music. Great white clouds will drift lazily down the avenues of the skies. How do we know this? These are the signs. Thus the believer does not quake at the thought of Christ's return. Ours prayers are being answered, "Thy kingdom come." Yes, "Come, Lord Jesus" (Revelation 22:20).

In 1997, Marshall Appelwhite led thirty-eight other people in a mass suicide near San Diego, California. Members of a New Age cult called "Heaven's Gate," Appelwhite and his followers lived together in a large house in anticipation of their final days on earth. They believed that a spaceship would come—right behind the Hale-Bopp comet—to take them to a "heavenly kingdom." Like numerous Christian and non-Christian groups throughout history, Heaven's Gate looked for specific signs that pointed to a "supernatural" rescue.

Sadly, some individuals have tried to figure out the date of the "last day" or the "end of the world." They have mixed the truth of God's Word with their own opinions, calculations, and false teachings. Many people have been deeply hurt. Some, like the members of Heaven's Gate, have taken their own lives—or even the lives of others.

In truth, Jesus will return. But the Bible simply does not provide exact dates and details about the second coming.

The Bible says, "But concerning that day or that hour, no one knows, not even the angels in heaven, nor the Son, but only the Father" (Mark 13:32).

Therefore stay awake—for you do not know when the master of the house will come, in the evening, or at midnight, or when the rooster crows, or in the morning—lest he come suddenly and find you asleep. (Mark 13:35–36)

The reason for Christ's exaltation is that I may be His own and live under Him in His kingdom and serve Him in everlasting righteousness, innocence, and blessedness.

The story is told from ancient Rome of a young girl who was placed on the public auction block. She was to be sold to the highest bidder. The girl was forced to turn around, front and back, that the audience might see and make an estimate. The bids came in rapid succession, for she was young and strong. Finally one man outbid all the others; he bought the girl. He immediately put down the money and took possession of his property. Then he turned to the slave girl and said, "You are free. I have bought you free. You may go your way."

She looked at him with her eyes wide open, with fear and apprehension. She did not understand. "Free," he said. "You may go; you are free. I have given you your freedom." The sincerity of his tone and the love in his eyes told her it was true. She fell at his feet, and, seized by gratitude, said, "Please, I don't want to be free. I want to serve you. Let me serve you not as a slave but as a friend."

Christ has redeemed me from the taskmaster—from sin, death, and the devil—that I might be His own and serve Him not out of compulsion but in love and gratitude.

Hymn

I know that my Redeemer lives;
What comfort this sweet sentence gives!
He lives, He lives, who once was dead;
He lives, my ever living head.

Prayer

O God, for our redemption You gave Your only Son to the death—even death on the cross! By His glorious resurrection You have delivered us from the power of the enemy and opened the way of eternal life. Help us, we pray, to die daily to sin that we may always live with Him in the joy of His resurrection; through Jesus Christ, Your Son, our Lord. Amen.

Bible Readings

1 Peter 3:18–19

Mark 16:1–14

Luke 24:50–53

Acts 7:55–60

Psalm 93

Matthew 25:31–46

2 Corinthians 5:15

Catechetical Review

1. What are the steps in the State of Exaltation? (He descended into hell, the third day He rose again from the dead, He ascended into heaven, and sits at the right hand of God the Father Almighty; from thence He will come to judge the living and the dead.)

2. When did Jesus descend into hell? (Sometime after He awakened and before He showed Himself to His disciples.)

3. What was His reason for descending into hell? (He wished to show Himself to hell as conqueror.)

4. When did the Lord step forth from the tomb? (On Easter Sunday.)

5. Why is the resurrection of Christ so comforting to us? (It proves [1] that He is the Son of God, [2] that His doctrine is true, [3] that God accepted the sacrifice of His Son, and [4] that we, too, will rise.)

6. Why is Easter an especially happy day for you? (I know that Jesus, the risen Christ, has saved me from sin, death, and the power of the devil.)

7. For how many days after His resurrection did Jesus show Himself alive to His disciples? (For forty days.)

8. Where did Jesus ascend to on the fortieth day? (Into heaven.)

9. Why did Jesus ascend into heaven? (To take possession of His glory, to be our Advocate with His Father, to prepare a place for us.)

10. Where is Jesus now? (Jesus is now at the right hand of God the Father Almighty; that is, He is everywhere, ruling as Lord of the universe.)

11. What is He doing there? (He is ruling all things, watching over the Church and praying for me.)

12. Will we ever see Jesus? Yes! (We will see Him on the Last Day and forever in eternity.)

13. When is the Last Day? (At the end of the world.)

14. Why will Jesus come back? (To judge the living and the dead, and to take all believers to heaven.)

15. How will Jesus return? (Jesus will return suddenly, visibly, and in great glory.)

16. Does anyone know the exact time when Christ will return? (No! Plain and simple!)

17. Why has God not revealed that to us? (He wants us to be prepared always.)

18. Why are we happy to know that Jesus will come again? (Because then we will live and reign with Him forever.)

19. Which prayer do you say for His return? ("Thy kingdom come!")

Bible Passages

1. For Christ also suffered once for sins, the righteous for the unrighteous, that He might bring us to God, being put to death in the flesh but made alive in the spirit, in which He went and proclaimed to the spirits in prison. (1 Peter 3:18–19)

2. And was declared to be the Son of God in power according to the Spirit of holiness by His resurrection from the dead. (Romans 1:4)

3. And if Christ has not been raised, your faith is futile and you are still in your sins. (1 Corinthians 15:17)

4. Yet a little while and the world will see Me no more, but you will see Me. Because I live, you also will live. (John 14:19)

5. Jesus said to her, "I am the resurrection and the life. Whoever believes in Me, though he die, yet shall he live, and everyone who lives and believes in Me shall never die. Do you believe this?" (John 11:25–26)

6. Men of Galilee, why do you stand looking into heaven? This Jesus, who was taken up from you into heaven, will come in the same way as you saw Him go into heaven. (Acts 1:11)

7. My little children, I am writing these things to you so that you may not sin. But if anyone does sin, we have an advocate with the Father, Jesus Christ the righteous. (1 John 2:1)

8. And He commanded us to preach to the people and to testify that He is the one appointed by God to be judge of the living and the dead. (Acts 10:42)

9. But the day of the Lord will come like a thief, and then the heavens will pass away with a roar, and the heavenly bodies will be burned up and dissolved, and the earth and the works that are done on it will be exposed. (2 Peter 3:10)

10. If anyone serves Me, he must follow Me; and where I am, there will My servant be also. If anyone serves Me, the Father will honor him. (John 12:26)

For Further Study

1. Study the Catechetical Review.

2. Memorize one or more Bible passages.

3. Review the Second Article and Luther's explanation.

Confirmation Builder—
Lesson 18

Sanctification

I believe in

1. the Holy Spirit,

2. the holy Christian church,

3. the communion of saints,

4. the forgiveness of sins,

5. the resurrection of the body,

6. and the life everlasting. Amen.

What does this mean?

I believe that I cannot by my own reason or strength believe in Jesus Christ, my Lord, or come to Him; but the Holy Spirit has called me by the Gospel, enlightened me with His gifts, sanctified and kept me in the true faith.

In the same way He calls, gathers, enlightens, and sanctifies the whole Christian church on earth and keeps it with Jesus Christ in the one true faith.

In this Christian church He daily and richly forgives all my sins and the sins of all believers.

On the Last Day He will raise me and all the dead, and give eternal life to me and all believers in Christ.

This is most certainly true.

The Holy Spirit

His Person

The Holy Spirit is the Third Person in the Holy Trinity; true God. He was present at creation, the history of Israel, the Baptism of Jesus, Pentecost, every Baptism. The Spirit inspired the "holy men of God." All Scripture is given by inspiration of the Holy Spirit. See the apostolic blessing (2 Corinthians 13:14).

His Name

He is called *Holy* Spirit, because He Himself is holy (without sin). He makes us holy.

When the Helper comes, whom I will send to you from the Father, the Spirit of truth, who proceeds from the Father, He will bear witness about Me. (John 15:26)

The Nicene Creed affirms that the Holy Spirit is "the Lord and giver of life, who proceeds from the Father and the Son, who with the Father and the Son together is worshiped and glorified, who spoke by the prophets."

The Father and the Son send the Spirit to do His divine work (John 14:15–26).

These words testify and prove that the Holy Spirit is not an ordinary spirit, such as a creature, or something apart from God and yet given to men by Him, nor merely the work He performs in our hearts, but that He is a Spirit who is essentially God Himself, who has His being from the Father, is not created or made but is One who proceeds from the Father and is also sent by Christ. (Martin Luther, What Luther Says, *§2043)*

His Work

He makes us Christians.

The Father gave His Son, the Son gave Himself, the Holy Spirit gives the fruits of Christ's redemption.

This is the office and work of the Holy Spirit: to reveal through the Gospel what great and glorious things God has done for us through Christ, namely, that He has redeemed us from sin, death, and the devil's power; has taken us into His grace and protection; and has given Himself utterly and entirely for us. (Martin Luther, What Luther Says, *§2045)*

Let's say there is a woman who is very sick; she cannot move or help herself. The doctor comes and, after a careful examination, writes a prescription. Does that make her well?

No. Someone must go and have the prescription filled.

Does that make her well? No, the sick woman must take the medicine.

The work of God in the healing of the sick woman is similar. The Father wrote the prescription: He made the plan of salvation. The Son filled the prescription by His suffering and death. The Holy Spirit applies Christ's saving work through Word and Sacrament. The Spirit converts us and renews us through the Gospel, through Baptism, and through the Lord's Supper.

- In Him you also, when you heard the word of truth, the gospel of your salvation, and believed in Him, were sealed with the promised Holy Spirit. (Ephesians 1:13)

- Jesus answered, "Truly, truly, I say to you, unless one is born of water and the Spirit, he cannot enter the kingdom of God." (John 3:5)

- For as often as you eat this bread and drink the cup, you proclaim the Lord's death until He comes. (1 Corinthians 11:26)

New York City has a marvelous water system. Upstate, there are large reservoirs, lakes. If someone asked, "What are these?" the answer is "These are the water supplies for New York City." "But the city is far away. How can this water be of any value to the people there?" The response: "The water is brought down to the city by means of aqueducts, and eventually led to each individual faucet."

Similarly, we can envision the great reservoir of God's love—the waters of life for many, all that Christ has procured for us through His life and death. But how can all this benefit us? The Holy Spirit, through the aqueduct of the spoken and visible Word (the Means of Grace), applies to our hearts the grace of God in Christ Jesus.

A. I cannot, by my own reason or strength, believe in Jesus Christ, my Lord, or come to Him.

I am by nature

John 15:5
"Apart from Me you can do nothing."

1. Spiritually blind. Of myself, I cannot see that I am so sinful, cannot see and understand why an innocent one should take my punishment in my place. The Holy Spirit removes the bandage from my eyes, endows me with spiritual power to see, understand, and appreciate the order of salvation.

Conversion. I am turned about from darkness to light.

2. Spiritually dead. "In trespasses and sins." The Holy Spirit makes alive, infuses new life, purifies thoughts and emotions, renews the will.

Conversion. I am brought from death to life.

Regeneration—born again, twice-born.

A man, 84 years old, was asked how old he was. He said, "Four years." How was that? "Four years ago, I became a Christian. I was regenerated, newborn. So I am only four 'years' old." Christians are twice-born people; first, according to the flesh; second, according to the Spirit.

Christ raises me from the dead: He gives me physical life, spiritual life, and eternal life.

3. An enemy of God.

Conversion: I am turned from God's enemy to God's friend.

St. Paul, for example, was turned from a person who hated Jesus and persecuted His Church to a disciple who loved His Lord and Savior and ministered to the Church throughout his life.

The prodigal son turned his back on his father. He rebelled against his father's ways and will. *Conversion!* The lost son returned to his father.

Once there was a briar growing in the ditch. A man came with a spade, and as he dug around it. The briar said, "What is he going to do with me? Doesn't he see that I am worthless?" In spite of that, the gardener dug up the briar and planted it in his garden among the finest flowers. Again the briar thought, "What a mistake to plant a good-for-nothing briar among such beautiful flowers." But the man, having planted the briar, went away, never heeding the words. After some time, he returned with a sharp knife, made a small slit in the briar, and grafted onto it a flower. In due time on that old briar bush began to bloom a great number of fragrant, beautiful flowers. Then the gardener said to the briar bush: "Your present beauty is not due to what came out of you, but what I put into you."

128

B. But the Holy Spirit has

1. called me [to Christ]—invited me to come, offering to me the blessings of Christ's redemption, and moving me to receive His gifts in faith . . .

by the Gospel—the visible or audible Word—not through dreams or visions; we do not necessarily have to have a strong feeling in order to be sure of our salvation; we cling to the promise of the Word.

Question: To convert an unbeliever, what do you do? *Answer:* Present the Word to him or her because through this means, the Spirit has promised to work.

2. enlightened me with His gifts—He sheds light on my understanding; that is, He enables me to grow in spiritual wisdom and knowledge.

3. sanctified—He has renewed my will and endowed my heart with new desires and inclinations, so that I am able to show my faith by doing good works.

Good works flow out of faith as naturally as flowers and fruit proceed out of a tree, or water out of a spring.

All the zeros placed to the left of a numeral are of no value. All the zeros placed to the right of a numeral increase the value. So all the works done before you have faith are valueless. But all the works done after you have faith, through Christ's strength, are pleasing to God.

The Holy Spirit *sanctifies*. He gives me power to

- resist sin;

- lead a Christian life; and

- do good works.

4. and kept me in the true faith—The Holy Spirit has kept me in the true faith through the Word and Sacrament. The Church is the Bethel, "the house of bread"; it is the armory of Christian warfare; it is the hearth where the fires of love are kept burning.

For by grace you have been saved through faith. And this is not your own doing; it is the gift of God, not a result of works, so that no one may boast. (Ephesians 2:8–9)

Parallel Doctrines

If saved—by the gracious work of the Holy Ghost
If lost—by your own fault

The Holy Spirit is ready and willing to work salvation in everyone who hears the Gospel, but many resist His work; they are thus lost through their own fault. A patient can refuse the best medicine the doctor offers.

You are lost in the wood. A guide finds you; he is able to lead you to safety and rescue. You can refuse to follow him. If you die, then it is your own fault. If you are brought safely to your destination, the guide gets the credit for your rescue.

Faith is like a plant. You can crush it with your heel, but you cannot make it grow.

The Spirit's Word

1. **calls**—plants seed in the heart;

2. **enlightens**—causes growth toward the light;

3. **sanctifies**—causes flowers and fruits (good works);

4. **keeps**—waters and nurtures the plant of faith so that it remains ever green.

The Spirit's Work among God's People, the Church

A man attended worship services at a local congregation. He was spiritually blind, dead, and an enemy of God. Then, as God's Spirit worked through the Word, he was moved in his heart to trust Christ for forgiveness. He did not know where faith came from; in truth, it came from the Holy Spirit. As a result, this man knew something better, higher, for the first time: comfort, peace, joy. He attended worship regularly for the remainder of his life.

1. **Called**—He heard the message of salvation. He realized his sinfulness and need of a Savior. By the Spirit's power, he turned from sin and received God's grace. He came up out of death into life. The Holy Spirit had called him by the Gospel. The seed of the Word was dropped into his heart. He was converted.

2. **Enlightened**—As this man continued coming to church, continued reading his Bible, his knowledge grew. More light was shed on his dark understanding; he gained a deeper and fuller understanding of God's love for sinful humankind. In other words, the seed of the Word grew toward the light. This, too, came from the Holy Spirit, who enlightened him with His gifts.

3. **Sanctified**—The neighbors began to talk about this man and say, "Have you noticed the changes in his life? He is a new person. He acts so different from the way he used to. He no longer does this and that; instead he is kind, decent, eager to help others." What happened? The plant brought forth flowers and fruits. The Holy Spirit began to sanctify the man, to renew his will, to lead him to do good and shun evil.

4. **Kept**—Only through the grace of God and the work of the Holy Spirit can this man be kept in the true faith to death.

Therefore, from beginning to end, this man's salvation is due to the work of the Spirit of God. This man did not contribute anything toward his salvation. He will never be able to pose as a little savior, never be able to sing the song of redemption in his own honor. But he will say, with all the saints, "To Him who sits on the throne and to the Lamb be blessing and honor and glory and might forever and ever!" (Revelation 5:13).

The Spirit's Work in Your Life

1. **Called**—You were called through the visible Word, namely, Baptism ("water included in God's command and combined with God's word"). If you were baptized as an infant, you may never recall a time when you were not a Christian.

2. **Enlightened**—This happened at home, by your parents, in a Christian day school, at Sunday School, through confirmation instruction, by church attendance, and through other opportunities for Christian instruction.

3. **Sanctified**—This shows in whatever you do, out of love toward God, by faith in Christ Jesus.

4. **Kept**—Thank His kindness. Go regularly to the supply house of spiritual strength.

Hymn

Holy Spirit, light divine,
Shine upon this heart of mine;
Chase the shades of night away,
Turn the darkness into day.

Prayer

May the outpouring of the Holy Spirit, O Lord, cleanse our hearts and change our lives so that we may serve You in our thoughts, words, and actions; through Jesus Christ, Your Son, our Lord. Amen.

Let Your mercy, O Lord, be upon me and the brightness of Your Spirit illumine my inward soul, that He may kindle my cold heart and light up my dark mind, through Jesus Christ, Your Son, our Lord. Amen.

Bible Readings

Psalm 53

_____

_____

Acts 2:1–13

_____

_____

Luke 14:16–24

_____

_____

Acts 16:25–34

_____

_____

Acts 5:1–11

_____

_____

Acts 7:51–60

_____

_____

Catechetical Review

1. Who is your Guide to Jesus? (My Guide to Jesus is the Holy Spirit.)

2. Who is the Holy Spirit? (The Holy Spirit is the Third Person of the blessed Trinity.)

3. What is the pathway through which the Holy Spirit leads you to Jesus? (The Word of God [spoken and visible—the Means of Grace].)

4. Why can you not find Jesus by yourself? (By nature I am spiritually blind, dead, and an enemy of God.)

5. What has the Holy Spirit done to bring you to Christ? (He has called me by the Gospel, enlightened me with His gifts, sanctified, and kept me in the true faith.)

6. Is the Holy Spirit willing to work this in everyone who hears the Gospel? (Yes!)

7. Why, then, are many people lost? (They resist the Holy Spirit.)

8. If, then, these people are lost, whose fault is it? (Their own fault.)

9. On the other hand, if a person is saved, who receives all the credit? (The Holy Spirit.)

10. Why is He called the "Holy" Spirit? (He Himself is holy, and He makes us holy.)

11. What are all those called who have been made holy by the Holy Spirit? (They are called Christians.)

12. What is a Christian? (A Christian is one who believes in Jesus, loves Him, and follows Him.)

13. Will the Christian do good works? (Yes, indeed; as the Holy Spirit evidences His power in the life of a Christian. A good work is "faith working through love" [Galatians 5:6].)

14. When were most of us made Christians by the Holy Spirit? (When we were baptized.)

Bible Passages

1. Therefore I want you to understand that no one speaking in the spirit of God ever says "Jesus is accursed!" and no one can say "Jesus is Lord" except in the Holy Spirit. (1 Corinthians 12:3)

2. To this He called you through our gospel, so that you may obtain the glory of our Lord Jesus Christ. (2 Thessalonians 2:14)

3. Jesus answered, "Truly, truly, I say to you, unless one is born of water and the Spirit, he cannot enter the kingdom of God." (John 3:5–6)

4. The natural person does not accept the things of the Spirit of God, for they are folly to him, and he is not able to understand them because they are spiritually discerned. (1 Corinthians 2:14)

5. And you were dead in the trespasses and sins. (Ephesians 2:1)

6. For the mind that is set on the flesh is hostile to God, for it does not submit to God's law; indeed, it cannot. (Romans 8:7)

7. For we are His workmanship, created in Christ Jesus for good works, which God prepared beforehand, that we should walk in them. (Ephesians 2:10)

8. The Lord is not slow to fulfill His promise as some count slowness, but is patient toward you, not wishing that any should perish, but that all should reach repentance. (2 Peter 3:9; see also 1 Timothy 2:4)

9. For by grace you have been saved through faith. And this is not your own doing; it is the gift of God, not a result of works, so that no one may boast. (Ephesians 2:8–9)

10. And without faith it is impossible to please Him, for whoever would draw near to God must believe that He exists and that He rewards those who seek Him. (Hebrews 11:6)

11. If you love Me, you will keep My commandments. (John 14:15)

For Further Study

1. Study the Catechetical Review.

2. Memorize one or more Bible passages.

3. Memorize the Third Article.

17 The Holy Christian Church

Confirmation Builder—
Lesson 18

The Invisible Church Is the Whole Company of Believers

1. The Gospel is preached in many denominations, in many languages, in many countries, to many people. The Holy Spirit calls people through the Gospel, makes them Christians through the Gospel.

2. Wherever the Gospel is in use, there will be found people who have saving faith in Christ (Isaiah 55:10–11).

3. All these believers, taken together, regardless of race, nationality, color, or station, form the one invisible, indivisible, universal Church of Christ, which He calls His Bride, His temple, His city, His flock, His Body (Romans 12:4–5; Colossians 1:18). This is the true Church of God, known on earth as the kingdom of grace, known in heaven as the kingdom of glory (or the Church Militant and the Church Triumphant).

4. This Church is invisible to us, for we cannot look into another's heart and see whether he or she has faith (Luke 17:20–21; 2 Timothy 2:19). For instance, by looking over the congregation of a Sunday morning, I cannot say, "The three persons in the first pew have saving faith, while the fourth one is a hypocrite." Nor can anyone else identify the true believers. Therefore, to us the Church is invisible. And so we rightly say, "I believe in the Holy Christian Church."

But God's firm foundation stands, bearing this seal: "The Lord knows those who are His," and "Let everyone who names the name of the Lord depart from iniquity." (2 Timothy 2:19)

---

5. This Church rests on Christ, the firm foundation, and is therefore called the Holy **Christian** Church. When Lutherans say, "I believe in the holy catholic church," we do not mean thereby the Roman Catholic or the Greek Catholic Church, but we mean the Church Universal, the Bride of Christ. The word *catholic* means "general" or "universal."

6. This Church is called the **Holy** Church. Why? Are the members holy? No and Yes.

   No. They are not sinless, either in their own estimation or in that of others. They still sin in thought, word, and deed, and will continue to do so as long as they live in a world contaminated by sin. All people are sinners; even the apostle Paul confessed his sinfulness.

   Yes. They are holy in the sight of God by reason of their faith in Christ. God, for Jesus' sake, forgives them their transgressions. Furthermore, they serve God with holy works.

We may therefore refer to them as a community, a gathering, of saints (Ephesians 5:25–27).

The Visible Church

1. The visible church is the local congregation, as in "St. Mark's Church."

2. It is composed of believers and, possibly, hypocrites; those who say they are Christians (Matthew 13:47–48; 22:11–12).

3. There are many, many visible churches. Some are true, some are not.

4. The true visible Church is an assembly of believers among whom the Gospel is preached and taught in truth and purity, and the sacraments are administered according to the Gospel (see Augsburg Confession IV).

A seven-year-old child knows what the Church is, namely, the holy believers and lambs who hear the voice of their Shepherd [John 10:11–16]. For the children pray, "I believe in one holy Christian Church." This holiness . . . [comes] from God's Word and true faith. (Martin Luther, Smalcald Articles III XII 2–3)

How to Determine Which Is the True Visible Church

Ten students copy a page out of a textbook. When the copies are compared, no two are alike. Each student maintains that his is the correct copy. How are we to determine which is the correct copy? By comparing each one with the original.

A favorite old game is Where Is the Button? One person went out of the room; the others hid the button. In she came and started her search. The farther away she was from the place where the button lay concealed the more the others assured her that she was "cold" or "ice cold." As she drew nearer, they said, "You are getting warmer, you are getting hot, you will soon burn yourself." Somewhat similarly, denominations stand in relation to the Bible. Some denominations are so far away from it that they are cold—ice cold! The church that stands on the Scriptures as God's Word, on the Gospel and the Sacraments, is the true church.

In Summary

1. Become a member of the invisible Church by believing in Christ (John 8:31–32).

2. Join the true visible Church by Baptism, confirmation, or profession of faith.

Don't cruise around from one church to another. Experience shows that "window-shoppers of religion," "spiritual vagabonds," soon lose whatever religion they have. Every Christian should be encamped with God's people.

You need the Church and the Church needs you. The Church is Christ's mystical body through which alone He can do His work of evangelizing the world. Certainly you don't want to hamper and hinder His work by staying away.

The Church is the one institution that will never pass away.

The Church has often been compared to a ship. In early Christian art, the Church is frequently depicted as a ship against which the personified winds are fighting, and the waves of the world are beating; but they do not succeed in crushing it. Many years ago, the Titanic made its maiden voyage across the ocean. It was called "The Floating Palace." Seamen were so sure of the Titanic's perfect safety that they failed to equip the ship with sufficient lifeboats. Then came the fatal night. Out in the bleakness of the dark, a cold, white object waited. Another moment, and the ship crashed against the iceberg and, trembling throughout its structure, descended into the icy deep. Women and children fled to lifeboats and were rowed to safety.

The Church of God, by comparison, is a small boat, but because Jesus is in it, it is a lifeboat, and it will ride triumphantly over the dark waters and come safely into the haven at last.

3. Give toward the support of the Church and toward missions (1 Corinthians 9:14; Matthew 28:19).

Everything we are and have comes from God; He has made us the stewards over His possessions. As the Holy Spirit works in us through the Means of Grace, He empowers us to return to God a portion of our time, talents and abilities, and possessions.

As God's Spirit changes us, He enables us to focus on Christ, rather than focus on self. By faith, He brings us truly to love Him who loved us and gave Himself for us. He moves us to respond to God with grateful hearts, without coercion.

If Christ has received you, He will also receive the gifts and actions dedicated to Him. First, He wants the giver—*you*—then the gifts. Let the love of Christ constrain you to give cheerfully, regularly, proportionately, and gratefully. Many Christians tithe; that is, they give 10 percent to church and charity. "Give as God has given to you" is an excellent principle by which to live.

4. Avoid false churches. Be loyal to your own (Matthew 7:15; 1 John 4:1; Romans 16:17).

The Church is like a great tree, which grows from the rich soil of the Gospel. But in its development through the centuries, many diseases affected the tree, damaging the branches. By the sixteenth century, the tree was enveloped in the darkness of false teachings. By God's grace, during the Reformation the pure light of the Gospel again shone brightly on the tree, allowing it to grow and flourish. The foundation in Jesus Christ was restored, and today the tree continues to grow and flourish—under God's blessing.

Therefore, as you received Christ Jesus the Lord, so walk in Him, rooted and built up in Him and established in the faith, just as you were taught, abounding in thanksgiving. (Colossians 2:6–7)

The Third Article

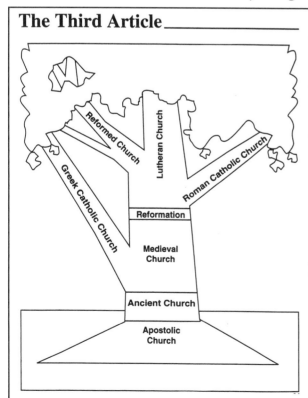

Hymn

The Church's one foundation
Is Jesus Christ, her Lord;
She is His new creation
By water and the Word.
From heaven He came and sought her
    To be His holy bride;
With His own blood He bought her,
and for her life He died.

Prayer

Lord, revive Your Church, beginning with me. Amen.

Almighty and everlasting God, we ask you humbly to shine down the bright beams of Your light on Your Church. Teach us daily to know and believe Your Gospel. Help us to walk in the light of Your truth. At the end of our life, bring us to glory with You, for into Your hands we commend ourselves, body and soul. Through Jesus Christ, our Lord. Amen.

Bible Readings

Psalm 46

Ephesians 2:19–22

1 Kings 8:1–21

Matthew 13:24–30

Matthew 7:15–20

Philippians 4:16–23

_____

_____

Catechetical Review

1. Through what means does the Holy Spirit make saints of sinners? (Through the Means of Grace.)

2. What are the Means of Grace? (The written and spoken Word of God and the Sacraments.)

3. Where are the Means of Grace to be found? (In the Christian Church.)

4. What is the Church? (The Church is the communion of saints, or the whole number of believers in Christ.)

5. Who are members of the Church? (All who have faith in Christ.)

6. How many such churches are there? (Only one.)

7. What denominational name does the Church bear? (None; it is the Bride of Christ.)

8. Is the Church limited to any place or age? (No, it is catholic, or universal.)

9. Why is the Church invisible to us? (We cannot look into another's heart and see whether he or she believes.)

10. Why is the Church called "holy?" (The members are holy by faith in Christ, and they serve God with holy works.)

11. Why is the Church called the "Christian" Church? (It is built upon Christ.)

12. What do you understand by the visible church? (A local congregation.)

13. Who are members of a local church? (Believers and possibly also hypocrites.)

14. How many visible churches are there? (There are a great many.)

15. Which must be the true visible church? (The church that is grounded in and focused on the Bible.)

16. What practical lessons can you gather from this doctrine of the Church?

_____ a. I want to be a member of the invisible Church.

_____ b. I want to be a member of the true visible church.

_____ c. I want to contribute toward the support of the church and missions.

_____ d. I will avoid false churches.

17. What are the fundamental teachings of the evangelical Lutheran Church?

_____ a. The Bible is the Word of God.

_____ b. Jesus is the only Savior.

_____ c. We are saved by believing in Jesus and being baptized.

Bible Passages

1. So we, though many, are one body in Christ, and individually members one of another. (Romans 12:5)

2. And He [Christ] is the head of the body, the church. He is the beginning, the firstborn from the dead, that in everything He might be preeminent. (Colossians 1:18)

3. For no one can lay a foundation other than that which is laid, which is Jesus Christ. (1 Corinthians 3:11)

4. But God's firm foundation stands, bearing this seal: "The Lord knows those who are His," and "Let everyone who names the name of the Lord depart from iniquity." (2 Timothy 2:19)

5. And I tell you, you are Peter, and on this rock I will build My church, and the gates of hell shall not prevail against it. (Matthew 16:18)

6. So Jesus said to the Jews who had believed in Him, "If you abide in My word, you are truly My disciples, and you will know the truth, and the truth will set you free." (John 8:31–32)

7. In the same way, the Lord commanded that those who proclaim the gospel should get their living by the gospel. (1 Corinthians 9:14)

For Further Study

1. Study the Catechetical Review.

2. Memorize one or more of the bible passages.

3. Memorize Luther's explanation to the Third Article.

18 The Forgiveness of Sins (Justification)

The worst thing in the world is sin.

The greatest blessing is the forgiveness of sin.

God for Christ's Sake, through the Gospel, Daily and Richly Forgives All the Sins of Me and All Believers

The story of salvation may be illustrated as follows:

Torn and disfigured— my sinful heart.

Restored by Christ— my Savior's blood has reclaimed my heart.

Empowered— my cleansed, motivated, and empowered heart.

This doctrine of justification, or the forgiveness of sins through Christ is the head and the cornerstone. It alone begets, nourishes, builds, preserves, and defends the church of God; and without the church of God cannot exist for one hour. (Martin Luther, What Luther Says, *§2195)*

Many people make a "Wordless Book." A Christian's book has three pages: a white page that has been scribbled upon, a red page, and clean white page. As you look at the scribbled page, recall Bible passages that tell us of our sin. As you look at the red page, recall Bible passages that tell us of Christ's sacrifice. As you look at the white page, recall Bible passages that tell us of our new life in Christ and His promise of eternal life in heaven.

A Map That Can Guide to Heaven

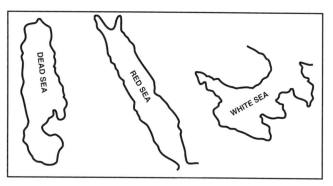

The DEAD SEA (in Israel) pictures the natural condition of the human heart, dead to God, to good. "Dead in trespasses and sins." We are born contaminated with the evil of sin, its results, its defilements; for "all have sinned."

The RED SEA (in the Middle East) reminds us of the "fountain filled with blood, drawn from Immanuel's veins." As the children of Israel passed from slavery in Egypt through the Red Sea, so we pass from the slavery of sin through the Red Sea of the Savior's blood into the Promised Land.

The WHITE SEA (in northern Russia) represents the sinner forgiven through Christ. "Purge me with hyssop, and I shall be clean; wash me, and I shall be whiter than snow" (Psalm 51:7).

God sees Christ and is satisfied; the sinner sees Christ and is satisfied.

The Sin-Bearer

All sin was carried by Christ to Calvary's cross and atoned for there. Sin is not counted against the sinner. The sinner is acquitted, declared free. "Not guilty" is the verdict. In Christ the sinner is justified.

Long ago, debtors who were unable to pay what they owed were thrown into prison. If another paid the debtor's bill, he or she would be released. The merit of another was counted as though it were the debtor's own.

In Old Testament times, the lamb was most frequently used in sacrifice. The priest laid his hand upon the creature offered for sin, and while the sinner confessed his iniquity over the head of the sacrifice, the sin was typically transferred to the victim, which was therefore called sin or guilt. Thus God laid upon His Son the iniquities of us all. He became SIN for us, that we might be made the righteousness of God in Him.

The Central Teaching

The central teaching of the Bible is that all who believe receive forgiveness of sins and are justified before God, not by works, but by grace, for Christ's sake, through faith.

After all, there are only two religions in this world, God's and human. Human religion, no matter under what name it may travel, is always based on self-righteousness. God's religion, the only religion the Bible knows, is based on Jesus' blood and righteousness. Human religion says, "First you must do, then you shall live." God's religion says, "First you must live, by grace through faith in Christ, then you shall do." Human religion says, "You are saved by character." God's religion says, "You are saved by grace."

The Resurrection of the Body

What happened to the house?

The tenant left.

When the soul leaves its earthly dwelling place, the body is vacant. Is that the end of the body? No, the distinctive teaching of Christianity is not merely that the soul is immortal, but that the body will be raised again.

Read 1 Corinthians 15; 2 Corinthians 5:1–5.

The Same Body, Yet Changed

The Mississippi River north of St. Louis is muddy. It passes through the Chain of Rocks water works. There water is collected in huge outdoor basins, drained off again and again, aerated, filtered through gravel and sand, and finally becomes clear and crystalline. It is the same water and yet not the same; it has been purified, changed.

So is it with the resurrection of the dead. What is sown is perishable; what is raised is imperishable. It is sown in dishonor; it is raised in glory. It is sown in weakness; it is raised in power. It is sown a natural body; it is raised a spiritual body. (1 Corinthians 15:42–44)

At the Last Day, every human being who has ever lived will rise. There is no annihilation of the wicked, or simple dissolution in the universe. The ultimate destiny of all is either heaven or hell.

It is difficult to illustrate the truth of the resurrection of the body. Consider, though, the tulip. It is an ugly bulb. Plant it in the ground, and God gives it a "body" as it has pleased Him. He gives to every seed, whether grain, flower, or plant, its own body. How are the dead raised up? By the command of the Lord. He who made our body in the first place in the secret chambers of darkness, He who fearfully and wonderfully fashioned us, He will give us the resurrection body.

In North India, a missionary was preaching in a bazaar when he was confronted by a Muslim. "You must admit," the Muslim said, "that we have one thing you do not, and it is better than anything you have. When we go to Mecca, we have a tomb to remember the Prophet. When Christians go to visit Jerusalem, you have nothing but an empty grave."

The missionary replied, "You are correct. But that is just the difference. Muhammad is dead. Muhammad is in his coffin. The founders of every religion or philosophy are dead today—except one! Jesus is alive. Jesus is risen from the dead. He is the living Savior. This is our faith!" (Adapted from Seasonal Illustrations for Preaching and Teaching, *p. 53.)*

A woman of Hanover, Germany, feared the resurrection of the body. She planned to frustrate God's attempt to raise her body. She had a strong vault built, with iron and concrete slabs. On the top she placed an inscription: "This shall never be opened." Yet time, sun, rain, wind, and cold wore away part of the stone. Dirt accumulated in a small crack. And in the dirt a seed of a poplar tree sprouted and grew. As the years went by, the immense stone was moved out of its original position and the grave was opened. How are the dead raised up? By the power of God.

One day in the laboratory of a famous scientist, a valuable silver cup was accidentally dropped into a vat of acid. Immediately the silver cup disintegrated, dissolving into the acid. The person who dropped the cup was frantic, but the great scientist assured him that everything would turn out all right. The scientist knew that silver was still present in the vat, hidden among the minute particles of the liquid acid. After pouring the right chemicals into the acid, the silver quickly began to appear in the solution. It was then gathered together and sent to a silversmith with a careful description of the original cup. In a few days, the cup reappeared in the laboratory, ready to be used and appreciated for its value again.

Just as the scientist was able to extract atoms of silver dissolved in a vat of acid, almighty God is easily able, at the Last Day, to bring together the matter that once comprised each person.

Life Everlasting

1. At death, the soul separates from the body.

2. The soul of the Christian goes to heaven; the body goes to the ground.

3. On resurrection day, the body will be raised, changed, glorified, and reunited with the soul.

4. The believer, body and soul, will live with Christ forevermore.

```
                          heaven | soul
                              to        joins
                          goes                body
                          soul                and
        Separation {                          } reunited
                          body                and
                          goes              raised
                              to              is
                          ground | body
```
(diagram center: "End of Time")

At Death

The soul does not die with the body.

It does not sleep in the grave.

It does not fly around in space for two thousand years, then return and become reincarnated, as the Egyptians believed, who for this reason embalmed the body and built pyramids with secret rooms.

It does not hover in the vicinity of its former home, endeavoring to guide or communicate with the living, as the spiritists claim.

But it is at once present with Christ.

Jesus told the criminal on the cross, "Truly I say to you, today you will be with Me in Paradise" (Luke 23:43).

The apostle John wrote, "And I heard a voice from heaven saying, 'Write this: Blessed are the dead who die in the Lord from now on.' 'Blessed indeed' says the Spirit, 'that they may rest from their labors, for their deeds follow them!'" (Revelation 14:13).

Paul wrote, "I am hard pressed between the two. My desire is to depart and be with Christ, for that is far better" (Philippians 1:23).

The early Christians did not celebrate the birthdays of their family and friends, but the anniversary of death. They believed that the death day of a Christian is really his or her birthday, a new birth into a true and abiding life.

The Blessedness of Heaven

1. **We shall see God face-to-face.** We shall "see Him as He is." We shall enjoy the blessed and exalted vision.

2. **We shall know the angels. We shall know ourselves. We shall know the saints in light.** Think of meeting the patriarchs; the prophets; the martyrs and apostles; Jesus Christ, our Elder Brother and divine Lord; our Christian relatives and friends.

3. **We shall be clothed about with the divine image.**

   Our intellect will be enlightened.

   Our will will be obedient to God's will.

   Our heart will be in love with the good.

4. **We shall be free from all ills.**

No sin, sorrow, and death.

No unfulfilled wants and desires.

No pricks of conscience.

5. **There will be degrees of glory** (1 Corinthians 15:41–42; 2 Corinthians 9:6).

Greater glory is given as a reward, not of merit, but of grace, to those who on earth showed their faith in consecrated service to the Lord and in many good works done to their neighbors.

In heaven, no earthly conditions and customs prevail, no division into families, no civil governments, no earthly vocations, no denominational divisions, no mission work, no Office of the Keys.

"For God so loved the world, that He gave His only Son, that whoever believes in Him should not perish but have eternal life" (John 3:16).

Eternal life begins here, in our hearts; for when we begin to believe in Christ, after we have been baptized, then, according to faith and the Word, we are liberated from death, from sin, and from the devil. Therefore we have the beginning of life eternal and its first fruits in this life, a sort of mild foretaste; we have entered the lobby; but soon, divested of this flesh, we shall fully appreciate all. (Martin Luther, What Luther Says, §1898)

Hymn

I lay my sins on Jesus,
    The spotless Lamb of God;
He bears them all and frees us
    From the accursed load.
I bring my guilt to Jesus
    To wash my crimson stains
Clean in His blood most precious
Till not a spot remains.

Prayer

O God, whose nature is ever to have mercy and forgive, hear our humble prayer. Though we are often overcome by our many sins, though we often doubt Your promises, pour out on us Your great and abundant mercy. Strengthen our faith. Renew our commitment. Enable us to serve You, and to share Your love with all people. For the sake of Jesus Christ, our Mediator and Advocate. Amen.

Bible Readings

Matthew 18:23–35

Numbers 21:1–9

_____

_____

Matthew 9:1–8

_____

_____

Luke 16:19–31

_____

_____

1 Kings 17:17–24

_____

_____

1 Corinthians 15:51–57

_____

_____

Revelation 21

_____

_____

Catechetical Review

The Forgiveness of Sins

1. Who forgives us our sins daily and richly? (God forgives us our sins daily and richly.)

2. Why does God forgive us our sins? (He is gracious and merciful.)

3. For whose sake does God forgive us our sins? (For Jesus' sake.)

4. What has Jesus done for you? (He has lived and died and now lives again for me.)

5. Is there anything in or about you to deserve forgiveness? (No, I receive forgiveness according to the riches of God's grace.)

6. For whom has Jesus won forgiveness? (For all people.)

7. Where does God tell us that He has forgiven us? (In the Gospel.)

8. Is the Gospel also in Holy Baptism and in the Lord's Supper? (Yes.)

9. Who receives the forgiveness that Jesus has won? (All who believe the promise of the Gospel.)

10. What then, is the central teaching of the Gospel? (This, that all who believe receive forgiveness of sins and are justified before God, not by works, but by grace, for Jesus' sake, through faith.)

The Resurrection and the Life Everlasting

1. What are the two parts of every person? (Body and soul.)

2. What takes place when a person dies? (The soul and body separate.)

3. Where does the soul of the Christian go? (Into the presence of God.)

4. Where does the body usually go? (Into the ground.)

5. At the end of time, what will take place with regard to the body? (The body will be raised again and be joined to the soul.)

6. With what kind of body will we be raised? (We will be raised with a glorified body.)

7. What is a glorified body? (A body like Christ's glorious body.)

8. Of what does the blessedness of heaven consist? (In this, that [a] we shall see God face-to-face; [b] we shall be clothed again with the divine image; [c] we shall be free from all ills; [d] we shall be eternally happy.)

9. To whom shall the blessedness of heaven be given? (To me and all believers.)

Bible Passages

1. Bless the LORD, O my soul, and forget not all His benefits, who forgives all your iniquity, who heals all your diseases. (Psalm 103:2–3)

2. That is, in Christ God was reconciling the world to Himself, not counting their trespasses against them, and entrusting to us the message of reconciliation. (2 Corinthians 5:19)

3. For our sake He made Him to be sin who knew no sin, so that in Him we might become the righteousness of God. (2 Corinthians 5:21)

4. For we hold that one is justified by faith apart from works of the law. (Romans 3:28)

5. And [Jesus] said to him, "Truly, I say to you, today you will be with Me in Paradise." (Luke 23:43)

6. And I heard a voice from heaven saying, "Write this: Blessed are the dead who die in the Lord from now on." "Blessed indeed," says the Spirit, "that they may rest from their labors, for their deeds follow them! (Revelation 14:13)

7. For I know that my Redeemer lives, and at the last He will stand upon the earth. And after my skin has been thus destroyed, yet in my flesh I shall see God, whom I shall see for myself, and my eyes shall behold, and not another. (Job 19:25–27)

8. But the one who endures to the end will be saved. (Matthew 24:13)

For Further Study

1. Study the Catechetical Review.

2. Memorize one or more Bible passages.

3. Review the Third Article and Luther's explanation.

Prayer

Prayer is to the soul what breath is to the body. When breathing becomes heavy and shallow, the body is sick. When praying becomes unpleasant or burdensome, the soul is sick. When the Christian stops conversing with heaven, then hell begins to speak.

What is prayer?

Prayer is a heart-to-heart talk with God. It is more wonderful than any other form of communication.

Prayer is a very precious medicine, one that helps and never fails. (Martin Luther)

Why should we pray?

1. God commands it.

2. God promises to hear us.

3. Because of our own and our neighbor's needs.

4. Out of gratitude for blessings received.

To whom should we pray?

Not to idols, not to saints, not to self, as if prayer were nothing more than a noble form of self-actualization, a helpful soliloquy, or a comforting monologue. We should pray to the triune God, for He alone *can* and *will* hear us. The Bible relates but one instance of "praying" to saints. The rich man in the torment of hell called upon Abraham. But this was the "prayer" of a lost soul, and it availed nothing. Revelation 19:10: "Then I fell down at his feet to worship him, but he said to me, 'You must not do that! I am a fellow servant with you and your brothers who hold to the testimony of Jesus. Worship God.'"

For what should we pray?

For spiritual and bodily blessings. When asking for bodily blessings, we add "If it be Your will."

A child asks for scissors and is refused. She sees the glitter, but her mother sees the sharp edge. There's an old saying, "If we had half the things we ask for, our troubles would be doubled."

How should we pray?

With confidence and in Jesus' name. He is the Go-between, the Mediator, the Intercessor, the Advocate, the Way that leads into the presence of God, the Ladder uniting heaven and earth. "In that day you will ask nothing of Me. Truly, truly, I say to you, whatever you ask of the Father in My name, He will give it to you" (John 16:23). Our request is inappropriate when we petition for something God has not promised to give or when we expect our prayers to be fulfilled by reason of our own merit or simply because we pray.

For whom should we pray?

1. For ourselves

2. For all others, even our enemies

3. Not for the souls of the dead

When and where should we pray?

Muslims pray five times a day, at certain hours. Whether they are with company or out shopping, when the set hour arrives, they turn their face toward Mecca and speak their prayer to Allah and his prophet. But the freedom of the Gospel does not bind us to any place or any hour of prayer.

We should pray at all times, but naturally some times are better than others, including morning, evening, and before and after meals.

O Lord, I call upon You; hasten to me! Give ear to my voice when I call to You! Let my prayer be counted as incense before You, and the lifting up of my hands as the evening sacrifice! (Psalm 141:1–2)

We should pray at all places, but naturally some places are better than others, as in church, in the company of family, in the privacy of our home.

When Stonewall Jackson was asked his understanding of the Bible command to "Pray without ceasing," he answered, "I can give you my idea of it by illustration, if you will allow it and not think that I am setting myself up as a model for others. I have so fixed the habit in my own mind that I never raise a glass of water to my lips without lifting my heart to God in thanks and prayer for the water of life. Then, when we take our meals, there is grace. Whenever I drop a letter in the post office, I send a petition along with it for God's blessing upon its mission and the person to whom it is sent. When I break the seal of a letter just received, I stop to ask God to prepare me for its contents and make it a messenger of good. When I go to my classroom and await the arrangement of the cadets in their places, that is the time to intercede with God for them. And so in every act of the day I have made the practice of prayer habitual."

What should be the posture in praying?

1. Fold hands. Folded hands will not be occupied doing other things. Crossed hands and fingers may remind us of the cross of Christ.

2. Close your eyes. This keeps you from distraction.

3. Bow your head.

4. Kneel.

5. Always think of what you are saying.

Which prayers should you use?

1. The traditional prayers of the Church, called "collects" and "prayers of the day."

2. The model prayer; that is, the Lord's Prayer.

3. Free prayers, prayers that come from the heart. Just talk to God as to your Savior, Friend, and Confidant.

A Christian is always praying, whether he is sleeping or waking; for his heart is always praying, and even a little sigh is a great and mighty prayer. (Martin Luther, What Luther Says, §3471)

The Model Prayer

The Lord's Prayer

See its symmetry: introduction, seven petitions, conclusion.

Head   **Body**   **Feet**

In the first three petitions, we ask for spiritual blessings;

in the fourth petition, for bodily blessings;

in the last three, for the turning aside of evil.

Hymn

What a friend we have in Jesus,
　　All our sins and griefs to bear!
What a privilege to carry
　　Ev'rything to God in prayer!
Oh, what peace we often forfeit;
　　Oh, what needless pain we bear—
All because we do not carry
Everything to God in prayer!

Prayer

O God of hope, the true Light of all the faithful: Grant that my heart may both offer You a worthy prayer and always glorify You with a life of praise; through Jesus Christ, Your Son, our Lord. Amen.

Luther's Morning Prayer

In the name of the Father and of the Son and of the Holy Spirit. Amen.

I thank You, my heavenly Father, through Jesus Christ, Your dear Son, that You have kept me this night from all harm and danger; and I pray You would keep me this day also from sin and every evil, that all my doings and life may please You. For into Your hands I commend myself, my body and soul, and all things. Let Your holy angel be with me, that the evil foe may have no power over me. Amen.

Bible Readings

1 Kings 18:17–40

Luke 18:9–14

Matthew 6:5–15

Matthew 15:22–28

Genesis 18:23–33

Luke 7:11–17

Daniel 6:10

Catechetical Review

1. Can we speak to God? (Yes, we can speak to God.)

2. What is this speaking to God called? (It is called prayer.)

3. To whom should we pray? (We should pray to the triune God: Father, Son, and Holy Spirit.)

4. What should move us to pray? ([a] God's command; [b] God's promise; [c] our own and our neighbor's need.)

5. In whose name do we pray? (We pray in the name of Jesus.)

6. Why do we pray in the name of Jesus? (Jesus is the Son of God, our Savior, and for His sake God will grant us all good things.)

7. For what do we ask God in our prayers? (We ask Him [a] to forgive us our sins; [b] to help us to be good; [c] to give us what we need; [d] to take us to heaven when we die.)

8. For whom should we pray? (For all people; for ourselves; for our loved ones; for our church, school, and country; even for our enemies.)

9. Does God always hear and answer prayers? (Yes, according to His will.)

10. In what three ways does God answer prayers? (By saying yes, by saying no, and by saying wait.)

11. When does God always answer yes to our prayers? (When we ask for spiritual gifts and for what He knows is good for us.)

12. What do we add to our prayers when we pray for earthly gifts? (We add: if it be according to Your will.)

13. When should we pray? (At all times, especially in times of trouble and temptations.)

14. When particularly ought we to pray? (In the morning and evening, and before and after meals.)

15. Where should we pray? (Everywhere, especially in church, school, and at home.)

16. What is the best prayer of all? (The Lord's Prayer.)

17. Why is it called the Lord's Prayer? (Our Lord Jesus Christ gave it to us.)

18. Why is the Lord's Prayer the best prayer of all? (It asks for the best things in the best way.)

19. With what word do we end our prayers? (We end our prayers with the word *amen*.)

20. What does *amen* mean? (*Amen* means "Yes, it shall be so." It means that we believe our prayers have been heard.

Bible Passages

1. Let the words of my mouth and the meditation of my heart be acceptable in Your sight, O LORD, my rock and my redeemer. (Psalm 19:14)

2. Ask, and it will be given to you; seek, and you will find; knock, and it will be opened to you. (Matthew 7:7)

3. And call upon Me in the day of trouble; I will deliver you, and you shall glorify Me. (Psalm 50:15)

4. In that day you will ask nothing of Me. Truly, truly, I say to you, whatever you ask of the Father in My name, He will give it to you. (John 16:23)

5. And this is the confidence that we have toward Him, that if we ask anything according to His will He hears us. (1 John 5:14)

6. Father, if You are willing, remove this cup from Me. Nevertheless, not My will, but Yours, be done. (Luke 22:42)

7. Pray without ceasing. (1 Thessalonians 5:17)

For Further Study

1. Study the Catechetical Review.

2. Memorize one or more Bible passages.

3. Memorize the Lord's Prayer.

The Lord's Prayer

20

The best form of prayer is in the Lord's Prayer, which Christ Himself has prescribed to us and has bidden us to pray. If you pray this prayer, you need not worry about having omitted anything. . . . For if Christ has prescribed the form of prayer, it follows that it pleases Him. . . . If He has promised to hear, it follows that He will hear. (Martin Luther, What Luther Says, §2462)

Confirmation Builder—
Lesson 19

The Introduction

Our Father Who Art in Heaven

(Our Father in heaven.)

What does this mean? With these words God tenderly invites us to believe that He is our true Father and that we are His true children, so that with all boldness and confidence we may ask Him as dear children ask their dear father.

Our

Mine and yours. In the Creed, we say "I," but here we say "Our," for we should pray for and with one another.

When I pray "Our" Father, I am praying

1. for those of the household of faith;

2. for those who are not yet the children of God.

A selfish prayer:	**Another selfish prayer:**
God bless me and my wife,	O Lord, send Your blessing upon our land.
Our son John and his wife,	If others want Your blessing, too.
Us four and no more.	Let them ask for it themselves.

An old proverb says, "He that prays for another is heard for himself." In the Lord's Prayer, we pray for others when we say, "*Our* Father."

Father

Jesus does not invite us to address God in vague and shadowy terms such as the Grand Architect, the Great Designer, the Unknowable One. He invites us to talk to God in the intimate language of family, as children speak to their father.

When applied to God, the word *Father* signifies fatherhood in perfection. God is the model, a picture for earthly fathers who work hard for the benefit of

153

their children, love them, and care for them as a paternal friend, counselor, and confidant. We need never be afraid to approach our heavenly Father and to tell Him our troubles. We know that He is always willing to help us.

God is our *Father*. We are God's children by right of creation, redemption, and sanctification. Jesus frequently addressed God as "Father": in the temple (Luke 2); in the Garden of Gethsemane (Luke 22); on the cross (Luke 23:34); and in the last word: "Father, into Your hands I commit My Spirit" (Luke 23:46).

If I understand these words [Our Father, who art in heaven] by faith: The God who holds heaven and earth in His hand is my Father, then I may conclude: Therefore I am Lord of heaven and earth, therefore Christ is my Brother, therefore everything is mine. (Martin Luther, What Luther Says, *§1684)*

Who Art in Heaven

God is not limited to heaven. These words remind us that our Father is Lord over all; He can both hear and grant our requests. He is "a very present help in trouble" (Psalm 46:1). Our extreme need is His opportunity.

The First Petition

Hallowed be Thy name

(Hallowed be Your name.)

What does this mean? God's name is certainly holy in itself, but we pray in this petition that it may be kept holy among us also.

How is God's name kept holy? God's name is kept holy when the Word of God is taught in its truth and purity, and we, as the children of God, also lead holy lives according to it. Help us to do this, dear Father in heaven! But anyone who teaches or lives contrary to God's Word profanes the name of God among us. Protect us from this, heavenly Father!

A. GOD'S NAME IS HOLY IN ITSELF

There is no spot or wrinkle attached to His name. The Greeks and Romans thought of their gods as magnified human beings, with plenty of weaknesses and foibles, even sins. But our God is not made after the likeness of human beings. He is absolutely holy. If He were not, we would not be interested in praying the other petitions of the Lord's Prayer.

B. GOD'S NAME SHOULD BE KEPT HOLY AMONG US

We ask God not only to guard us against the sin of cursing. The petition *Hallowed be Thy name* means "May Thy name be kept holy." What is God's name? God's name is a short revelation of Himself. Suppose a person had never seen a Bible, had never been in church, and had never been told anything about the Christian religion. One day, an airplane circled over his wilderness home and dropped a piece of paper with these words

THE NAMES OF GOD ARE—

YAHWEH (I am that I am, the eternal One)

JESUS (Savior)

GOD (The Source and Dispenser of all good)

The person would have a pretty fair idea of God; for God's names are a condensed revelation of His nature and activity in the world.

But we have larger revelations of God:

a. NATURE reveals His power and wisdom.

b. CONSCIENCE reveals His wrath against sin (Romans 2:14–15).

c. THE BIBLE reveals all we know of God; it is our fullest revelation of Him.

Therefore, when we pray, "Hallowed be Thy name," we ask that the Bible be kept holy.

HOW IS THE BIBLE KEPT HOLY?

When it is **PREACHED PROPERLY** and **LIVED PROPERLY**.

In this petition, we pray for pastors that they may preach and expound God's Word in all its truth and purity, and we pray for pastor and people that they may live according to God's Word. When this is done, God's name is hallowed among us.

The Second Petition

Thy Kingdom Come

Confirmation Builder—
Lesson 21

(Your kingdom come.)

What does this mean? The kingdom of God certainly comes by itself without our prayer, but we pray in this petition that it may come to us also.

How does God's kingdom come? God's kingdom comes when our heavenly Father gives us His Holy Spirit, so that by His grace we believe His Holy Word and lead godly lives here in time and there in eternity.

A THREEFOLD PRAYER

There are three kingdoms:

1. **The kingdom of power:** the kingdom through which God evidences His power; nature, the world, the universe

2. **The kingdom of grace:** the kingdom through which God evidences His grace in Christ Jesus; that is, the Church on earth, called the Church Militant

3. **The kingdom of glory:** the kingdom through which God evidences His glory; that is, the Church in heaven, called the Church Triumphant

When we pray, "Thy kingdom come," we are not asking that the kingdom of power should come, for it is here now! We are, rather, asking that the kingdom of grace should come (1) into my heart; (2) into the hearts of others; and (3) that all should come to glory.

We are praying, "May the Christian Church grow on earth, and may Jesus come at last to take His Church to heaven."

A ship springs a leak, and goes down; you are in the water. What is your wish when the rescue ship draws near?

1. You want to be saved yourself.

2. You want others to be saved.

3. You want the ship to reach the home harbor.

Thus, when you pray, "Thy kingdom come," you are asking for the following:

1. That you might get aboard the rescue ship of the Church.

2. That others might likewise get aboard.

3. That the ship might soon reach its haven.

This petition is a great missionary prayer.

LIVING THE PRAYER

Many years ago, Hans Egede braved the rigors of the Arctic climate in Greenland in order to preach the Gospel to the Inuit. David Livingston went to Africa. His friend H. M. Stanley tried to persuade him to return to England to enjoy a well-deserved rest, but Livingston plunged once more into his missionary work. Adoniram Judson, the apostle of Burma, languished for months in a prison that was so notorious for its cruelty that it was known as "Let-ma-yoon" ("Hand, don't resist" *committing suicide*).

Similarly, today Christians are living for Christ at home and around the world. The sun never sets on God's people who through their lives and witness endeavor to bring the Gospel to those who do not yet believe. As God's people, we desire that this petition be fulfilled in our midst: "Thy kingdom come."

The Third Petition

Thy Will Be Done on Earth as It Is in Heaven

(Your will be done on earth as in heaven.)

What does this mean? The good and gracious will of God is done even without our prayer, but we pray in this petition that it may be done among us also.

How is God's will done? God's will is done when He breaks and hinders every evil plan and purpose of the devil, the world, and our sinful nature, which do not want us to hallow God's name or let His kingdom come; and when He strengthens and keeps us firm in His Word and faith until we die.

This is His good and gracious will.

A. GOD'S WILL IS DONE INDEED WITHOUT OUR PRAYER

His will is done each day in the world of nature. The sun rises and sets with marked regularity, the tides come and go, the stars that occupy the great spaces have their appointed courses, and even the comets must obey when the Monarch of the universe summons them to appear before His throne. On all sides, His will is being done. People call it the "reign of law," but since there cannot conceivably be a law without a lawgiver, we may rightly view the laws as the will of God in operation.

His will is done **in the lives of individuals**, even though "the nations rage and the peoples plot in vain" (see Psalm 2).

An old proverb states, "Man proposes, but God disposes." In the case of Joseph, God's will was done despite the actions of his ten brothers.

I am not the captain of my soul, master of my destiny. I may make my plans and map out my career, but if He who sees the end from the beginning has other plans for me, I shall soon enough realize what is meant by the statement "God's will be done."

His will is done **in the kingdom of grace.**

Some people bitterly oppose the Church. Even so, God's will *will* be done. The gates of hell, which means the best of Satan's forces, will not prevail against the Church. The Gospel will be preached and the Church will grow until time shall be no more.

B. WE PRAY IN THIS PETITION THAT GOD'S WILL MAY BE DONE AMONG US ALSO

What is the will of God?

"[God] desires all people to be saved and to come to the knowledge of the truth" (1 Timothy 2:4).

"For this is the will of My Father, that everyone who looks on the Son and believes in Him should have eternal life, and I will raise Him up on the last day" (John 6:40).

"For this is the will of God, your sanctification" (1 Thessalonians 4:3).

It is the will of God that we shall *believe* in His Son, Jesus Christ, and *love one another,* as He commanded His disciples.

THE HOLY THREE VERSUS THE UNHOLY THREE

The angels do God's bidding. Their will is aligned with His. On earth there are three wills opposing God's will, namely, the wills of the devil, the world, and our flesh. In this petition, we ask God to break the will of the unholy three and lead us to accept and do His will.

FATHER, NOT MY WILL, BUT YOURS, BE DONE

Furthermore, "Thy will be done," though dark the way may be. His will is the best. All things work together for good to them that love Him. It is only by submission to God's will that we find peace.

Our life is like a tapestry woven on the loom of time. We see the underside with its jumbled threads and dizzying knots. God views from above, and the picture is complete.

The Fourth Petition

Give Us This Day Our Daily Bread

(Give us today our daily bread.)

What does this mean? God certainly gives daily bread to everyone without our prayers, even to all evil people, but we pray in this petition that God would lead us to realize this and to receive our daily bread with thanksgiving.

What is meant by daily bread? Daily bread includes everything that has to do with the support and needs of the body, such as food, drink, clothing, shoes, house, home, land, animals, money, goods, a devout husband or wife, devout children, devout workers, devout and faithful rulers, good government, good weather, peace, health, self-control, good reputation, good friends, faithful neighbors, and the like.

Temporal Blessings

This petition stands in the middle of the seven. It is the only one asking for temporal blessings. The Lord's Prayer is 6–1 in favor of spiritual blessings. When we make a prayer, we often reverse the order, 6–1 in favor of temporal blessings.

GIVE—All that we have in earthly things is a gift of God. He gives without our asking, even to all the wicked. The difference between the Christian and the non-Christian is this: Though both receive good things from God, the Christian acknowledges the gift as coming from God, whereas the non-Christian does not. God's people honor Him by praying before and after meals.

US, OUR—We should eat our own bread, not stolen bread. We should share our bread with those in need.

THIS DAY, DAILY—We should not worry and fret about the future. God will provide each day.

Remove far from me falsehood and lying; give me neither poverty nor riches; feed me with the food that is needful for me, lest I be full and deny You and say, "Who is the Lord?" or lest I be poor and steal and profane the name of my God. (Proverbs 30:8–9)

God fed the children of Israel with manna from heaven (Exodus 16). He fed Elijah in a miraculous way, both at the brook and in the home of the widow (1 Kings 17).

BREAD. Everything we need: food, shelter, clothing, happy home, peace, good weather, and all other blessings.

The Fifth Petition

And Forgive Us Our Trespasses, As We Forgive Those Who Trespass against Us

(Forgive us our sins as we forgive those who sin against us.)

What does this mean? We pray in this petition that our Father in heaven would not look at our sins, or deny our prayer because of them. We are neither worthy of the things for which we pray, nor have we deserved them, but we ask that He would give them all to us by grace, for we daily sin much and surely deserve nothing but punishment. So we too will sincerely forgive and gladly do good to those who sin against us.

FORGIVENESS—Received, Paid Out

We are guilty of many trespasses. We have many *debts*: sins of commission and omission, sins against self, against others, against God.

Our debts pile up like a mountain before us. God, for Jesus' sake, removes our mountain of sins. In His grace and strength, we also remove the molehill of our neighbor's sins against us. If we refuse to forgive our neighbor, and then, in the evening, pray, "Forgive as I forgave," are we not mocking God's forgiveness to us?

We are to forgive even our enemies as Jesus did on the cross when He spoke the intercessory prayer "Father, forgive them, for they know not what they do" (Luke 23:34). Empowered by the Holy Spirit, believers have followed Jesus' example in their own lives. Stephen, when pummeled by stones, kneeled and cried with a loud voice, "Lord, do not hold this sin against them" (Acts 7:60). We think of John Hus, who prayed from the flames that encircled him, "Lord, for Thy mercy's sake, forgive all my enemies." Louis XII of France placed a cross before the names of his enemies as a constant reminder of the cross of Christ and His love for all people.

Forgiveness is a perfume the flower gives back to the foot that has crushed it.

Confirmation Builder—
Lesson 25

"For if you forgive others their trespasses, your heavenly Father will also forgive you, but if you do not forgive others their trespasses, neither will your Father forgive your trespasses." (Matthew 6:14–15)

The Sixth Petition

And Lead Us Not into Temptation

(Lead us not into temptation.)

What does this mean? God tempts no one. We pray in this petition that God would guard and keep us so that the devil, the world, and our sinful nature may not deceive us or mislead us into false belief, despair, and other great shame and vice. Although we are attacked by these things, we pray that we may finally overcome them and win the victory.

What does *temptation* mean?

"God tested Abraham" (Genesis 22:1). God does not tempt anyone (see James 1:13). Is this a contradiction? The word *temptation* has two meanings in the Bible.

1. *Temptation* means a leading into sin. Such a temptation can never come from God.

2. *Temptation* means a testing of faith. "God tested Abraham" means "God put Abraham's faith on trial."

A weight is attached to a rope not to break it but to test it. A rocket motor is tested repeatedly to demonstrate its reliability. Each level of a video game gets more difficult to test the player's abilities. Testing is intended to do more than merely prove; it is meant to improve. When a sailor has to navigate his ship under a heavy gale and in a difficult channel, or when a general has to fight against a superior force and on disadvantageous ground, skill and courage are not only tested but improved. So faith grows stronger during tests—trials and hardships—and God enables us to trust Him in the midst of struggles.

When we pray,

Lead us not into temptation,

we ask,

Do not let Satan tempt us, and, if he does, give us power to resist.

The Seventh Petition

But Deliver Us from Evil

(But deliver us from evil.)

What does this mean? We pray in this petition, in summary, that our Father in heaven would rescue us from every evil of body and soul, possessions and reputation, and finally, when our last hour comes, give us a blessed end, and graciously take us from this valley of sorrow to Himself in heaven.

PRAYERS

O Lord,

- spare us from every harm of body, soul, property, and honor, and, above all, save us from an ungodly death;

- give us strength to bear up under the trials we at times must face;

- remove the burden from our back, or strengthen us to bear the burden.

O Lord, You are the Savior of all who trust in You; keep us always in Your love and care and grace. Preserve us through our life's end. Keep us free from pain and in peace, gather us together unto those faithful who have gone before us, when You desire, and as you desire. In Jesus' holy name we pray. Amen.

The Conclusion

For Thine Is the Kingdom and the Power and the Glory Forever and Ever. Amen.

(*For the kingdom, the power, and the glory are Yours now and forever.* Amen.*)

What does this mean? This means that I should be certain that these petitions are pleasing to our Father in heaven, and are heard by Him; for He Himself has commanded us to pray in this way and has promised to hear us. Amen, amen means "yes, yes, it shall be so."

*These words were not in Luther's Small Catechism.

FOR THINE IS THE KINGDOM—All things belong to You, God.

THINE IS THE POWER—You have the power to give all things to us.

THINE IS THE GLORY—All honor belongs to You; we thank You for Your bountiful goodness toward us.

AMEN—It shall be so. All that I ask in faith, God will give me in His way and at His appointed time.

Hymn

Our Father, who from heav'n above
    Bids all of us to live in love
As members of one family
    And pray to you in unity,
Teach us no thoughtless words to say
But from our inmost hearts to pray.

Prayers

Almighty God, You know that we are weak. But You are strong, and we trust in Your power to save us from sin, death, and Satan. Surround us with Your loving kindness in Christ. Be present in our lives, here in time and forever in eternity; through Jesus Christ, Your Son, our Lord. Amen.

O God, from whom come all holy desires, all good counsels, and all just works, give to us, Your servants, that peace which the world cannot give, that our hearts may be set to obey Your commandments and also that we, being defended from the fear of our enemies, may live in peace and quietness; through Jesus Christ, Your Son, our Lord, who lives and reigns with You and the Holy Spirit, one God, now and forever. Amen. (*Lutheran Service Book*, p. 313)

Bible Readings

Luke 12:1–13

_____

_____

Matthew 5:14–16

_____

_____

Genesis 50:15–21

_____

_____

Matthew 18:23–35

_____

_____

Matthew 4:1–11

_____

_____

Genesis 22:1–19

_____

_____

Luke 2:25–35

_____

_____

The Lord's Prayer

1. Why do we say "Our" Father and not "My" Father? (Through faith in Christ, God is the Father of us all, we belong to one family, and therefore we pray with and for one another.)

2. Why has Christ told us to address God as our "Father"? (Christ wants us to approach God without fear or doubting.)

3. Of what is the phrase "who art in heaven" to remind us? (That God is over all; He can help us in every trouble.)

4. What do we ask of God in the First Petition? (That His Word be preached properly and lived properly.)

5. What do we ask of God in the Second Petition? ([a] That we may come into God's kingdom; [b] that others may come into His kingdom; [c] that Christ may come soon to take His children to heaven.)

6. What do we ask of God in the Third Petition? (That God may break the will of the unholy three and lead us to do His will.)

7. What do we ask of God in the Fourth Petition? (That we may receive the necessities of life with thankfulness.)

8. What do we ask of God in the Fifth Petition? (That He forgive us our sins.)

9. Since God forgives us our sins, what do we promise? (That we will forgive our neighbor his or her sins.)

10. What do we ask of God in the Sixth Petition? (That He may help us to overcome the temptations of the devil, the world, and our flesh.)

11. What do we ask of God in the Seventh Petition? (That He may spare us from every evil of body and soul, and especially from an evil death.)

12. What are the words of the Conclusion to the Lord's Prayer? ("For Thine is the kingdom and the power and the glory forever and ever.")

13. What is the meaning of *Amen*? (*Amen* means "Yes, it shall be so." All that I ask in true faith, God will give me in His way and at His appointed time.)

Bible Passages

1. For in Christ Jesus you are all sons of God, through faith. (Galatians 3:26)

2. Sanctify them in the truth; Your word is truth. (John 17:17)

3. [Jesus said] "The time is fulfilled, and the kingdom of God is at hand; repent and believe in the gospel." (Mark 1:15)

4. [God] desires all people to be saved and to come to the knowledge of the truth. (1 Timothy 2:4)

5. For this is the will of God, your sanctification. (1 Thessalonians 4:3)

6. The eyes of all look to You, and You give them their food in due season. You open Your hand; You satisfy the desire of every living thing. (Psalm 145:15–16)

7. "And whenever you stand praying, forgive, if you have anything against anyone, so that your Father also who is in heaven may forgive you your trespasses." (Mark 11:25–26)

8. But the Lord is faithful. He will establish you and guard you against the evil one. (2 Thessalonians 3:3)

9. The Lord will rescue me from every evil deed and bring me safely into His heavenly kingdom. To Him be the glory forever and ever. Amen. (2 Timothy 4:18)

For Further Study

1. Study the Catechetical Review.

2. Memorize one or more Bible passages.

3. Select and memorize one of Luther's explanations.

21

The Sacrament of Holy Baptism

What Is a Sacrament?

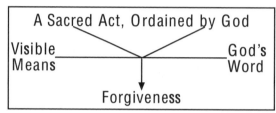

A Sacred Act, Ordained by God

Visible Means — Forgiveness — God's Word

Is marriage a sacrament?

A sacred act? Yes.
Instituted by God? Yes.
Any visible means? Yes.
Does it offer forgiveness? No.
Therefore, NOT a sacrament.

Is confirmation a sacrament?

A sacred act? Yes.
Instituted by God? No.
Any visible means? No.
Does it offer forgiveness? No.
Therefore, NOT a sacrament.

Is Baptism a sacrament?

A sacred act? Yes.
Instituted by God? Yes;
    Matthew 28:19.
Any visible means? Yes; water.
Does it offer forgiveness? Yes.
Therefore, it IS a sacrament.

Is the Lord's Supper a sacrament?

A sacred act? Yes.
Instituted by God? Yes; e.g.,
Matthew 26:26–28.
Any visible means? Yes; bread
    and wine.
Does it offer forgiveness? Yes.
Therefore, it IS a sacrament.

Only two sacraments: Holy Baptism and Holy Communion.

The Sacrament is a ford for us, a bridge, a door, a ship, a [carriage], in which and by which we pass from this world into eternal life. Therefore everything depends on faith. (Martin Luther, What Luther Says, §3958)

1. The Nature of Baptism

What is Baptism?

Baptism is not just plain water, but it is the water included in God's command and combined with God's Word.

Which is that Word of God?

Christ our Lord says in the last chapter of Matthew: "Therefore go and make disciples of all nations, baptizing them in the name of the Father and of the Son and of the Holy Spirit." [Matthew 28:19]

"In the name of the Father and of the Son and of the Holy Spirit" is not a magic formula, but the quintessence of the divine Word, the Gospel spoken in a breath. The divine majesty is present as always, in the Word.

The Seat of the Doctrine: Matthew 28:18–20

Christ says	—He ordained this sacred act.
Go	—Ordinarily, ministers are to baptize, but any Christian may baptize in case of emergency.
Make disciples	—Make believers, followers.
All nations	—Adults and children, men and women, young and old.
Baptizing	—Applying water by sprinkling, pouring, washing, or immersing.
Teaching	—Instruction in the Word of God, Law and Gospel.

In the name of the Father and of the Son and of the Holy Spirit.

Children should be baptized, because

1. they belong to all nations (Matthew 28:19; Acts 2:38–39);

2. they are sinful and need cleansing (John 3:5–6);

3. they are brought to faith and receive forgiveness of sins only through Baptism;

4. they believe God's promises (Matthew 18:6);

5. the miracle the Holy Spirit works in regenerating children is the same as He works in adults; as Luther points out, adults too cannot be reborn except by the Holy Spirit.

A great king of France received his crown at the city of Reims, and it was a custom in those days that kings would call themselves after the city in which they received their crown. But this king called himself Louis of Poitiers, because he was baptized there.

We, too, can value our Baptism highly, for through Baptism we were made "a kingdom, priests to His God and Father" in Christ (Revelation 1:6).

But you are a chosen race, a royal priesthood, a holy nation, a people for His own possession, that you may proclaim the excellencies of Him who called you out of darkness into His marvelous light. Once you were not a people, but now you are God's people; once you had not received mercy, but now you have received mercy. (1 Peter 2:9–10)

Sponsors

1. serve as witnesses that the child has been properly baptized;

2. will see to it that the child is given a Christian education, especially should the parents die or prove neglectful;

3. will remember the child in their prayers.

Which Mode of Applying Water Is Correct?

The Greek word for "baptize" is *baptizo*, and means "to wash, pour, sprinkle, or immerse." Any of these modes of applying water is correct.

Wash

Hebrews 9:10: "various washings," literally, "diverse baptizings."

Mark 7:4: "And when [the Pharisees] come from the marketplace, they do not eat unless they wash. And there are many other traditions that they observe, such as the washing of cups and pots and copper vessels and dining couches."

Some religious leaders immersed the cups and pots and brazen vessels; they probably did not regularly immerse themselves in water.

Pour

On the day of Pentecost, when all were filled with the Holy Spirit, Peter recalled the prophecy then fulfilled, "I will pour out My Spirit on all flesh" (Acts 2:17).

John the Baptist prophesied of Christ's gift of the Spirit: "He will baptize you with the Holy Spirit and fire" (Matthew 3:11).

Sprinkle

Sprinkling is a valid mode of baptizing; we are sprinkled with the blood of atonement (Hebrew 10:22; 1 Peter 1:2).

Immerse

Some denominations lay great stress on the mode of Baptism, accepting immersion only and rebaptizing those not fully immersed in water. They insist that *baptize* means only "to immerse," and that in the early days of Christianity Baptism was always administered by immersion.

Baptism by immersion was indeed known in the apostolic age: "And they both went down into the water, Philip and the eunuch, and he baptized him. And when they came up out of the water, the Spirit of the Lord carried Philip away" (Acts 8:38–39). The eunuch may have been immersed, but Philip may also have poured water over his head.

It is not at all certain, however, that immersion was always practiced in the apostolic age. It seems unlikely that, when three thousand were added to the Church in one day, all were immersed.

Moreover, in the conversion of the Philippian jailer (Acts 16) it is unlikely that a place convenient for immersion was found in his house or in many other homes where Baptism was administered. But even if the early Christians had employed only immersion, their example alone would not prove that we must do so also, or we should have to do many other things they did.

The argument resolves itself into this question: "What does *baptize* mean?" And the answer is this: *Baptize* means to apply water by washing, pouring, sprinkling, or immersing. The amount of water does not matter, whether it is a trickle or a stream, nor does whether it is running water or still water. The Lord said, "Baptize," apply water, without specifying the quality, the quantity, or the mode of application, leaving all this to Christian freedom. For convenience's sake, many congregations have chosen the mode of sprinkling or pouring. The important thing is that the water be applied in the name of the triune God.

There is on earth no greater comfort than Baptism. (Martin Luther, What Luther Says, *§164)*

Hymn

Baptized into Your name most holy,
O Father, Son, and Holy Ghost,
I claim a place, though weak and lowly,
Among Your saints, Your chosen host.
Buried with Christ and dead to sin,
Your Spirit now shall live within.

Prayer

I thank You, gracious Father, that You have received me through Holy Baptism into the covenant and kingdom of Your grace, in which we have forgiveness of sin and everlasting life. Grant Lord that, buried with Christ in Baptism, I may daily die to sin and live to righteousness, that in the end, together with my parents and all saints, I may obtain the promised inheritance in heaven: through Jesus Christ, Your Son, our Lord. Amen.

Bible Readings

Matthew 3

Acts 16:12–15

_____

_____

Acts 16:16–34

_____

_____

Acts 8:26–40

_____

_____

Acts 22:1–16

_____

_____

Mark 10:13–16

_____

_____

Luke 7:30

_____

_____

Catechetical Review

1. What is a sacrament? (A sacrament is a sacred act, instituted by God, through which we receive the forgiveness of sins.)

2. How many sacraments are there? (Two: Holy Baptism and the Lord's Supper.)

3. Which are the visible elements in the two Sacraments? (The visible element in Baptism is water. The visible elements in the Lord's Supper are bread and wine.)

4. What is joined to the visible elements? (The Word of God.)

5. What is offered, given, and sealed to us in the Sacraments? (Forgiveness of sins, life, and salvation.)

6. What is Baptism? (Baptism is "water included in God's command and combined with God's word.")

7. Who instituted Baptism? (Christ our Lord.)

8. To whom is the command to baptize given? (To the Church.)

9. How is this command carried out by the Church? (The Church calls pastors, who ordinarily baptize.)

10. Who may and should baptize in case of emergency? (Any Christian.)

11. How is Baptism administered? (By applying water in the name of the Father and of the Son and of the Holy Spirit.)

12. Why is immersing in water not the only correct way of applying water in Baptism? (Because in ordaining Baptism, Christ used a word which simply means "apply water.")

13. How may water be applied in Baptism? (By washing, pouring, sprinkling, or immersing.)

14. How do we usually apply water in Baptism? (By sprinkling or pouring.)

15. Who is to be baptized? (All nations.)

16. Who is meant by "all nations"? (Children and adults.)

17. What answer should be given to those who deny that children are to be baptized? (Children are to be baptized because [a] children are included in "all nations"; [b] children are born sinful and need Baptism for the washing away of their sins; [c] children are brought to faith and receive forgiveness of sins only through Baptism; and [d] children, too, believe God's promises.)

18. Why do we have sponsors at the Baptism of infants? ([a] The sponsors are to serve as witnesses that the child has been properly baptized; [b] they are to help in the Christian training of the child, especially should the parents die or become neglectful; [c] and they are to remember the child in their prayers.

Bible Passages

1. Go therefore and make disciples of all nations, baptizing them in the name of the Father and of the Son and of the Holy Spirit, teaching them to observe all that I have commanded you. And behold, I am with you always, to the end of the age. (Matthew 28:19–20)

2. And Peter said to them, "Repent and be baptized every one of you in the name of Jesus Christ for the forgiveness of your sins, and you will receive the gift of the Holy Spirit. For the promise is for you and for your children and for all who are far off, everyone whom the Lord our God calls to Himself." (Acts 2:38–39)

3. But when Jesus saw it, He was indignant and said to them, "Let the children come to Me; do not hinder them, for to such belongs the kingdom of God." (Mark 10:14)

For Further Study

1. Study the Catechetical Review.

2. Memorize one or more Bible passages.

3. Memorize Luther's first and second Catechism questions about the Sacrament of Holy Baptism and his answers.

22

Holy Baptism (Continued)

2. The Blessings of Baptism

What benefits does Baptism give?

It works forgiveness of sins, rescues from death and the devil, and gives eternal salvation to all who believe this, as the words and promises of God declare.

Which are these words and promises of God?

Christ our Lord says in the last chapter of Mark: "Whoever believes and is baptized will be saved, but whoever does not believe will be condemned." [Mark 16:16]

Benefit of Baptism: Forgiveness (Acts 2:38)

Deliverance

Eternal life (Mark 16:16)

Through Baptism, we become the children of God. Baptism is the seal of the covenant.

Can anyone be saved without Baptism? The principle is that we must be baptized (John 3:5–6). If, however, one did not have an opportunity to be baptized, yet still believes in Christ, then he or she will be saved. It is faith that saves, as demonstrated, for example, in the thief on the cross. But if one says, "I believe in Christ, but I won't be baptized," such an attitude demonstrates that he or she does not believe in Christ. If I believe in Christ, I also believe in Baptism, for Baptism was commanded by Christ, my Savior and Lord.

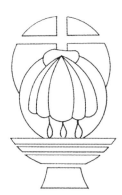

Whoever is baptized in Christ is baptized through His suffering and blood, or, to state it more clearly, through Baptism he is bathed in the blood of Christ and cleansed from sin. . . .

Holy Baptism has been purchased for us by the same blood which Christ shed for us and with which He paid for our sin. This blood, with its merit and power, He has deposited in Baptism. . . . For the person who is receiving Baptism in faith is in effect actually being visibly washed with the blood of Christ and cleansed from sin. (Martin Luther, What Luther Says, *§127, 128)*

Have you ever seen two trees or bushes growing so close together that you can't distinguish which fruit belongs to which tree? That is the way it is now with us and Christ. God is pleased with our fruit because our limbs have intermingled with the tree of Christ. Our lives, our limbs, are so intertwined with Christ that our fruit is Christ's fruit, and Christ's fruit is our fruit.

Baptism is how it all got started. Jesus' life and death were applied to you when you were still a dead piece of wood which the pastor was holding over the baptismal font. But God's Word and the water changed all that. In a split second, in the blink of an eye, while angels watched you and the sanctuary was filled with the sound of their wings, God made you alive. He changed you from a dead piece of wood to a live young tree. God spoke the words "You are mine" as the pastor said, "I baptize you in the name of the Father and of the Son and of the Holy Spirit." Heaven applauded, for once more the life of God became the life of a child. Once more death was swallowed up in victory. Once more hell wept and heaven rejoiced because you were made one with your Father through the blood of Jesus Christ. That's what happened in your Baptism. (Adapted from Windows into the Lectionary, *by Donald L. Deffner, pp. 63–64.)*

3. The Power of Baptism

How can water do such great things?

Certainly not just water, but the word of God in and with the water does these things, along with the faith which trusts this word of God in the water. For without God's word the water is plain water and no Baptism. But with the word of God it is a Baptism, that is, a life-giving water, rich in grace, and a washing of the new birth in the Holy Spirit, as St. Paul says in Titus chapter three:

"He saved us through the washing of rebirth and renewal by the Holy Spirit, whom He poured out on us generously through Jesus Christ our Savior, so that, having been justified by His grace, we might become heirs having the hope of eternal life. This is a trustworthy saying." [Titus 3:5–8]

Power of Baptism

Word of God . . . in and with the water.

Faith . . . trust in God's Word in and with the water.

An unsigned check reads, "*Pay to the order of* Alissa Suzanne . . . One Thousand Dollars."

How much is the check worth? Nothing!

If I sign my name on the signature line, however, the check is valuable—worth $1,000 (provided, of course, that I have the amount in the bank). A valid, signed check indicates that I possess the power to back up my promise to pay. How much is the piece of paper then worth? $1,000!

But if the recipient does not believe that I am able to do what I have promised, and she does not go to the bank and cash the check, it is has no value *to her*.

So it is with Baptism. Here is water—simple water, worth no more than a piece of paper. But Jesus says, "Through this water, in the name of the triune God, I give you complete forgiveness of your sins." The power lies not in the water itself but in Jesus, who stands behind His promises, who sealed His promises with His sacrifice on the cross.

The water has God's power for me as I believe.

The Word of God gives Baptism its power. Faith is the hand that receives the blessing and power of Baptism.

At the baptismal font, two hands are present.

1. The Word of God is the "divine hand" that places the pearl of forgiveness into the water.

2. Faith is the "human hand" that receives the pearl in the water.

4. The Significance of Baptizing with Water

What does such baptizing with water indicate?

It indicates that the Old Adam in us should by daily contrition and repentance be drowned and die with all sins and evil desires, and that a new man should daily emerge and arise to live before God in righteousness and purity forever.

Where is this written?

St. Paul writes in Romans chapter six: "We were therefore buried with Him through baptism into death in order that, just as Christ was raised from the dead through the glory of the Father, we too may live a new life." [Romans 6:4]

SIGNIFICANCE OF BAPTISM

Unclean ⟶ Water and Word ⟶ **clean**. Baptism.

Unclean ⟶ Word ⟶ **clean**. Repentance and remembrance of Baptism.

Our baptismal calling is to serve God by a Christian life day by day.

Our Baptism abides forever. Even though someone should fall from Baptism and sin, still we always have access to it. So we may subdue the old man again. But we do not need to be sprinkled with water again [Ezekiel 36:25–26; Hebrews 10:22]. Even if we were put under the water a hundred times, it would still be only one Baptism, even though the work and sign continue and remain. Repentance, therefore, is nothing other than a return and approach to Baptism. We repeat and do what we began before, but abandoned. (Martin Luther, Large Catechism IV 77–79)

Hymn

All who believe and are baptized
Shall see the Lord's salvation;
Baptized into the death of Christ,
They are a new creation;
Through Christ's redemption they will stand
Among the glorious heav'nly band
Of ev'ry tribe and nation.

Prayer

Almighty God, we give thanks that Your Son, Jesus, suffered and died for our sins. We celebrate with joy His resurrection from the dead and ascension into heaven. We are grateful for the work of Your Holy Spirit in us, which brought us to faith by Baptism. We know that You are faithful in Your covenant with us. Keep us faithful as well. Show us the way You would have us live. In Jesus, our blessed Savior. Amen.

Bible Readings

John 3:1–21

_____

_____

Galatians 3:26–27

_____

_____

Mark 16:15–16

_____

_____

Romans 6:1–11

_____

_____

Titus 3:3–7

_____

_____

Luke 6:36–45

_____

_____

Exodus 14:21–22

_____

_____

Catechetical Review

1. What blessings does Baptism give? (Forgiveness of sins, life, and salvation.)

2. Who receives the blessings of Baptism? (All who believe.)

3. In whose name were you baptized? (In the name of the Father and of the Son and of the Holy Spirit.)

4. Whose child have you become through Baptism? (Through Baptism, I have become a child of God, a member of the Church, and an heir of heaven.)

5. How could water do all this for you? (It was not the water merely, but the Word of God and faith.)

6. What emotions does Baptism evoke among the people of God? (Baptism brings joy and contentment to the children of God.)

7. How often were you baptized? (Only once; but each day I should remember and affirm my Baptism.)

8. What is the baptismal vow? (I renounce the devil and all his works and all his ways. I believe in God the Father, Son, and Holy Spirit. I will follow Christ and live as His child, in the Spirit's grace and power, to death.)

Bible Passages

1. And Peter said to them, "Repent and be baptized every one of you in the name of Jesus Christ for the forgiveness of your sins, and you will receive the gift of the Holy Spirit." (Acts 2:38)

2. Rise and be baptized and wash away your sins. (Acts 22:16)

3. For in Christ Jesus you are all sons of God, through faith. For as many of you as were baptized into Christ have put on Christ. (Galatians 3:26–27)

4. Baptism, which corresponds to this, now saves you, not as a removal of dirt from the body but as an appeal to God for a good conscience, through the resurrection of Jesus Christ. (1 Peter 3:21)

5. And such were some of you. But you were washed, you were sanctified, you were justified in the name of the Lord Jesus Christ and by the Spirit of our God. (1 Corinthians 6:11)

6. Husbands, love your wives, as Christ loved the church and gave Himself up for her, that He might sanctify her, having cleansed her by the washing of water with the word. (Ephesians 5:25–26)

For Further Study

1. Study the Catechetical Review.

2. Memorize one or more Bible passages.

3. Memorize Luther's third and fourth questions about the Sacrament of Holy Baptism and his answers.

The Office of the Keys

23

Confirmation Builder—
Lesson 30

*What is the Office of the Keys?**

The Office of the Keys is that special authority which Christ has given to His church on earth to forgive the sins of repentant sinners, but to withhold forgiveness from the unrepentant as long as they do not repent.

*Where is this written?**

This is what St. John the Evangelist writes in chapter twenty: The Lord Jesus breathed on His disciples and said, "Receive the Holy Spirit. If you forgive anyone his sins, they are forgiven; if you do not forgive them, they are not forgiven." [John 20:22–23]

*What do you believe according to these words?**

I believe that when the called ministers of Christ deal with us by His divine command, in particular when they exclude openly unrepentant sinners from the Christian congregation and absolve those who repent of their sins and want to do better, this is just as valid and certain, even in heaven, as if Christ our dear Lord dealt with us Himself.

*This question may not have been composed by Luther himself but reflects his teaching and was included in editions of the catechism during his lifetime.

The Office of the Ministry

Jesus gave the Church the power to

- preach the Gospel;
- administer the Sacraments;
- forgive and retain sins.

This special authority "belongs to" the Church. The government does not have this right, but it is the privilege of the Church in general and of every local congregation in particular.

(1) **CHRIST** gave the power to the (2) **CHURCH**, the church to the (3) **PASTOR** to carry out the Office of the Keys publicly and on behalf of the congregation.

Preach the Gospel

Christ gave this power to the Church. The congregation calls a pastor to act as its representative, as its mouthpiece, and by a formal installation service recognizes him as a "Servant of the Word." To him, the congregation delegates the power it received from Christ. So then, when the pastor proclaims the Gospel, he does so *for* the congregation and *in the stead and by the command* of Christ.

Note. The pastoral office is a divine institution (Acts 20:28; Ephesians 4:10–12).

Note. Living, professing, and sharing the Gospel is the right, privilege, and obligation of every Christian, not only the pastor.

Administer the Sacraments

Christ gave this power to the Church. So the congregation chooses, calls, and installs a pastor to officiate at Baptisms and the distribution of Holy Communion. And to him, the congregation transfers the power it received from Christ. So then, when the minister baptizes or celebrates Holy Communion, he (no. 3) does so in the name of the congregation (no. 2) in the name of Christ (no. 1).

CHRIST   CONGREGATION   MINISTER

Forgive or Retain Sins

While Jesus was on earth, He spoke these words to people: "Your sins are forgiven" (e.g., Matthew 9:1–8).

Before leaving this earth, He gave to the Church the power to forgive and retain sins (John 20:22, 23).

So the congregation delegates Christ's power to the pastor. When, therefore, the pastor forgives sins, he (no. 3) does so in the name of the congregation (no. 2) in the name of Christ (no. 1).

This power is called, in picture language, the Office of the Keys. A key unlocks or locks a door. Sin closes the door of heaven. Forgiveness of sins unlocks the door of heaven.

Whose Sins Are to Be Forgiven?

The sins of penitent sinners, those who turn from sin (with sorrow) and turn to Christ (with joy).

Whose sins are to be retained?

The sins of impenitent sinners, those who are not heart-sorry for their sins or do not believe. These sins are to be retained (that means, not forgiven) so long as these persons do not repent.

How does this work out practically in a congregation?

Church Discipline

Take the case of an openly unrepentant sinner. He or she should be won from the error of unbelief and sin. Unrepentant sin is an affront to God and a scandal—a cause for stumbling—to the members of the congregation. What should the Church do? The Church has the power to administer the Office of the Keys. There are four steps to be taken, according to Matthew 18:15–17.

If your brother sins against you, go and tell him his fault, between you and him alone. If he listens to you, you have gained your brother. But if he does not listen, take one or two others along with you, that every charge may be established by the evidence of two or three witnesses. If he refuses to listen to them, tell it to the church. And if he refuses to listen even to the church, let him be to you as a Gentile and a tax collector. Truly, I say to you, whatever you bind on earth shall be bound in heaven, and whatever you loose on earth shall be loosed in heaven. (Matthew 18:15–18)

1. A Christian who is aware of a fellow Christian's sin is to admonish him or her. The church member should not *at first* tell anyone, not even the pastor. If the erring person heeds the admonition, the matter is resolved. No one else is to be informed about the situation.

But if he or she does not heed, then the second step—

2. The member takes with him or her one or two trustworthy, mature Christians, that "every charge may be established by the evidence of two or three witnesses."

If the unrepentant person acknowledges his or her sin in repentance and faith, the matter is dropped. If he or she does not listen, then the third step—

3. The church is informed. The church invites the unrepentant person to attend the meeting in which the congregation holds before the person his or her sinfulness. If he or she repents, the matter is settled; he or she is a member in good standing. If not, then the fourth step—

4. The church excommunicates the person, which means puts him or her out of communion, out of fellowship, regards him or her as a lost person, outside of the church, in need of the Law and the Gospel.

Or, if the person refuses to attend the meeting, he or she excommunicates himself or herself.

The congregation then tells the person through its pastor, "Your sins are retained." And this holds true in heaven also, as if Christ Himself dealt with the unrepentant person.

If, after a while, the person repents, asks for forgiveness and reinstatement, the congregation would through its pastor forgive the person's sin and again recognize him or her as a brother or sister in Christ.

Note. While there are three grades of admonition, the Lord does not say that we should merely be satisfied to admonish a sinner three times; we may do so more frequently.

Hymn

Jesus sinners doth receive;
Oh, may all this saying ponder
Who in sin's delusions live
And from God and heaven wander!
Here is hope for all who grieve:
Jesus sinners doth receive.

Prayer

Almighty, merciful, and most gracious God and Father, we ask you to turn the hearts of all who wandered from Your truth, to strengthen the faith of all who experience doubt and temptation, and to guide those who endure hardship and suffering. Keep them in Your fatherly care, and help us to be Your light and comfort in this dark world. In the name of Jesus, we pray. Amen.

Bible Readings

John 20:19–23

_____

_____

Psalm 130

_____

_____

Luke 15:11–32

_____

_____

Luke 18:9–14

_____

_____

Matthew 26:69–75

_____

_____

Matthew 18:15–20

_____

_____

2 Corinthians 2:4–10

_____

_____

Catechetical Review

1. What powers has Christ given to the Church? (The powers [a] to preach the Gospel; [b] to administer the Sacraments; [c] to forgive and retain sins.)

2. To whom has Christ given the power to forgive or retain sins? (To the Church.)

3. Why is this power called the Office of the Keys? (The Church by this office has the power to lock or unlock the door of heaven.)

4. Recite the Bible verse in which Christ gave this power to the Church. ("If you forgive the sins of any, they are forgiven them; if you withhold forgiveness from any, it is withheld." [John 20:23].)

5. Whose sins are to be forgiven? (The sins of the penitent sinners.)

6. Who are penitent sinners? (Penitent sinners are those who are sorry for their sins and believe in Christ as their Savior from sin.)

7. Whose sins are to be retained? (The sins of the impenitent.)

8. Who are impenitent sinners? (Impenitent sinners are those who are not sorry for their sins and do not believe in Christ.)

9. What happens to the door of heaven when sinners do not repent? (The door is shut.)

10. What is the church's dealing with impenitent sinners called? (Church discipline.)

11. What is the last step of church discipline called? (Excommunication.)

12. What is the meaning of "excommunication"? (To put out of communion, out of fellowship.)

13. What Christian privileges are denied to an excommunicated person? (He or she is not permitted to commune, cannot be a sponsor, and cannot receive Christian burial.)

14. What is the real purpose of excommunication? (To get the excommunicated person to repent so that he or she feels sorry for his or her sins, asks for forgiveness and for reinstatement as a member of the church.)

15. To whom does a church entrust the Office of the Keys? (The church entrusts the Office of the Keys to its pastor.)

16. In whose name does the pastor use the Office of the Keys? (In the name of the church and in the name of Christ.)

Bible Passages

1. I will give you the keys of the kingdom of heaven, and whatever you bind on earth shall be bound in heaven, and whatever you loose on earth shall be loosed in heaven. (Matthew 16:19)

2. Repent therefore, and turn again, that your sins may be blotted out. (Acts 3:19)

3. The sacrifices of God are a broken spirit; a broken and contrite heart, O God, You will not despise. (Psalm 51:17)

4. And they said, "Believe in the Lord Jesus, and you will be saved, you and your household." (Acts 16:31)

5. This is how one should regard us, as servants of Christ and stewards of the mysteries of God. (1 Corinthians 4:1)

For Further Study

1. Study the Catechetical Review.

2. Memorize one or more Bible passages.

3. Memorize Luther's explanation to "What is the Office of the Keys?"

24 Confession and Absolution

Confirmation Builder—
Lesson 29

How Christians should be taught to confess

What is Confession?

Confession has two parts.

First, that we confess our sins, and

second, that we receive absolution, that is, forgiveness, from the pastor as from God Himself, not doubting, but firmly believing that by it our sins are forgiven before God in heaven.

What sins should we confess?

Before God we should plead guilty of all sins, even those we are not aware of, as we do in the Lord's Prayer; but before the pastor we should confess only those sins which we know and feel in our hearts.

Which are these?

Consider your place in life according to the Ten Commandments: Are you a father, mother, son, daughter, husband, wife, or worker? Have you been disobedient, unfaithful, or lazy? Have you been hot-tempered, rude, or quarrelsome? Have you hurt someone by your words or deeds? Have you stolen, been negligent, wasted anything, or done any harm?

Confession embraces two parts:

1. To admit or confess a wrong.

2. To be forgiven.

   If you step on another person's foot, you say,

1. "Excuse me," or "I beg your pardon."

2. We receive his or her pardon.

   When we disobey God's Word

1. We confess our sins.

2. We receive God's forgiveness or absolution.

Absolution is nothing else than the preaching and proclaiming of the forgiveness of sins. . . . Because it is necessary to preserve such preaching in the church, absolution, too, should be retained. For there is only this difference between the two: While through preaching the Gospel we publish this forgiveness everywhere and tell it to all in general, in absolution we tell it specifically to one or more desiring it. (Martin Luther, What Luther Says, *§1)*

---

1. Confession

The difference between confessing before God and the pastor is the difference between

MUST	and	MAY
Before God,		Before the pastor,
we **MUST**		we **MAY**
confess all sins.		confess certain sins.

Private Confession enables you to unburden your heart, to receive spiritual guidance and advice from your pastor, and to obtain the comfort of personal Absolution. The pastor is bound to silence by the seal of the confessional.

One reason for our custom of "registering" or "announcing" for Holy Communion is to afford our members an opportunity, if they wish to embrace it, of making private confession. Of course, a Christian must under all circumstances confess his or her sins to a neighbor whom he or she has offended and grieved (Matthew 5:23–24).

It is a good practice to consult frequently with the pastor regarding the sins and guilt that disturb us. When anything is wrong with us physically, we go to the doctor. When our souls are troubled, we also need help. If we are wise, we will go to Jesus to consult with Him. We may also go to our pastor, whom Jesus has given to His Church to help His people. A pastor is often known as an "undershepherd of souls." His ministry is the care of souls. We will tell him our trouble—all and honestly. He will sympathize with us and help us to resolve issues and explore solutions. Indeed, if we do not quite know where the trouble lies, he will help us to find it. Then, out of the Word of God, he will prescribe the remedy. And we shall go forth with new health in our soul. Sometimes, of course, we shall have to return for more treatments, as we do in the case of some physical upsets.

It is a good practice to consult with our pastor, our soul physician, just as soon as we begin to notice signs of soul disorders coming over us. Make your pastor your confessor, your best friend.

Great is the benefit derived from the use of the keys and private absolution. By it the conscience can be quieted. Therefore I do not want it rejected. (Martin Luther, What Luther Says, §18)

What Sins Should We Confess?

Examine yourself according to the Ten Commandments. Ask yourself the following:

1. Have I placed God first in my life? Have I avoided all idolatrous and superstitious practices? Have I laughed at religion, or the Church, or God's representatives in the holy ministry?

2. Have I taken God's name in vain by cursing, swearing falsely, or using an oath in trivial matters? Have I angered others so as to make them curse or blaspheme God? Have I gone to fortune-tellers or toyed with horoscopes, astrology, and the powers of the darkness?

3. Have I attended church and Holy Communion regularly? Have I paid attention while in church, listened, believed, and lived accordingly? Have I neglected my daily devotions?

4. Have I honored my parents and those in authority over me? Have I shown reverence to persons who are older?

5. Have I harbored hatred against my neighbor? Desired revenge? Am I "on the outs" with someone? Have I hurt someone in body, mind, or feelings? Have I helped the sick and needy?

6. Have I associated with bad companions? Did I entertain dirty thoughts, sing lewd songs, tell or listen to unclean stories, or look at indecent pictures? Did I dress modestly? Have I fled fornication, in thought, word, or deed?

7. Have I stolen anything? Or damaged property? Or been dishonest?

8. Have I given false testimony? Spoken evil of my neighbor? Engaged in gossip and slander? Judged harshly?

9/10. Have I coveted unjustly anything that belonged to my neighbor? Have I been envious?

2. Absolution

The Absolution is spoken by the pastor (no. 3) in the name of the congregation (no. 2), in the name of God (no. 1). It holds true in heaven also.

The first part of the Order of the Holy Communion is the confessional service called "The Preparation." It contains the Confession and the Absolution.

Hymn

Amazing grace—how sweet the sound—
That saved a wretch like me!
I once was lost but now am found,
Was blind but now I see!

Prayer

I confess to God Almighty, the Father, the Son, and the Holy Spirit, and before all the company of heaven, that I have sinned in thought, word, and deed, through my fault, my own fault, my own most grievous fault; wherefore I pray Almighty God to have mercy upon me, to forgive me all my sins, and to make clean my heart within me.

May the Almighty and merciful Lord grant me pardon and forgiveness of all my sins, a spirit of true repentance, amendment of life, and the grace and comfort of the Holy Spirit! In Jesus' name I pray. Amen.

Bible Readings

Psalm 51

_____

_____

1 John 1:5–10

_____

_____

2 Samuel 12:1–14

_____

_____

1 Samuel 7:1–6

_____

_____

1 Kings 8:33–40

_____

_____

Daniel 9:1–19

_____

_____

Matthew 5:23–24

_____

_____

Catechetical Review

1. What are the two parts of Confession? (That we confess our sins and that we receive Absolution or forgiveness.)

2. Before whom _must_ we confess our sins? (Before God.)

3. Must we confess our sin to a neighbor whom we have offended and grieved? (Yes, indeed.)

4. Before whom _may_ we confess our sins? (Before the pastor.)

5. When the pastor forgives sins, in whose name does he do so? (In the name of Christ.)

6. How certain is his Absolution? (It holds true in heaven also.)

7. Is private Confession obligatory? (No, but it is good for the soul.)

8. What added benefit does one receive from private Confession? (The comfort of individual Absolution from particular sins.)

9. What service precedes the celebration of Holy Communion? (The confessional or preparatory service.)

10. What are the two main parts of the confessional service? (Public Confession of sins and public Absolution of sins.)

Bible Passages

1. If we say we have no sin, we deceive ourselves, and the truth is not in us. If we confess our sins, He is faithful and just to forgive us our sins and to cleanse us from all unrighteousness. (1 John 1:8–9)

2. Therefore, confess your sins to one another and pray for one another, that you may be healed. The prayer of a righteous person has great power as it is working. (James 5:16)

3. So if you are offering your gift at the altar and there remember that your brother has something against you, leave your gift there before the altar and go. First be reconciled to your brother, and then come and offer your gift. (Matthew 5:23–24)

4. Truly, I say to you, whatever you bind on earth shall be bound in heaven, and whatever you loose on earth shall be loosed in heaven. Matthew 18:18

For Further Study

1. Study the Catechetical Review.

2. Memorize one or more Bible passages.

3. Memorize Luther's questions and answers on Confession and Absolution.

The Sacrament of the Altar

25

The Sacrament of the Altar

Confirmation Builder—
Lesson 31

What is the Sacrament of the Altar?

It is the true body and blood of our Lord Jesus Christ under the bread and wine, instituted by Christ Himself for us Christians to eat and to drink.

Where is this written?

The holy Evangelists Matthew, Mark, Luke, and St. Paul write:

Our Lord Jesus Christ, on the night when He was betrayed, took bread, and when He had given thanks, He broke it and gave it to the disciples and said: "Take, eat; this is My body, which is given for you. This do in remembrance of Me."

In the same way also He took the cup after supper, and when He had given thanks, He gave it to them, saying, "Drink of it, all of you; this cup is the new testament in My blood, which is shed for you for the forgiveness of sins. This do, as often as you drink it, in remembrance of Me."

Various Names

Sacrament of the Altar—Celebrated on and received at the altar.

Lord's Supper—The supper He prepares; He gives the heavenly food. Supper is the evening meal. We light the eucharistic candles in commemoration of this.

Lord's Table—the table He spreads. He is the Host.

Breaking of Bread—The Passover bread originally used was unleavened bread, crisp, brittle, and therefore had to be broken. A biblical term (Acts 2:42).

Holy Supper—In distinction from the common supper.

Eucharist—Spoken blessing, giving of thanks. "When He had given thanks." This name sets forth the joyous character of the celebration.

Holy Communion—Oneness, union of bread with Christ's body, of wine with His blood. Furthermore, "we are all one bread and one body, even as we are all partakers of this one bread and drink of this one cup" (Close Communion).

Mass—An ancient term, sometimes used in the sense of a worship service with Holy Communion, or with reference to the Ordinaries: Kyrie, Gloria in Excelsis, Credo, Sanctus, and Agnus Dei, as in Bach's *Mass in B Minor*. The term is also used in our Lutheran Confessions (see Augsburg Confession XXIV: "The Mass") and forms part of the word *Christmas*.

What Is the Lord's Supper?

Two elements are present: The visible and the invisible.

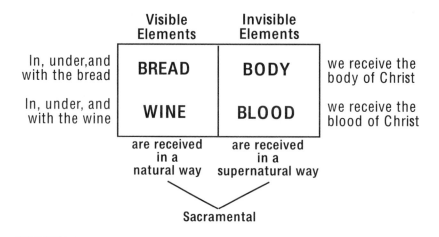

I certainly love it with all my heart, the precious, blessed Supper of my Lord Jesus Christ, in which He gives me His body and blood to eat and to drink orally, with the mouth of my body, accompanied by the exceedingly sweet and gracious words: Given for you, shed for you. (Martin Luther, What Luther Says, §2464)

Three Views

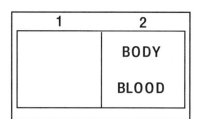

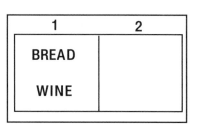

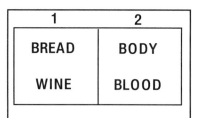

The Roman Catholic Church places the emphasis on column 2 (the invisible elements). The **Reformed Churches** place the emphasis on column 1 (the visible elements). The **Lutheran Church** places the emphasis on *both* columns, in faith and in obedience to the Lord's words.

Roman Catholics say the bread and wine are changed—*transubstantiated*—into the body and blood of Christ. The bread is no longer bread, the wine is no longer wine. They furthermore teach the Sacrifice of the Mass; that is, the priest "re-presents" the sacrifice of Jesus in reparation for the sins of persons living and dead and for blessings in heaven and life.

The **Reformed Churches** say the bread and wine "signify," "represent," "picture" Christ's body and blood. They say, "When we see the minister break the bread, we think of how Christ's body was broken in death. When we see the wine or the grape juice poured from the flagon, we think of how Christ's blood was poured out on the cross. The Lord's Supper is a memorial feast, a beautiful ceremony of remembrance."

The **Lutherans** teach the real presence, that "I receive with the bread the true body, and with the wine the true blood, of Christ." Reasons:

1. The words of Christ (Matthew 26:26–28; Mark 14:22–24; Luke 22:19–20; 1 Corinthians 11:24–25).

2. The apostles' constant teaching (1 Corinthians 10:16; 1 Corinthians 11:27).

3. It is a testament—a *will*—in which Jesus gave Himself.

To us, the Lord's Supper is both a memorial feast and a Sacrament—that is, a Means of Grace—whereby God offers, gives, and seals to us the forgiveness of sins which Christ has earned for us.

We should attend Holy Communion regularly, prompted by the desire for forgiveness. How often do Lutheran congregations celebrate it? Some every Sunday, some once, twice, or three times a month.

The Sacrament is instituted for the very purpose of giving us comfort and strength. Therefore you should let nothing keep you from it. If you feel your weakness, blessed are you; for you must indeed feel your shortcomings. (Martin Luther, What Luther Says, *§2531)*

Hymn

Draw near and take the body of the Lord,
And drink the holy blood for you outpoured;
Offered was He for greatest and for least,
Himself the victim and Himself the priest.

Prayer

Blessed Jesus, as You come to me in the blessed Sacrament of Your body and blood, prepare my heart and grant that, having received You, I may never be separated from You. I give You thanks and praise as You live and reign with the Father and the Holy Spirit, one God, world without end. Amen.

Bible Readings

Matthew 26:26–30

Mark 14:22–25

Luke 22:14–20

1 Corinthians 11:23–29

Acts 2:41–47

Luke 24:28–35

_____

_____

Matthew 11:28–30

_____

_____

Catechetical Review

1. Who instituted the Lord's Supper? (Christ our Lord.)
2. What two kinds of elements are present? (The visible and the invisible elements.)
3. What are the visible elements? (Bread and wine.)
4. What are the invisible elements? (The body and blood of Christ.)
5. What do you receive with the bread? (The body of Christ.)
6. What do you receive with the wine? (The blood of Christ.)
7. In what manner do you receive the bread and wine? (In a natural manner.)
8. In what manner do you receive the body and blood? (In a supernatural manner.)
9. What is this union of the bread with the body, of the wine with the blood, called? (A sacramental union.)
10. Is the Lord's Supper a memorial feast or a sacrament? (It is both.)
11. Why should Christians receive the Sacrament often? (Christ's command, His promise, and our need.)

Bible Passages

1. The cup of blessing that we bless, is it not a participation in the blood of Christ? The bread that we break, is it not a participation in the body of Christ? (1 Corinthians 10:16)

2. In the same way also He took the cup, after supper, saying, "This cup is the new covenant in My blood. Do this, as often as you drink it, in remembrance of Me." For as often as you eat this bread and drink the cup, you proclaim the Lord's death until He comes. (1 Corinthians 11:25–26)

3. Come to Me, all who labor and are heavy laden, and I will give you rest. (Matthew 11:28)

For Further Study

1. Study the Catechetical Review.
2. Memorize one or more Bible passages.
3. Memorize Luther's first and second questions about the Sacrament of Holy Communion and his answers.

The Sacrament of the Altar (Continued)

26

The Benefits of the Lord's Supper

Confirmation Builder—
Lesson 31

What is the benefit of this eating and drinking?

These words, "Given and shed for you for the forgiveness of sins," show us that in the Sacrament forgiveness of sins, life, and salvation are given us through these words. For where there is forgiveness of sins, there is also life and salvation.

The Benefits of the Lord's Supper

1. It gives and seals the forgiveness of sins, strengthening our faith in the Savior. The assurance that Christ died for us is made doubly sure when we receive the same body and blood He gave and shed on the cross for our forgiveness and life.

2. It strengthens us to love God and our neighbor.

3. It draws believers together in the oneness of faith—that is, in Christian "commun-ity."

A boy often visited his grandparents' farm during the summer. He loved to wander around in the large back yard and nearby woods, and to eat the grapes growing in the garden. Many times he would pick the grapes to see if they were ripe. They usually were not. And he would return to the house, sit down at the table, and ask his grandmother to help him get rid of the sour taste in his mouth. Her answer was always the same. She would give the boy a swallow of wine. It was sweet and took care of the problem without clashing with the sour grape taste. It simply removed it and brought refreshment.

Our Lord Jesus has a similar, but greater, cure. When we have been eating the "sour grapes" of our sinful thoughts and actions and want to be forgiven, He invites us to His table. There in His blood, truly present in, with, and under the wine, and in His body, truly present in, with, and under the bread, He removes our sin and guilt. He gives His body and blood to cover our many failures, to renew us and strengthen us for living. He frees us from the bitterness of our disobedience and foolishness. We are new creations. (Adapted from Windows into the Lectionary, *by Donald L. Deffner, pp. 73–74)*

The Power of the Lord's Supper

How can bodily eating and drinking do such great things?

Certainly not just eating and drinking do these things, but the words written here: "Given and shed for you for the forgiveness of sins." These words, along with the bodily eating and drinking, are the main thing in the Sacrament. Whoever believes these words has exactly what they say: "forgiveness of sins."

The Salutary Use of the Lord's Supper

Who receives this sacrament worthily?

Fasting and bodily preparation are certainly fine outward training. But that person is truly worthy and well prepared who has faith in these words: "Given and shed for you for the forgiveness of sins."

But anyone who does not believe these words or doubts them is unworthy and unprepared, for the words "for you" require all hearts to believe.

Worthy

What makes a person "worthy" to receive Holy Communion? Some people think it is the way we dress for worship. Some think it depends on what we have thought and done during the past week. Instead, it is faith in Christ's offer and promise of forgiveness.

Not by any preparation or work of your own do you become worthy and fit to partake of the Sacrament. This takes place through faith alone. For only faith in the Word of Christ justifies, makes alive, makes a person worthy and well prepared. (Martin Luther, What Luther Says, *§2526)*

Fasting and Bodily Preparation

Some Christians prefer not to eat before receiving the Sacrament. Others go to much trouble in bodily preparation. But fasting and bodily preparation alone will not make a person worthy. Faith does; faith in the real presence, faith in the forgiveness.

Self-Examination

Questions to ask . . .

1. Do I believe I am a sinner?

2. Am I sorry for my sins?

3. Do I believe in Christ as my Savior and Lord?

4. Do I believe that His body and blood are truly present in the Sacrament?

5. Do I plan, with the help of the Spirit, to change my sinful thoughts and actions and to follow Christ?

Who Should Not Receive?

1. Those who do not confess Christ, and also the unrepentant.

2. Those of a different confession of faith.

3. Those who are unforgiving; those who carry a grudge in their heart and refuse reconciliation.

4. Those who cannot examine themselves, such as infants; persons who have not received instruction in the faith; persons who are unconscious.

Confirmation

Confirmation is both a period of instruction in the Christian faith and a public rite for baptized persons to make confession of their faith.

Confirmation instruction for both youth and adults usually focuses on the Bible, Luther's Small Catechism ("The Six Chief Parts"), and other important teachings and practices in the Lutheran Church.

Confirmation as a rite allows the baptized Christian, after a period of instruction, to publicly affirm God's gifts of forgiveness, life, and salvation bestowed in Baptism. It also usually indicates that the confirmed member has been received in communicant and voting membership of the Church.

"Be faithful unto death, and I will give you the crown of life." (Revelation 2:10)

Hymn

O Jesus, blessed Lord, to Thee
My heartfelt thanks forever be;
Who hast so lovingly bestowed
On me Thy body and Thy blood.

Prayer

O Lord Jesus Christ, strengthen me with Your holy body and precious blood. O Lord Jesus Christ, as You have saved me through Your holy life and innocent death in my place, let nothing ever separate me from You. Against the evil foe defend me; in true faith keep me, that with all the redeemed saints I may bless and glorify You, here in time and forever in heaven. Amen.

Bible Readings

Matthew 6:16–18

_____

_____

Matthew 5:23–24

_____

_____

1 Corinthians 10:16–21

_____

_____

Matthew 22:1–14

_____

_____

Mark 7:24–30

_____

_____

Revelation 3:10–13

_____

_____

Revelation 7:9–17

_____

_____

Catechetical Review

1. What is the benefit of such eating and drinking? (That is shown us by these words, "Given and shed for you for the remission of sins.")

2. What blessing do we receive through the Sacrament? (The forgiveness of sins.)

3. How is this offered to us? (Through the words in the Sacrament.)

4. And what seal does Christ affix to the words in the Sacrament? (His body and blood.)

5. Is there then any reason why you should waver in your assurance of sins forgiven? (No; on the contrary, my assurance is made doubly sure.)

6. How can bodily eating and drinking do such great things? (It is not the eating and drinking indeed that does them.)

7. What is it then? (The Word of God and faith.)

8. Who is a worthy communicant? (He or she that has faith in these words, "Given and shed for you for the forgiveness of sins.")

9. May a person whose faith is weak go to the Lord's Table? (By all means.)

10. What questions should a communicant ask before receiving the Sacrament? ([a] Do I believe I am a sinner? [b] Am I sorry for my sins? [c] Do I believe in Christ as my Savior and Lord? [d] Do I believe that His body and blood are truly present in the Sacrament? [e] Do I plan, with the help of the Spirit, to change my sinful thoughts and actions and to follow Christ?)

11. What rite does the church observe, in order to enable members to examine themselves? (The Rite of Confirmation.)

12. What, in brief, is the vow you make at confirmation? (To remain faithful to God and His Church to death.)

13. What is God's promise to those who keep this vow? (He will give them a crown of life.)

14. Why should you remain a faithful member of the evangelical Lutheran Church? (It teaches the truth of justification by grace, through faith, for the sake of Jesus Christ, based on the teachings of the Bible alone.)

Bible Passages

1. Immediately the father of the child cried out and said, "I believe; help my unbelief!" (Mark 9:24)

2. All that the Father gives Me will come to Me, and whoever comes to Me I will never cast out. (John 6:37)

3. Let a person examine himself, then, and so eat of the bread and drink of the cup. For anyone who eats and drinks without discerning the body eats and drinks judgment on himself. (1 Corinthians 11:28–29)

4. I am coming soon. Hold fast what you have, so that no one may seize your crown. (Revelation 3:11)

For Further Study

1. Study the Catechetical Review.

2. Memorize one or more Bible passages.

3. Memorize Luther's third and fourth questions about the Sacrament of Holy Communion and his answers.

Martin Luther, His Life and Work

By Alfred Faulstick

1

The Formation of the Church

Christ commanded His disciples to go into all the world and preach the Gospel. They were to wait in Jerusalem until the Holy Spirit had been poured out on them. This wonderful act occurred on the day of Pentecost, when three thousand people became Christians. From that day and place onward, the preaching of the Gospel has reached every country of the globe.

Congregations must necessarily be established in order to spread the Good News of the grace of God in Christ Jesus. The apostles established many congregations. The greatest missionary was the apostle Paul. The Book of Acts records his missionary journeys throughout the Mediterranean.

The congregations were called "churches," and all Christians—that is, all believers in Christ—were called "the Church" (invisible Church). The church visible was the local congregation, believers who called pastors (1 Timothy 3:2; 2 Timothy 2:24) and maintained their living (Galatians 6:6). The mission of the Church was and is to "make disciples of all nations." The institution of the Church has scriptural foundation. Of course, we must always bear in mind that the Church does not exist for its own sake, but for the sake of its message. First the message, then the Church; that is the order of importance.

The Deformation of the Church

Originally, the church was a martyr institution, bitterly persecuted by the world on account of its message, the preaching of Christ and Him crucified, "a stumbling block to Jews and folly to Gentiles" (1 Corinthians 1:23). In time, however, the world began to "patronize" or support the church; the church then became more concerned about its own interests and organization. The result was that the "message" was moved further into the background.

Under Constantine the Great (Roman emperor, died 337), the church was united with the empire and became established as a world power. Ambition seized some among the clergy. The bishops in the larger cities, as in Rome, Jerusalem, Constantinople, Alexandria, and Antioch, began to exercise more influence and power than the others. The bishop of Rome and the bishop of Constantinople became the most powerful bishops. When both wanted to be supreme, a split occurred in the church, and Christendom was divided into the Roman Catholic

Church and the Greek Orthodox Church. The bishop of Rome declared himself head, or father, of the church, "the Pope."

Soon after the establishment of the papal authority, the church began to show signs of deterioration and decay. Worldly life and corrupt morals found their way into all classes of society; more and more confidence was placed in the intercession of saints, outward church services, and good works. False teachings became common. The Bible lost its authority. It was no longer the absolute norm of faith and life. Human traditions were placed on a level with or even above the authority of the Bible. The sweet, glowing Gospel of Christ, the Savior who yielded His life in love for His people and the world, was shrouded in mist. Christ was depicted as a stern judge. Sinners would have to address Him through His mother. False doctrines and practices crept into the life of the church and God's people. The church was *de*-formed; it was in need of a *re*-formation.

The Reformation of the Church

Some years before Luther, a number of attempts at reform were made. John Wycliffe (1326–84) testified in England, Girolamo Savonarola (1452–98) in Italy, John Hus (1372–1415) in Bohemia. For their efforts, Savonarola and Hus were burned at the stake. Wycliffe, the "Morning Star of the Reformation," was forced to retire from his teaching position at Oxford University. He died of a stroke before the full weight of Rome could be brought against him. In 1415, after it had ordered that Hus be burned at the stake, the Council of Constance also ordered that Wycliffe's bones be disinterred, burned, and their ashes scattered to the four winds. Such was the church's response to reform.

The efforts of Wycliffe, Savonarola, and Hus paved the way for a later reformer, who by the grace of God, called the church back to the Gospel. That man was Martin Luther, known in history as the "Father of the Reformation."

2

Birth—Schooling—Ordination—Journey to Rome

Birth

Martin Luther was born in Eisleben, Germany, on November 10, 1483. He was baptized the next day, and, since that was St. Martin's Day, he received the name of Martin. His parents were Hans and Margarethe Luther. They were pious, but quite strict, parents.

Schooling

At the age of six, he went to the little hillside school at Mansfeld. Rigid discipline was maintained at school, with little, if any, display of kindness. He learned to know Jesus not as a loving Savior but as a stern judge whom one must fear and respect. He was taught to pray to the saints and the Virgin Mary to turn away the anger of Jesus.

At the age of fourteen, he went to the high school at Magdeburg. He had to sing from house to house to get something to eat. He later continued his studies at Eisenach.

In 1501 he entered the University at Erfurt. He earned the degree of bachelor of arts in 1502, and the master of arts in 1505.

Luther was devoutly religious. He was deeply conscious of his sin. He was afraid of death. He cried to the Virgin Mary when one day he cut a deep gash in his leg with a short sword. Later on, in the summer, he was almost struck by lightning. He fell on his knees in terror, crying, "Help, dear Saint Anne." He vowed that, should he be spared, he would become a monk. He entered the monastery of St. Augustine, becoming a monk on July 17, 1505. He tried hard to find peace by doing all sorts of menial tasks, by fasting, and by spending nights in prayer. But all his "good works" did not quiet the unrest of his soul.

In the monastery, Luther found a complete edition of the Bible. He read it eagerly. The blessed Gospel greatly quieted him. Dr. Staupitz, the prior of the monastery, also pointed him to Jesus, the loving Savior, whose blood cleanses from sin.

Professor at the University

In 1507, Luther was ordained to the priesthood. In 1508, he was appointed to lecture on philosophy at the University of Wittenberg. It was not long before he began to preach in the chapel of the monastery. His preaching attracted great attention.

In 1509, he was transferred to the University of Erfurt. While there, he was commissioned to make a journey to Rome. He was glad of the chance to visit the "holy city," but he was disappointed in what he saw and learned there.

Upon his return from Rome, he was transferred back to the University of Wittenberg. This time, he was asked to teach theology. How happy he was that he could devote all his strength and time to the study of the Sacred Scriptures. He distinguished himself as a theologian. The university awarded him the degree of doctor of divinity (1512).

3

The Sale of Indulgences—Ninety-Five Theses—Burning the Papal Bull—Worms—Wartburg

The Diet at Worms

Leo X was pope. He needed much money for St. Peter's Church in Rome. John Tetzel was one of the men commissioned to sell indulgences. Tetzel made quite a stir in Germany. Some of Luther's parishioners went to buy indulgences, and because they thought they had bought remission of sins, they refused to confess their sins before going to Communion. Luther knew that this was wrong; he knew from the Bible that the life of a Christian should be one of daily and continual repentance. He wished to have this matter discussed publicly.

Every Friday afternoon, public debates were held in the Castle Church, and it was the custom to post the topics of debate on the door of the church. And so Luther prepared ninety-five points of discussion, called the Ninety-Five Theses, and, on October 31, 1517, he posted these on the door of the Castle Church at Wittenberg. These theses flew like the wind through all of Germany and beyond. The pope heard about them, too, but he passed the matter up as "a monkish squabble." Before long, however, he thought it necessary to take action. He ordered Luther to appear before Cardinal Cajetan, his representative, at a diet (a public assembly) that was soon to be held at Augsburg. He went in October 1518.

At Augsburg, Luther was ordered to revoke everything he had written touching the matter of indulgences. This he could not do, because he was certain that his writings were in agreement with Scripture. Thus, gradually, Luther came to see the errors of the Roman Church, and he began to publish other documents and books in which he again set forth the truth of the Bible. The pope then issued a bull (formal letter) in which he commanded Luther to repent within sixty days of all he had written against the Roman Church, or else he would be condemned as a heretic. However, Luther felt bound by his conscience to continue his teaching as before and to publish what he knew to be God's Word.

To show that he regarded God's Word more than man's word, Luther burned the papal bull outside the city walls, in the presence of a group of students. (To this day, the spot is shown in Wittenberg where this daring act was done. A tablet is erected there that reads: "Dr. Martin Luther burned at this place, on December 10, 1520, the papal bull.") By this act, Luther completed his break with the Roman Church. He was subsequently summoned to the Diet at Worms, in April 1521, to appear before Pope Leo X and Emperor Charles V. Luther's friends feared for his life, claiming that he would not return alive, but Luther was sure that it was his duty to go there in the name of Christ and to confess the truth. He was so certain of the truth and so confident of God's protection that he replied to the pleadings of his friends: "And if they will build a wall of fire between Wittenberg and Worms that will reach up to heaven, I will still go in God's name and tread between the teeth in the mouth of Behemoth and confess Christ!"

At four o'clock in the afternoon of the first day after his arrival in Worms, Luther was conducted into the hall where the diet was in session. The streets were so crowded that he had to make his way through the backyards and alleys. Just before he entered the hall, an elderly gentleman, Captain George Frundsberg, tapped him on the shoulder and said: "Little monk! Little monk! You are now on your way to take a stand such as I and many another general have not taken in the most desperate battles, but if you are sincere and sure of your cause, go in God's name and be of good cheer, God will not forsake you."

Upon his appearance before the diet, Luther was asked two questions: first, whether the books lying on the table before him were his, and, second, whether he would retract what he had written in them. To the first question, Luther answered, "Yes." To the second question, he did not give an immediate answer, but asked for time to consider the question. An allowance of twenty-four hours' time was given him, and Luther spent all night in prayer over the matter.

On the following day, at four o'clock in the afternoon, he was again summoned to the diet. When he was asked whether he would retract, Luther replied with a long address, which he delivered in Latin and repeated in German. He was then requested to give a shorter answer. This he did, saying in part: "Unless I am convinced by the testimony of Holy Scripture . . . I cannot and will not recant, since it is neither safe nor advisable to do anything against conscience. Here I stand; I cannot do otherwise! God help me! Amen."

Luther was now excommunicated—excluded from the church as a heretic. Emperor Charles, furthermore, signed the Edict of Worms, a decree, drawn up by Luther's foes, forbidding everyone to aid or shelter him and ordering his books to be burned. This probably would have meant the death of Luther had it not been for his good friend the Elector Frederick of Saxony, who planned his rescue.

In the Black Forest of Saxony was an isolated fortress called the Wartburg. As Luther's wagon entered the forest on its way home from Worms, it was suddenly surrounded by a group of horsemen, who brought the wagon to a stop, seized Luther, and took him away to the Wartburg. Here he was commanded to wear the clothes of a hunter and let his beard grow so that no one could recognize him. This was the Elector's successful plan of sparing Luther.

Luther remained ten months at the Wartburg. While there, he began to translate the New Testament into the language of the people. Later on, he also translated the Old Testament, and in 1534 he published the entire Bible in German.

The Fanatics

Meanwhile, Wittenberg was the scene of religious fanaticism. Under the leadership of Dr. Carlstadt, people stormed into the churches and threw out pictures and crucifixes, and abolished organ and choir music, thinking they could reform the church in this way. Moved by the extreme teaching of the Roman Church regarding the words of Christ in the Lord's Supper, "This is My body," namely, that the bread changed into the body of Christ (transubstantiation), Dr. Carlstadt went to the other extreme and taught that the bread merely represents the body of Christ. There was also another group of fanatics who came from the town of Zwickau in West Saxony, Germany, and who were called the "Zwickau prophets." Besides trying to reform the church in the manner in which Carlstadt attempted it, they also taught false doctrines regarding the Sacrament of Baptism, namely, that Baptism is merely an act of initiation into the Church, but does not work forgiveness of sin, life, and salvation. Because they demanded that everyone baptized as a child must be baptized again in adult life, they were called "Anabaptists."

Luther at first tried to correct the matter through writing, but with no results. Finally, he returned from the Wartburg, and through his influence, preaching every day for eight days, this fanatical spirit was checked in Wittenberg and the Word of God and common sense prevailed. Of course, this fanaticism continued in other places, and its leaders brought about a rebellion among the peasants of Germany, who welcomed this fanaticism because they long had been oppressed. Luther, on the other hand, put forth every effort to stem this rebellion; but unfortunately, Luther's advice was not accepted, and the result was the Peasants' War.

At this time also, two men appeared in Switzerland: Ulrich Zwingli in German Switzerland and John Calvin in French Switzerland. Both men preached against the errors of the Roman Church, but they also tried to bring about a reformation in a rash and fanatical manner similar to that of Carlstadt and the Zwickau prophets. Both men taught essentially the same errors regarding the Lord's Supper and Holy Baptism as Carlstadt and the Zwickau prophets had done.

A meeting was arranged at Marburg between Luther and Zwingli, known as the Colloquy of Marburg. Zwingli maintained that the Lord could not be bodily present at the same time at the many different places at which the Lord's Supper is celebrated in one day; that the body of Christ is not present in the Sacrament, but is received only in a spiritual way; and that the bread represented the presence of the body. Over against this teaching, Luther maintained that when Christ said, "This is My body," He knew and meant what He said, and that we dare not deny His word. Nothing came of this meeting, for Zwingli continued in his error. Those who continued this spirit and these teachings, chiefly under the influence of Zwingli and Calvin, founded the Reformed Church, which continues to this day under various denominational names.

The Augsburg Confession

In the course of time, those who believed as Luther did (mockingly called "Lutherans") found it necessary to outline their faith in writing. And when they were summoned to state their belief before the Emperor and officials of the Roman Church, they presented the document they had prepared. It was read on June 25, 1530, in the city of Augsburg, and therefore it is called the Augsburg Confession. Previously, Luther had also published his Small Catechism, in 1529, in order to help the people, and especially the children, in learning God's Word, for they knew so little about it. Luther also believed that the people should take part in the services at church; therefore, he introduced singing by the congregation, and he himself also composed several hymns, the most famous of them being "A Mighty Fortress Is Our God."

Family Life—Death—Legacy

When Luther became a monk, he vowed to remain unmarried. However, he had come to see that it is contrary to God's Word for the pope to forbid priests, monks, and nuns to marry. In order to testify against this error by his own example, he entered holy matrimony on June 13, 1525, with Katharina von Bora, a nun who had been converted by reading his writings. She became his devoted wife. They had six children: Hans, Elizabeth, Magdalene, Martin, Paul, and Margaret. Magdalene died at an early age. Luther was a kind and devoted father and spent much time with his children.

Luther's Death

The time was coming when Luther's life on earth was drawing to a close. For several years, he had not been well. In January 1546, Luther was asked to attend a meeting in Eisleben, the place of his birth, in order to settle a dispute. While there, he complained about pains in his chest. He went to his room and lay down on a couch, but the pains continued. After about an hour's sleep, he awoke and went into his bedroom, praying: "Into Your hands I commit my spirit; You have redeemed me, O Lord God of truth." After midnight he had another attack. Death was approaching, and he knew it.

He arose, walked into the next room, lay down on the couch again, and prayed this beautiful prayer: "O my heavenly Father, one God and Father of our Lord Jesus Christ, God of all comfort, I thank You that You have given for me Your dear Son, Jesus Christ, in whom I believe, whom I have preached and confessed, loved and praised. . . . I pray You, dear Lord Jesus Christ, let me commend my soul to You. I am certain that I shall be with You forever and that no one can ever, ever tear me out of Your hands. . . . Father, into Your hands I commend my spirit. You have redeemed me, faithful God."

Luther repeated to himself other passages of Scripture. When his friends saw that he was about to pass away, Dr. Jonas approached him and said: "Venerable father, will you die steadfastly adhering to Christ and the doctrines you have preached?" Luther answered distinctly, "Yes!" He passed away between two and three o'clock on Thursday morning, February 18, 1546, and was buried near the pulpit in the Castle Church in Wittenberg.

Conclusion

Luther's great work of the Reformation may be summed up in these words: Luther restored the message of the Christian Church in its original truth and purity. Luther did not wish to abolish the outward forms of Christian worship, nor did he want to start a new church; he wished to cleanse the church of its false doctrine. To him, the critical issue was the Gospel, and it was a matter of greatest importance to him that the message be the entire truth, and nothing but the truth, of God's Word. His two great principles were *Sola Scriptura*—"the Bible alone," and *Sola Gratia*—"by grace alone." In summary, we are saved by grace, through faith, for Christ's sake. This truth is the heart and center of Lutheran doctrine and life.

Drills for the Books of the Bible

Rev. H. W. Prange

1. Ask for the books of any group by going in rotation around the class.

2. Teacher names a book; a student gives the category.

3. One student names a book, other students name the book that precedes and follows it.

4. Teacher calls for "first Law book" or "third historical book" or such.

5. Play at arranging a library. Ask each pupil to bring (in imagination) any set of books; ask for the title of each book of the set he or she has brought. Ask where this set must find its place on the shelf and similar questions.

6. Teacher names a book; the pupils look for it in their Bibles. The first one to find it rises and reads the first verse or any given verse. (Give the class frequent practice in this drill.)

7. Competitive drill: Divide the class into two divisions and have them spell the books of the Bible on the plan of the old-fashioned spelling bee.

"Synod"

Christians are banded together into congregations not only for worship but also for mission and ministry. In union, there is strength. Just as a congregation of Christians can do the Lord's work better and more efficiently than an individual Christian, so a group of congregations organized into a synod is better able to carry on the work of the Lord—for example, the work of missions.

The principal work of our Synod is proclaiming the Gospel throughout the world and training pastors and teachers to preach and teach the Gospel.

The work carried on by our Synod cannot be done without a great amount of planning and supervision. The Synod, therefore, meets in convention every three years. The convention elects the officers of the Synod: a president, five vice-presidents, a secretary, a treasurer, a board of directors, and various committees to supervise the work that it decides should be done.

Just as our nation is divided into states, so our Synod is divided into districts. Officers and committees are elected by each district to supervise and carry out its work. Each district meets in convention every three years. Each congregation sends a pastor and a lay representative to the district convention.

Worshiping with Angels and Archangels: An Introduction to the Divine Service

By Scot A. Kinnaman

The Divine Service uses two distinct elements that create a framework for our worship each time we gather together. Those parts of the liturgy that do not change each week are called the Ordinary, because they are ordinarily present each week in the Divine Service. The Ordinary reflects the changeless and time-less texts of the liturgy, some of which have been in continuous use for more than 1,500 years. The second element of our worship consists of the changeable texts, known as the Propers. The Propers bring variety as they follow the seasons of the Church Year and the associated Scripture readings. The Propers carry the message or theme for the day, which is often taken from the Holy Gospel.

The Preparation

The Preparation has not always been part of the Divine Service. Yet, Confession and Absolution have always been seen as proper preparation for those who desire to participate in Holy Communion.

Invocation. The Divine Service begins with the name of God. Invoking His name orders our worship, making it clear that this is His service to us, not our service or someone else's. We call upon God to bless that which will be done in His name. Here, at the beginning of the service, the Invocation also recalls us to our own baptismal beginning.

INVOCATION: From the Latin for "call upon."

Confession. In the **Confession**, we are saying "amen," or "yes, yes, this is true," to God's righteous judgment against our sin. But the Lord is present with us and ready to forgive. After all, this is the reason the Lord gathers His people together in the Divine Service, to give them His mercy and grace.

CONFESSION: The act by which one admits or confesses sin and the guilt of sin.

- **Absolution**. Our Lord declares through the mouth of His servant, the pastor, that by His grace and mercy our sins are forgiven. The **Absolution** speaks the Gospel into our ears in a personal way. Through these Gospel words, we receive the salvation earned by Christ upon the cross of Calvary; every sin is covered by His blessed death.

Service of the Word

After the Confession and Absolution, the Divine Service continues with the **Service of the Word**. The purpose of the Service of the Word is to present Christ to the assembled congregation as the people prepare to meet Him in His Supper.

Introit. The **Introit**, one of the Propers (the verses chosen are different each Sunday), is sung by the congregation or choir. The Introit is a collection of passages from the Psalms that sets the tone for our worship and introduces the rest of the Divine Service, in which Christ comes to us in His Word and His Sacrament.

INTROIT: Latin for "enter."

Kyrie. As we move toward the reading of God's Word, we join with all believers through the ages, in heaven and presently on earth, and ask the Lord for mercy. The **Kyrie** is the first prayer of the gathered congregation. It is a cry for mercy that our Lord and King hear us and help us in our needs and troubles.

KYRIE: A shortened form of the Greek words Kyrie eleison, *which mean "Lord, have mercy."*

Hymn of Praise. Confident that the Lord is merciful, we join the whole Church in singing the **Hymn of Praise**. In the traditional Hymn of Praise, the **Gloria in Excelsis**, the pastor begins with the angelic hymn in Luke 2:14: "Glory to God in the highest, and on earth peace." In the Gloria, the Church celebrates Christmas all year long, and we, along with the shepherds, are invited to go and see Jesus in the Scripture readings that follow.

GLORIA IN EXCELSIS: Latin for "glory [to God] in the highest."

The Divine Service also offers a second Hymn of Praise, **"This Is the Feast."** This Easter hymn to the crucified and risen Savior is based on passages from Revelation 5:12–13 and 19:5–9. Because of its resurrection theme, this hymn is used more frequently during the Easter season and on the festivals of Christ celebrated throughout the Church Year.

Salutation. The **Salutation** is a special greeting between the congregation and its pastor.

Collect. The **Collect of the Day** "collects" in a concise and beautiful manner the Gospel message for the day. Most of these prayers have been in continuous use in the Church for more than 1,500 years. In the Collect, we join with the great body of believers, the communion of saints, and with the generations yet to come. The congregation makes the Collect its own with its "amen."

AMEN: The congregation's declaration that what has been said is true and worthy of agreement; "yes, yes, this is most certainly true."

Old Testament/First Reading. Through the history of Israel and the words of the prophets, the **Old Testament Reading** teaches us about God's work in the time before Christ.

Gradual. Hearing the Word of God, the people respond with words of praise. The **Gradual** is a Proper. It is a portion of a psalm or other Scripture passage that provides a response after the Old Testament Reading.

Epistle/Second Reading. The **Epistle** gives us God's counsel on how His gracious Word is applied to the hearer and the Church.

Alleluia. Like the Gradual, the **Alleluia and Verse** provide a transition between the readings. The word *alleluia* is Hebrew for "praise the Lord." The Verse prepares us to meet the Christ of God in His Word, hearing of His life, ministry, death, and resurrection for the salvation of all.

Holy Gospel. The **Holy Gospel** always contains the very words or deeds of Jesus. This makes the reading of the Holy Gospel the summit of the Service of the Word, and we recognize this by surrounding our Savior's words with songs of glory and praise and by standing to receive His gracious words.

Hymn of the Day. God's people have been encouraged to sing their prayers, praise, and thanksgiving to God. The **Hymn of the Day** is the principal hymn of the Divine Service and relates to the theme of the day from the Holy Gospel.

Sermon. Our Lord sent His apostles into the world to preach that forgiveness of sins, life, and salvation are found through Him. In the preaching of the **Sermon**, that apostolic Word is proclaimed among us today.

SERMON: The pastor's proclamation, usually based on the Scripture readings for the day.

Creed. Having received the Word of the Lord, we respond by confessing the Christian faith. This statement of faith is called a **Creed** (from the Latin word *credo*, "I believe"). By confessing one of the Church's historic creeds, we express our unity in the faith—the same faith that the entire Church has confessed throughout the world and across the ages.

Prayer of the Church. It is both our duty and our privilege as God's children to bring our concerns before Him. In the **Prayer of the Church,** we pray not only for our own needs but also for our neighbor. This is seen in the traditional invitation: "Let us pray for the whole people of God in Christ Jesus and for all people according to their needs."

Offering. Just as we respond to the hearing of God's Word in prayer, praise, and thanksgiving, we also respond in the **Offering** by returning to God a portion of the treasure He has given us.

Offertory. The **Offertory** is sung as the congregation's offering is brought forward and presented before the altar. During the singing of the Offertory, the altar is prepared by the pastor for the celebration of Holy Communion.

Service of the Sacrament

The **Service of the Sacrament** is the celebration of the Sacrament of the Altar. The Sacrament was instituted by Jesus Christ for the forgiveness of sins. It is to be celebrated by all Christians until Christ comes again on the Last Day.

Preface. The Service of the Sacrament begins with the **Preface**, an ancient dialogue or conversation between the pastor and the people.

Sanctus. As a Hymn of Praise was sung at the beginning of the Service of the Word, so now a song of praise is sung before the Sacrament. The **Sanctus** is the angelic hymn described in the heavenly vision of Isaiah 6. In this vision the seraphim are gathered around the throne of God, proclaiming His holiness and glory. In the hosannas of the second half of the Sanctus, we worship Jesus who comes in His Holy Supper (Matthew 21:9).

SANCTUS: Latin for "holy."

The Words of Our Lord. The pastor speaks the **Words of Our Lord** to consecrate, or set apart, the bread and the wine for God's special use. In the Sacrament of the Altar, Christ gives His true body and true blood under the forms of consecrated bread and wine. Once again, God's grace comes to us in the Divine Service. Jesus Himself is present and forgives our sins. This is the Good News because Jesus' Word does what it says.

The Lord's Prayer. The chief prayer of the Christian Church is the **Lord's Prayer**, and it is prayed here at the chief event of the Divine Service. As children of God, we call upon "our Father" as we prepare to encounter Jesus in His Supper, acknowledging that in the Sacrament He will answer our petitions.

Pax Domini. The pastor holds the body and blood of Jesus before the congregation and speaks the **Pax Domini** as Christ Himself did on that first Easter when He stood in the midst of His disciples.

PAX DOMINI: Latin for "the peace of the Lord."

Agnus Dei. John the Baptist foresaw Jesus' death on Calvary, and at Jesus' Baptism, John cried out, "Behold, the Lamb of God, who takes away the sin of the world!" (John 1:29). In Jesus' presence, we, too, cry out and sing the praise of Christ, the "Lamb of God," who in His death on Calvary bore our sins, even the sins of the whole world. It is this Christ who has washed us clean by His blood, bringing us His merciful salvation and peace (Revelation 7:14).

AGNUS DEI: Latin for "Lamb of God."

Distribution of the Lord's Supper. At the altar, the pastor distributes first the body and then the blood of Jesus. After all have communed, the pastor dismisses those at the altar by making the sign of the cross and saying: "The body and blood of our Lord Jesus Christ strengthen and preserve you in body and soul to life everlasting. Depart in peace. Amen."

Post-Communion Canticle. At the close of Holy Communion, as the pastor closes the sacred vessels and covers them with a veil, the congregation stands to sing the **Nunc Dimittis**. The Nunc Dimittis is Simeon's prayer of thanksgiving for being allowed to see the Messiah before he died. With the incarnate Christ in his arms, Simeon rejoiced and made his confession (Luke 2:28–32).

Having seen Christ in the Sacrament—receiving Him in our mouths and so into our souls—we join Simeon in his inspired song.

Post-Communion Collect. The prayer "collects" our grateful thoughts into one prayer, asking that the gifts received in the Divine Service, and specifically in the Lord's Supper, would strengthen our faith toward God and would carry into our lives and callings as we deal with one another.

Benediction. In the Old Testament, God gave Aaron and his sons who followed him in the priesthood His very name to use as a blessing for the Israelites (Numbers 6:22–27). So also today in the **Benediction**, the Lord blesses His people with His holy name.

We end the Divine Service as we began—in the name of the Lord and with a threefold speaking of God's holy name.

Christian Symbols

By Walter M. Schoedel and David W. Christian

The Holy Blessed Trinity

In the Athanasian Creed we confess "And the catholic [universal Christian] faith is this, that we worship one God in Trinity and Trinity in Unity" (*Lutheran Service Book*). We hear God in the Scriptures speaking of Himself as being three persons (Father, Son, and Holy Spirit), but the three persons are only one God. That is why we refer to Him as the Trinity, which means "three in one."

The **triangle** has served as the common symbol for the Trinity. Each equal side represents a person of the Godhead. Together the sides form one complete Being.

The **shield** is found in many different forms, yet the message of each is the same: the Father is God, the Son is God, and the Holy Spirit is God. The distinct character of each person is indicated by the words *is not*.

To communicate the concept of the Trinity, the church's symbols have also included the designs of three equal arcs, **three interwoven circles**, and a flower like a **shamrock**. Tradition tells the story of how St. Patrick saw a shamrock, a yellow flower with three leaves. He picked it and said, "God is like this flower; this flower has three petals, and the three petals form this shamrock. So God consists of three persons, and yet He is one God."

God the Father

The hand, appearing in various forms, is the most common symbol of God the Father. The Old Testament speaks frequently of the hand of God; for example, "my times[, O Lord,] are in Your hand" (Psalm 31:15). The hand signifies power, protection, and possession, as the Israelites sang after God saved them from the Egyptian army: "Your right hand, O Lord, glorious in power, Your right hand, O Lord, shatters the enemy" (Exodus 15:6).

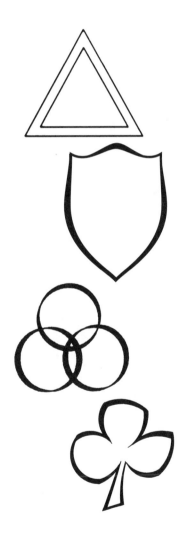

The **hand** of God is seen emerging from a cloud reaching down to bless His people. The hand of God with a circle depicts God as being eternal with an eternal concern for His people.

The **eye** is another common symbol for God the Father. It conveys the message that He sees us. "Behold, the eye of the Lord is on those who fear Him, on those who hope in His steadfast love" (Psalm 33:18).

The **eye of God** signifies God's loving care and concern for His creation. It also reminds us that God sees everything we do. Jesus reminds us that God notices our faithful Christian actions even when no one else does: "Pray to your Father who is in secret. And your Father who sees in secret will reward you" (Matthew 6:6).

God the Son

There are many symbols to represent God the Son, Jesus Christ, our Lord and Savior. There are monograms representing His name, crosses representing His crucifixion, and pictures depicting events during His ministry.

The **monograms**. A monogram is usually two or more letters, such as initials, that identify a person. The early Christians made use of monograms to acknowledge that they belonged to Jesus.

IHS are the first two letters and the last letter of the Greek name for Jesus written in Greek capital letters, *IHSOYS*. *Jesus* means "the Lord saves." The monogram *IHS* is often written on altars and paraments.

Chi Rho (pronounced key row) are the first two letters of the Greek word for Christ, *Xristos*. *Christ* means "Anointed One." Old Testament prophets and kings were anointed—olive oil was poured on their heads—to consecrate them to God. Christ was consecrated for His ministry at His Baptism.

INRI stands for the Latin *Iesus Nazarenus Rex Iudaeorum*—"Jesus of Nazareth, King of the Jews"—the title Pilate ordered to be placed above the cross.

Alpha and Omega are the first and last letters of the Greek alphabet. Jesus said, "I am the Alpha and the Omega, the first and the last, the beginning and the end" (Revelation 22:13; see also Revelation 1:8; 21:6). Jesus is the beginning and the end of all things; the world was created through Him (John 1:3), and one day He will come again to bring this world to a close (Revelation 22:12).

The Cross

More than **four hundred various shapes** of the cross have been used by Christians down through the centuries. Some of them have become identified with a particular community of Christians. The cross reminds us of the words of the apostle Paul, "We preach Christ crucified" (1 Corinthians 1:23). The Romans used many different types of crosses for crucifying, and we simply do not know exactly which type was used to crucify Jesus Christ, because the Bible does not describe it in detail.

The **Latin Cross** is the most common form of cross. There are many variations of this design.

The **Jerusalem Cross** represents the five wounds of our Lord in His hands, feet, and side from the spear. The four small crosses may also indicate the four corners of the earth to which the message of the cross is to be proclaimed.

The **Celtic Cross** with a circle around the middle signifies that the message of the cross is eternal.

The Pictures

Jesus referred to Himself as the Vine, the Bread, the Door, and other symbols. Christian artists down through the centuries have drawn pictures to communicate the message of Jesus Christ.

The **butterfly** is a symbol of Christ's resurrection and of eternal life for believers.

The **phoenix** rising from flames is another symbol of Christ's resurrection. A nonbiblical Greek legend says that the phoenix, an imaginary bird, lived several hundred years in a row before dying. The bird was then burned up, but would rise again from its own ashes and live several more hundred years before repeating its death and "resurrection." Christians borrowed this pagan myth and applied it to Christ.

The **lamb** illustrates Jesus as "the Lamb of God, who takes away the sin of the world" (John 1:29). Sometimes the Lamb of God is pierced with His blood flowing into a chalice, showing that He gives us His blood, shed for us for the forgiveness of sin, in the Lord's Supper.

The **Shepherd** symbolizes Jesus the Good Shepherd (John 10:11), who guides, protects, and gives His life for the sheep, His flock.

God the Holy Spirit

In contrast to the large number of symbols for Jesus Christ, there are few for God the Holy Spirit. There are fewer direct references in the Bible to the Spirit than to the Father and the Son, and it is more difficult to picture the Spirit because the Spirit usually is not described in physical terms. The words of Christ indicate the difficulty of "pinning down" the Spirit through a symbol: "The wind blows where it wishes, and you hear its sound, but you do not know where it comes from or where it goes. So it is with everyone who is born of the Spirit" (John 3:8; in both Hebrew and Greek, the same word can mean either "wind" or "Spirit").

The **descending dove** is the most common symbol of the Holy Spirit. In creation, the Spirit hovered over the waters (Genesis 1:2; the same Hebrew verb is used of a bird hovering in Deuteronomy 32:11). At the Baptism of Jesus, the Spirit descended bodily in the form of a dove (Luke 3:22).

The **seven-fold flame** commemorates the coming of the Holy Spirit in the form of tongues of fire on Pentecost (Acts 2:14). In the Bible (particularly in Revelation), the number seven often represents the holiness and perfection of God. The one Holy Spirit is often described as sevenfold (Revelation 4:5; 5:6) and as bestowing seven gifts or fruits (see Isaiah 11:2 and Galatians 5:22–23).

The Four Evangelists

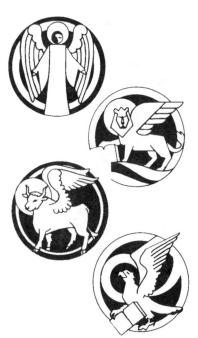

The writers of the four Gospels are called evangelists because they proclaim the Good News of Jesus Christ. Symbols for the four Gospel writers have existed since the earliest days of the Church. The artists were influenced by the vision of the prophet Ezekiel, who saw four creatures supporting the throne of God: "As for the likeness of their faces, each had a human face. The four had the face of a lion on the right side, the four had the face of an ox on the left side, and the four had the face of an eagle" (Ezekiel 1:10). John saw a similar vision of four creatures resembling a man, a lion, an ox, and an eagle (Revelation 4:7).

The **winged man** represents St. Matthew because his Gospel emphasizes the manhood or humanity of Christ. It begins by listing the human ancestors of Jesus.

The **winged lion** represents St. Mark because his Gospel emphasizes the power and miracles of Christ.

The **winged ox** represents St. Luke because his Gospel emphasizes the sacrificial death of Christ, and oxen were often used as sacrificial animals.

The **winged eagle** represents St. John because his Gospel emphasizes the deity of Christ. The eagle soars higher than any other animal up toward heaven.

Tradition tells us that these four symbols represent major events in Christ's life: the winged man, His incarnation; the winged ox, His death; the winged lion, His resurrection; and the eagle, His ascension.

The Means of Grace

To bring the Gospel message of love and forgiveness into our lives, God has given us His Holy Word and His blessed Sacraments, Baptism and the Lord's Supper. Because God conveys His grace to us through the Word and the Sacraments, we speak of them as the Means of Grace. There are many symbols depicting the use and message of the Means of Grace.

The **lamp** is a reminder of the words of the psalmist, "Your word is a lamp to my feet and a light to my path" (Psalm 119:105). The open Bible indicates that the Bible is to be read. "In Thessalonica; they received the Word with all eagerness, examining the Scriptures daily" (Acts 17:11).

The **shell** with three drops of water reminds us of Baptism, when water was poured on us three times in the name of the Father and of the Son and of the Holy Spirit.

The **chalice** is a reminder of the cup our Lord blessed at the Last Supper, which we share in the Lord's Supper.

The Church

The Church is the body of believers in Christ who have been called by God in their Baptism to be His very own and are nurtured in the faith through the Word of God and the Lord's Supper. Through the Holy Spirit, each member receives gifts for building the Church. Through the years, numerous symbols for the Church have been developed. The following are most familiar:

The **rock** points us to God, our Rock and Redeemer (Psalm 19:14).

The **vine and branches** recall the words of Jesus, "I am the vine; you are the branches" (John 15:5). This speaks of the Church's dependence on Christ for her life and growth.

The **ark with the rainbow** reminds us of God's covenant with Noah (Genesis 9:13) and the new covenant He made with us in Jesus Christ (Luke 22:20).

The **cross and orb** represent the mission of the Church to proclaim the Gospel throughout the world. This design also depicts the triumph of the Gospel over the world.

The **ship** depicts the Church carrying the faithful safely across the stormy seas of life.

The **cross on the mast** symbolizes the message of Jesus Christ that empowers and guides the Church. The term for the part of the church where the congregation sits, the *nave*, means "ship."

Stars and Candles

Lights, particularly oil lamps and candles, have been used for both practical and symbolic purposes in the church from the earliest times. Today candles are still used in the church because of their symbolism. They stand for Christ, who is the light of the world.

Stars with different numbers of points have always had symbolic meanings.

The **six-pointed star** is the *Creator's star*, a symbol of creation because God completed His work in six days.

The **five-pointed star** is known as the *Bethlehem star*, and it reminds us of the Wise Men to whom God revealed the Christ (Matthew 2:1–11).

The **two candles** on the altar emphasize the two natures of Christ, divine and human.

The **seven candles** in the candelabras beside the altar symbolize the seven gifts of the Holy Spirit (Revelation 5:12) and the seven churches (Revelation 1:20).

Additional Symbols

The **fish** is one of the oldest symbols for Christ. The Greek word for fish is *IXThYS*. The *I* stands for *Iesous*, Jesus; the *X* stands for *Xristos*, Christ; the *Th* (one letter in Greek) stands for *Theou*, or God; the *Y* stands for *Yios*, Son; and the *S* stands for *Soter*, Savior. Therefore, the fish stands for "Jesus Christ, Son of God, Savior."

An **angel** is always associated with a message from God, such as the birth of Christ, which the angels announced to the shepherds on the first Christmas (Luke 2:8–20).

The **rose** can represent Jesus Christ (see Song of Solomon 2:1). It can also serve as a reminder of Isaiah's prophecy that the desert shall blossom as a rose at the coming of the glory of God (Isaiah 35:1).

Crowns can represent the Wise Men, the kingdom of God, and the suffering of Christ on the cross.

A **lily** can be a symbol of purity, and of the Virgin Mary in particular. However, it is used most often at Eastertime as a symbol of resurrection. The lily bulb looks lifeless, but it produces a beautiful flower, symbolizing life emerging from death.

Luther's Coat of Arms is a cross within a heart, resting on a rose representing Christ, surrounded by a gold circle. Luther himself described its meaning as follows: The cross in the heart signifies that faith in Christ crucified within our heart saves us. The heart is on a white rose to show that faith gives peace and joy. The rose is on a sky-blue background to show that our joy now is a small taste of the future joy of heaven. The gold circle indicates that joy in heaven is endless and more precious than gold. There is a little poem about this symbol: "The Christian's heart is resting on roses, Even while beneath the cross it reposes."

A **scroll** reminds us of the many writings of the prophets, apostles, and the evangelists. Many parts of the Bible were originally written on scrolls (Jeremiah 36).

A **sword** represents the Word of God, as is associated with the Holy Spirit (Ephesians 6:17) and Law and Gospel (Hebrews 4:12–13).

An **anchor** is a reminder of hope in Christ, stability and support in the face of adversity and change.

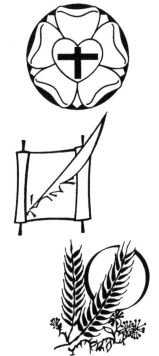

A **sheaf** of wheat can be used to depict God's blessings, a spiritual harvest, or the bread used in the Lord's Supper.

Trumpets in the Bible are used to call people to worship and to announce glorious messages, the Day of Judgment, and the resurrection.

Torches signify witnessing for Christ. As Christ said, "Let your light shine before others, so that they may see your good works and give glory to your Father who is in heaven" (Matthew 5:16).

The Church Building

1. Nave. The main part of the building, where the congregation sits. From the Latin for "ship."

2. **Chancel.** The front part of the church, where the altar, pulpit, lectern, and Communion rail are located. It is often raised.

3. Altar. Usually made of marble or wood, it is located in the center of the chancel. Since sacrifices were made on altars in the Old Testament, it reminds us of the sacrifice of Jesus for the sins of the world. It also serves as the "table" for the Lord's Supper.

4. Pulpit. A large, enclosed podium, where the pastor usually preaches the sermon.

5. Lectern. A small podium, where the lector ("reader") reads the Scripture lessons.

6. Paraments. The cloth decorations in the chancel on the altar, pulpit, and lectern. The paraments are changed to match the color for the season of the Church Year.

2 Appendix

Luther's Small Catechism

The Six Chief Parts

The Ten Commandments

As the head of the family should teach them in a simple way to his household

The First Commandment

You shall have no other gods.

What does this mean? We should fear, love, and trust in God above all things.

The Second Commandment

You shall not misuse the name of the Lord your God.

What does this mean? We should fear and love God so that we do not curse, swear, use satanic arts, lie, or deceive by His name, but call upon it in every trouble, pray, praise, and give thanks.

The Third Commandment

Remember the Sabbath day by keeping it holy.

What does this mean? We should fear and love God so that we do not despise preaching and His Word, but hold it sacred and gladly hear and learn it.

The Fourth Commandment

Honor your father and your mother.

What does this mean? We should fear and love God so that we do not despise or anger our parents and other authorities, but honor them, serve and obey them, love and cherish them.

The Fifth Commandment

You shall not murder.

What does this mean? We should fear and love God so that we do not hurt or harm our neighbor in his body, but help and support him in every physical need.